# MASS CORRUPTION VOLUME 1: THE COPS

By Howie Carr
Frandel LLC 2025

Copyright © 2025 Howie Carr

ISBN: 978-0-9861933-3-0

Library of Congress Control Number: 2025947342

All rights reserved. This book or any portion thereof may not be reproduced or used in any manner whatsoever without the express written permission of the author/publisher, except for the use of brief quotations in a book review.

Printed in the United States of America.

# Table of Contents

**Introduction** . . . . . . . . . . . . . . . . . . . . . . . . . . . . . . . . . . . . . . . . . . . v
**Chapter 1**  "Pin It on the Girl" . . . . . . . . . . . . . . . . . . . . . . . . . . . 1
**Chapter 2**  Who's Who in the Karen Read Trials . . . . . . . . . . . . . 4
**Chapter 3**  The Trials of Karen Read. . . . . . . . . . . . . . . . . . . . . . 10
**Chapter 4**  Calling All Canton Coneheads. . . . . . . . . . . . . . . . . 47
**Chapter 5**  Trooper Michael Proctor, Badge Number 3863 . . . . . . 52
**Chapter 6**  Meet Hank Brennan . . . . . . . . . . . . . . . . . . . . . . . . . 63
**Chapter 7**  Welcome to Norfolk County . . . . . . . . . . . . . . . . . . 75
**Chapter 8**  Rubber Duckies Everywhere . . . . . . . . . . . . . . . . . 100
**Chapter 9**  Copland . . . . . . . . . . . . . . . . . . . . . . . . . . . . . . . . . 109
**Chapter 10** BPD . . . . . . . . . . . . . . . . . . . . . . . . . . . . . . . . . . . . 119
**Chapter 11** BPD Hall of Shame . . . . . . . . . . . . . . . . . . . . . . . . 136
**Chapter 12** Jameson and Ginger . . . . . . . . . . . . . . . . . . . . . . . . 140
**Chapter 13** Sandra Birchmore: "Suicide" in Canton . . . . . . . . . 150
**Chapter 14** Juston Root: 31 Shots in 3 Seconds . . . . . . . . . . . . 159
**Chapter 15** Annie and Sonja . . . . . . . . . . . . . . . . . . . . . . . . . . . 162
**Chapter 16** MSP: A Long Way from Norman Rockwell . . . . . . . 169
**Chapter 17** MSP Hall of Shame . . . . . . . . . . . . . . . . . . . . . . . . 180
**Chapter 18** MSP: To Protect and Steal . . . . . . . . . . . . . . . . . . . 186

| | | |
|---|---|---|
| **Chapter 19** | Trooper Leigha Genduso, Badge Number 3800 | 213 |
| **Chapter 20** | FBI | 222 |
| **Chapter 21** | "Not So Honorable" | 234 |
| **Chapter 22** | Fred Weichel: Another Norfolk County Frame-up | 241 |
| **Chapter 23** | Rotten Boroughs | 246 |
| **Chapter 24** | High Sheriffs in Low Places | 261 |
| **Epilogue** | | 267 |
| **Acknowledgments** | | 275 |
| **Index** | | 277 |

# Introduction

Massachusetts law enforcement has always been corrupt, but until Karen Read's trials, most people never thought much about it.

Everybody understood at least vaguely how certain politically connected families like the Kennedys or the Bulgers had for generations gotten away with, literally, murder, or at least manslaughter. They'd read or heard about the unending scandals in the Massachusetts State Police (MSP). But it was mostly background noise, not something to worry about daily—unless you or someone close to you got ensnared in the deeply rotten system.

Massachusetts was like something out of Don Henley's song about local TV news, "Dirty Laundry." You didn't really want to know what was going on. Just leave well enough alone . . .

Then Karen Read went on trial for second-degree murder in Norfolk County. It was live streamed, not just on broadcast and cable TV, but on the internet. You could follow the trial at your workplace, you could listen to it in your car, or on earphones while out walking your dog—in whatever state you were in.

It dominated the state's conversation, but very little of the information came from traditional media. Local TV news had long since devolved into irrelevance—sinkholes in Florida, high-speed car chases in LA, basically chewing gum for the eyes, as they used to say of television.

Two days after the death of John O'Keefe, the local CBS affiliate—Channel 4, WBZ-TV—ran a bogus story saying that the MSP had ring-camera video of Karen Read striking her boyfriend with her SUV. For most people, that was it. Case closed. WBZ wouldn't have made up a story out of whole cloth, would it?

Channel 4 didn't retract the story for two and a half years.

The idea of framing an innocent woman to protect a band of drunken good ol' boys—"Neanderthals," as Karen Read privately termed them—seemed beyond the pale. Of course, innocent people had been framed in Norfolk County before.

Did the names Sacco and Vanzetti ring a bell for anyone? Maybe not. They don't teach history, or much of anything else, in public schools in Massachusetts anymore.

The local newspapers were almost as bad as TV news. The *Boston Globe* had zero interest in Karen Read, a heterosexual white woman born in Massachusetts. For the out-of-state women who ran the *Globe* as a vanity project for another out-of-state billionaire's trophy wife, it lacked any of the elements that mattered:

Illegal aliens

Transgenders

Donald Trump

Plus, the case was being prosecuted by a loyal member of the local Democrat nomenklatura, who had been on one public payroll or another continuously since 1976. If you couldn't trust a loyal party apparatchik like Michael Morrissey, who could you trust? He was a Kamala Harris delegate to the Democrat convention in Chicago.

Good people, in other words. The best.

Exposing the frame-up of Karen Read was left to a handful of unconnected people, most notably a former high-school history teacher from Worcester County named Aidan Kearney, who ran a news blog under the name Turtleboy.

When Kearney started getting close to the truth, he was locked up in the county jail for two months. Norfolk County—where due process went to die.

As the two trials unfolded a year apart, the people, the non-insiders, got a crash course in political corruption. The cops lied, they didn't

Aidan "Turtleboy" Kearney: He broke the story.

investigate their fellow cops, they didn't care about chains of custody, search warrants, or due process.

Evidence mysteriously appeared weeks after the crime. Cops destroyed their cell phones just ahead of preservation orders from the courts. Surveillance videos were altered without explanation. Other possibly exculpatory video just vanished or was never sought by Morrissey's investigators.

Then, at the end of the first trial in 2024, when Karen Read was acquitted of the two murder charges, the judge simply refused to accept the verdicts. The state's highest court declined to reinstate the not-guilty verdicts. Karen Read was forced to stand trial a second time—double jeopardy.

It had always been this way in Massachusetts. It's just that it was never so widely discussed, at least not in polite society.

Now everyone could see what had been true all along. The cops—and the courts—were crooked, top to bottom. Not all of them, of course, but a disproportionate number. For example, until Karen Read, outside of a civics class or textbook, who had ever heard of a real-life case of *double jeopardy*—being tried twice for the same crime, after being acquitted the first time?

It seemed unimaginable, until it wasn't. At least in Norfolk County.

Karen Read was twice found not guilty of murder—of the same murder.

This book is a brief examination of the corruption that has become an accepted way of life in too much of Massachusetts.

To illustrate the problem, I have collected many of my recent columns in the *Boston Herald*, most about the two Karen Read trials and the unending corruption in the MSP. You will read them pretty much as they were written, although in some articles, I have made edits or updates. The date they originally ran is at the beginning of each column.

I've tried to cut out some repetitious material that appears from column to column, although you'll notice repeated references to, say, Sgt. Bukhenik's $211,080 salary. Also, there may be a few phrases unfamiliar to those readers who didn't follow the trials day to day. For instance, when Jennifer McCabe at 2:27 a.m. that fateful morning inquired on Google about death by freezing, she typed, "Hos long to die in cold?" Not "How long" but "Hos long." It became a recurring theme on social media—and in my columns: "Hos long?"

In this volume I've also attempted to catalog other miscarriages of justice—different frame-ups, and not just in Norfolk County, as well as the state's drug-lab scandals and the law enforcement corruption afflicting other cities and towns across the Commonwealth.

What I call the "hackerama" also plays a role in this cancer. Without all the political jobs that politicians like District Attorney Michael "Meatball" Morrissey and his cronies control on public payrolls, they could not build the kind of organizations that allow them to retain power, decade after corrupt decade, in elections with miniscule turnouts.

I have also included chapters about the three generations of corruption in the Boston FBI office, and how more recently public officials who were falsely portrayed in the mainstream media as "incorruptible," specifically Robert Mueller, covered up their actions.

More recently, of course, the local FBI and US attorney's office have been instrumental in uncovering the rot permeating Norfolk

County, but this is a relatively new phenomenon. As you will learn, the scandalous behavior of past local G-men predated even Whitey Bulger.

Some readers may complain that I have overlooked scandals in other law enforcement agencies across the state. But I am just one writer in a very, very crooked state.

And this is, after all, only volume 1 of *Mass Corruption*.

This is just the way things are here. In my first book, *The Brothers Bulger*, I quoted from Edwin O'Connor's final 1966 novel, *All in the Family*. In the wake of the Karen Read trials, O'Connor's description of public life in Massachusetts seems at least as appropriate now as it was sixty years ago:

> *Corruption here had a shoddy, penny-ante quality that it did not have in other states . . . Here everything was up for grabs and nothing was too small to steal . . . In our politics there seemed to be a depthless cushion of street-corner cynicism, a special kind of tainted, small-time fellowship which sent out a complex of vines and shoots so interconnected that even the sleaziest poolroom bookie managed in some way, however obscure, to be in touch with the mayor's office or governor's chair.*

Perhaps the names—and sexual preferences—have changed. But not much else. It's still crooked, from top to bottom.

Decades ago, Whitey Bulger instinctively understood this. He and his partner Stevie Flemmi had at least six FBI agents on their payroll. Like the G-men, the local cops expected payoffs, especially at Christmas. Whitey would always put the cash in envelopes, so as not to embarrass the police. That's what all the wiseguys did. It was professional courtesy.

"Christmas," Whitey used to say, "is for cops and kids."

The old governor's councilor, Patrick "Sonny" McDonough, sometimes used cops as his bagmen to collect payoffs for pardons, or political appointments.

"I hate it when a cop delivers me $300," Sonny would say, between puffs on his cigar, "because I never know if they've stolen $200 or $700. The problem with cops is, they think whatever they get is theirs."

The larger problem is, with so many cops running rackets of their own, it doesn't leave them much time for actually, you know, stopping crime. Enforcing the law. Making arrests. Keeping neighborhoods safe. That kind of stuff is for squares.

The effectiveness of investigative police work has always been overrated. It's much easier for cops (not to mention reporters) to just develop sources, or "snitches." The snitch gives the cops (or reporters) information to arrest or expose the unconnected (and potential rivals). Additionally the thugs may cut the cops (if not the reporters) in on some of their scores, or at least pay them off to look the other way if anything untoward turns up that could be used against them.

Think of it as the Whitey Bulger business model.

Whatever, the fact remains that next to no significant arrests are ever made by any local or state cops in Massachusetts. Almost all the heavy lifting is done by the G-men, whether FBI, ATF, IRS, DEA, or nowadays, ICE.

Consider the case of one Joe Ponzo, a police officer in suburban Stoneham for many years. He had sticky fingers: He was embezzling funds from the local cop union. Finally, one of the honest cops in town was fed up enough to pay a visit to the main FBI office in Chelsea.

The honest cop's account of chicanery piqued the interest of the new-breed, honest G-men. They got search warrants for Mr. and Mrs. Ponzo's bank accounts. They quickly discovered that although the statute of limitations had expired on his nickel-and-dime con, Officer Ponzo was sitting on $7 million in unexplained funds.

Next, they figured out that Joe Ponzo was a mere junior partner to his brother, a contractor named Christopher who was an auxiliary police officer in Stoneham. Chris stole $36 million.

All the stolen loot came from a single state program, Mass Saves,

Joe Ponzo, Stoneham cop, stole $7 million.

under which the Commonwealth assesses an ever-rising fee on consumers' monthly utility bills as an "energy-efficiency fee." Mass Saves is a local offshoot of what President Trump calls the "Green New Deal Scam."

In the indictments of the cop Ponzo brothers, the feds described Mass Saves as a "public-private partnership," which traditionally means that something public is about to disappear into some private pockets. In this case, the Ponzo brothers' pockets.

Chris Ponzo, auxiliary Stoneham cop, stole $36 million.

For almost a decade, they converted Mass Saves into Mass Steals. Joe Ponzo alone stole more money than any of the more famous LEO crooks you will soon be reading about—all the crooked Boston FBI agents, the MSP embezzlers and other assorted thieving troopers, the Boston cops running overtime rackets, the bank burglars in Medford.

And for more than a decade, their crimes went utterly undetected by anyone in state government, especially the Ponzos' fellow cops.

On a cop's salary, Joe Ponzo had a million-dollar home in Stoneham; an $830,000 waterfront condo in Marco Island, Florida; and a lakefront condo in Laconia, New Hampshire.

And what did the ratepayers get in return?

"They got a crooked cop," said the feds in their sentencing memorandum earlier this year, "who, for years, paid hundreds of thousands of dollars in bribes in return for millions of dollars in lucrative and inflated contracts under the Mass Saves program."

His brother Chris used his $36 million to buy "multiple properties, vehicles, a boat, a Cessna airplane, and his own aircraft hangar."

And to repeat, Massachusetts law enforcement, like Sgt. Schultz on *Hogan's Heroes*, knew nothing.

They didn't have a clue what was going on under their noses. Neither the local cops, nor the district attorney, nor the attorney general (who for most of that time was Maura Healey, now the governor). The state's inspector general saw nothing, nor did the state auditor. Neither did any of the so-called watchdog legislative committees with subpoena power.

Nobody wanted to rock the boat.

More than a century ago, the Ponzi scheme in Boston was a worldwide scandal. It's still studied as the model for how to run a pyramid scheme. But Ponzi generated short money compared to the Ponzo scheme a few miles north in Stoneham.

Yet in the end, the Ponzos got little more than slaps on the wrist—twenty-seven-month prison sentences each, for stealing $43 million in public funds.

Unlike Ponzi scheme, the Ponzos barely made the Boston outlets, let alone worldwide media. Obviously, like the Karen Read case, the Ponzos' decade of uninterrupted, unnoticed looting did not reflect well on the Democrat power structure that the Boston media are part of. And so the Ponzos were all but ignored in the Boston press.

But afterward, US Attorney Leah Foley did issue a statement after Joe Ponzo's sentencing, noting his lengthy career in Massachusetts law enforcement.

"He chose," Foley said, "greed over integrity."

He wasn't the only one, and that's what this book is all about.

# CHAPTER ONE

# "Pin It on the Girl"

That's how defense attorney Alan Jackson described what the cops in Norfolk County were attempting to do to Karen Read, from day one.

"Pin it on the girl."

On the morning of January 29, 2022, a dead Boston cop was lying on the snow-covered lawn of another Boston cop, who refused to come outside at dawn after the body of his alleged friend was discovered.

The dead cop's girlfriend, Karen Read, drunk the night before, wasn't sure what had happened. She was quickly arrested, taken to an MSP barracks, and handcuffed to a radiator. Her attorney, David Yannetti, just as clueless about the actual circumstances of John O'Keefe's death, expressed his condolences to the dead man's grieving family.

But a day or so later, Yannetti got a call from a connected person who told him that there was a lot more to the case than the local police were letting on. And that was the beginning of a three-and-a-half-year struggle to win justice for Karen Read.

Perhaps the most appalling part of the persecution—and that's what it was—were the text messages from Trooper Michael Proctor wishing that Karen Read would commit suicide. Sixteen hours into the investigation, he told his pals she was going down, and that the Boston cop who wouldn't come outside would have no problems, because he was . . . a Boston cop.

A Boston cop from Canton. Like Proctor himself. Like the acting superintendent of the Boston Police Department (BPD), whose wife served as a state judge with Judge Beverly Cannone, who would do her best, or worst, to deny Karen Read a fair trial—twice.

And then it turned out that Cannone's brother, like her a second-generation public defender, had once represented the brother of Brian Albert, Chris Albert. As a young man Chris Albert had killed a foreign exchange student in a late-night car accident. After killing the student, he fled from his vehicle and hid for eighteen hours before turning himself in to the police.

Following serving six months in prison for vehicular homicide, Chris Albert had been elected selectman in Canton. A third brother, Kevin Albert, was a detective on the Canton Police Department, where he got drunk at least once with his fellow townie Michael Proctor—so drunk, as it turned out, that he left his badge in Proctor's MSP cruiser (and at first thought he'd lost his gun as well).

These were the people who were trying to put Karen Read in prison for twenty years, even though she hadn't hit her boyfriend with her car. Over the course of the morning, after she had supposedly run him over and killed him, she left more than fifty hysterical, drunken voicemails on his cell phone, shrieking at him.

So what, the cops said. She was just one devious . . . cunt, as Michael Proctor called her to his friends. A whack job, with a "weird Fall River accent." And that was a large part of it: She wasn't from Canton. She was from the next county over, thirty-seven miles south. As far as the Canton townies were concerned, she might as well have been from Mars.

Same thing with John O'Keefe. Sure, he owned a house in Canton, but he hadn't really been local either. He was from Braintree. Eleven miles away.

In his text messages to his Canton High School buddies and fellow MSP thugs just hours after O'Keefe's death, Proctor went on and on about how he was going to get Karen Read, a "babe." A "girl." He told his buddies he was searching her cell phone but "no nudes yet." His sergeant gave him a thumbs-up emoji for that text.

He texted his sister about his loathing of Karen Read: "Hopefully she kills herself."

FBI agents found the texts while investigating yet another unsolved cop-related murder in Canton. When he read them in court in 2024, Proctor instantly became the poster boy for the corruption in Massachusetts law enforcement.

Not only did he drive his cruiser drunk, not only did he solicit "gifts" for his wife from his same sleazy townie pals that he refused to interview or even consider as suspects, he was also an incompetent investigator. He couldn't be bothered interviewing possibly exculpatory witnesses, he didn't turn over evidence for weeks or months at a time, and he couldn't have cared less about maintaining chains of custody.

Karen Read was quickly charged with murder, even though the state medical examiner listed the cause of John O'Keefe's death as "undetermined." Proctor was angry about that. He called the medical examiner a "whack-job cunt" too, just like Karen Read. At a federal grand jury, Proctor was asked to explain why, in a case he claimed to believe was a murder, he would admit the actual cause of death was "undetermined."

"I said at the time," he stammered to defense attorney Alan Jackson, "it was kind of like not figuratively of course, it's an of course like I had never really seen that before in a homicide."

There are no MENSA chapters in the barracks, let's leave it at that.

Before the columns on the trials, let's look at the key players in both 2024 and 2025.

# CHAPTER TWO

# Who's Who in the Karen Read Trials

## The Defense

Back row, attorneys Robert Alessi, Alan Jackson, and David Yannetti. Front row, back to camera, attorney Elizabeth Little and Karen Read.

Outside court, 2024, Jackson did most of the talking.

In the courtroom, they often conferred.

Elizabeth Little, left, always there with Karen and Alan.

AJ pensive, as when Judge Cannone sustained the forty-ninth consecutive objection to his questions in a half hour.

AJ, not so pensive.

Three "first-chair" defense lawyers on the same team in 2025: Alessi, Jackson, and Yannetti.

The 2024 team: Yannetti, Read, and Jackson

## The "Persecution"

Judge Beverly "Auntie Bev" Cannone.

District Attorney Michael "Meatball" Morrissey.

Special Prosecutor Hank Brennan.

# CHAPTER THREE

# The Trials of Karen Read

## "Nefarious" a Constant Refrain in Karen Read Retrial

Jen McCabe: Tooth decay . . . and truth decay.

*May 2, 2025*

Hos long must this trial continue?

Over the last few days, the prosecution's star witness, Jen McCabe, has been demolished, despite the best efforts of the second-generation hack judge, Beverly Prescott Cannone, to stop the bleeding.

If this trial were a phone call, it would be a butt-dial—something that should never have been made. You know, like the seven butt-dials that Jen McCabe made to the murder victim, John O'Keefe, right before or immediately after he became a murder victim.

Seven butt-dials! And those are just in addition to all the butt-dials made less than two hours later by the two McAlbert cops back and forth on the cell phones they both decided to destroy just before they were ordered by the court not to destroy them.

Oddly, the "butt-dials" from Jen to John O'Keefe were discovered only on O'Keefe's phone. Somehow they'd disappeared from McCabe's phone before she turned it over to the police. Hmmmmm . . .

If this trial were a prize fight, and there was a real ref in the ring, it would already be over. And then somebody would be passing the hat to take up a collection for cab fare to send Jen McCabe back home, along with her magical butt-dialing, call-deleting cell phone.

This whole trial is nefarious, to use one of the words of the day first introduced into the record by Jen McCabe herself, who returned to the courthouse Friday wearing her little cross for the first time since Tuesday.

Too late, Jen.

Nefarious made its first appearance when defense attorney Alan Jackson asked Jen about yet another previously undisclosed phone call she made to her sister, Coco, at 5:07 a.m. It was an hour before John O'Keefe's body was found outside 34 Fairview Road that snowy morning.

Jackson asked Jen why in her grand jury testimony she'd never bothered to mention the 5:07 a.m. phone call to the death house.

"There's nothing nefarious," she harrumphed. "I remembered who I called. I didn't go back and look at phone records."

Alan Jackson looked perplexed about her abrupt dropping of the other n-word.

"I didn't say it was 'nefarious,'" he said. "Why would you use the word 'nefarious'?"

"Because," she said, "there's nothing about me calling my sister that is nefarious and I feel like you're insinuating that it might be, and it's not."

Jackson saw his opportunity and he took it.

"Do you use that word because it sounds nefarious?"

"No," she said, "I just used the word 'cause I think that's the way you're trying to portray it."

"Do you use the word because you think that's how it's coming across—nefarious?"

"Uh, no, not that at all."

The moral of the story: When you're denying that your statements are nefarious, you're sounding more than somewhat nefarious. You're losing.

It sounds as nefarious as saying, when confronted with holes in her earlier testimony, Jen answers, as she did several times yesterday: "To be honest, I had completely forgotten."

Maybe she also forgot her own name when the FBI first approached her and asked her to identify herself. Her first answer to the G-men was "I'm Nicole."

At the end of her testimony, though, Jen McCabe again forgot—about all the lies she'd already admitted to the jury that she'd told the FBI.

"I helped clear up some misconceptions," she bragged, "that they had been told."

Sure, Nicole, er Jen, sure you did.

So much reasonable doubt is piling up that you wonder if a lot of it isn't going over the jurors' heads, it's coming in so fast.

How about the group chats among the McAlberts? Consider Jen's husband Matt McCabe, obviously overcome with grief for his dead pal, whom he calls "the guy" in the chats, as in "Tell them the guy never went into the house."

Again, that would be the death house, 34 Fairview.

Then Matt McCabe muses to the family about whether Karen Read will cop to lesser charges that will make everything go away.

Before they all must testify. Under oath.

"If she pleads out," Matt says, "it will end. If she fights it, it will be an episode."

Welcome to the episode. A very nefarious episode.

At another point, in the McAlbert group chat, Jen asks sister Coco: "Any update?"

To which Coco, Mrs. Brian Albert, the owner of the death house at 34 Fairview, replies:

"Will get more info tomorrow. Don't want to text about it."

Don't want to text about it? That doesn't sound at all nefarious, does it?

Defense attorney Jackson kept asking McCabe about her earlier testimony to multiple state and federal grand juries. She would feign forgetfulness, ask Jackson for "the pa-pah." She would then appear to study the transcript and then look up.

"The pa-pah says I did it. I don't remem-bah it."

Jackson would hand her another transcript.

"I see what I—I read, sorry, I saw what I just read. I don't remember my exact words of every testimony, but I did read that, yes."

Mark Twain once summed up the problem with lying: "If you tell the truth, you don't have to remember anything."

Jen McCabe spent the months between the trials working on her tooth decay. But not nearly so much work with another much more profound flaw—truth decay.

Hos long until somebody stops this fight?

## Meet Conehead #4: Trooper Joseph Paul

*June 18, 2024*

How corrupt and incompetent are the MSP?

Trooper Joseph Paul is one of their "experts," and he was the third MSP knucklehead that the corrupt prosecutors from Norfolk put on the stand to . . . do something.

Mostly, to even further destroy their frame-job case against Karen Read.

Trooper Paul made $130,000 last year. Yesterday in court he described "debris" as "'bree." He pronounced "constrained" as "cu-strained."

Over and over again he said he couldn't say anything "definitely," only he always used the non-word "da-finely."

Here's just one back-and-forth between Paul and Karen Read's lawyer, Alan Jackson. Paul was the third consecutive conehead to testify for the MSP, and the fourth chrome dome over all.

Jackson, the defense attorney, asked Trooper Paul—Conehead #4—exactly who or what he was relying on to come to his incoherent, preposterous conclusions about the victim's magic cocktail glass, among other impossibilities.

> CONEHEAD #4: "It's what was told me as evidence."
>
> JACKSON: "By whom?"
>
> CONEHEAD #4: "The crime scene there, it was glass from the cup."
>
> JACKSON (incredulously): "Who told you?"
>
> CONEHEAD #4: "It was told to me by the crime scene when I was at my inspection, that initial inspection . . ."
>
> JACKSON: "So what you meant by 'that's what was told to me' is that the crime scene talked to you?"
>
> CONEHEAD #4: "Yes."
>
> JACKSON: "Did the crime scene say anything else?"
>
> CONEHEAD #4: "I don't know what you want me to say."

To repeat, this is the MSP expert. He has an associate's degree from a community college in "administration of justice."

The defense's accident-reconstruction experts, who have yet to testify, were first hired by the FBI.

The witnesses from the FBI may turn out to be boring. But I doubt the jurors will be openly laughing at them the way they were at Conehead #4 yesterday.

He first stumbled onto the witness stand late Friday afternoon. He quickly made an impression on the jury when he forgot how long he'd been on the job.

"Eight and a half years," he began. "I mean, twelve and a half years, sorry."

Yes, you are. Sorry, that is.

It's really bad right now for the MSP. They're no longer called "troopers." Their new nickname is "Proctors," as in, "I saw some Proctors heading east going fast on the Pike."

Until last week, the *Boston Globe* had been defending the proctors' sleazy behavior. One of their blow-in columnists even suggested last Sunday that only racists supported Karen Read. But then, that's the *Globe*.

The *Globe*'s motto is and always has been, "Comfort the comfortable and afflict the afflicted."

Of course, if Karen Read were a lesbian, or black, or both, the *Globe* would have long ago turned her into Emmett Till, or Rosa Parks, or both.

Yesterday, though, after Michael Proctor was forced to read his own X-rated text messages on live TV, the *Globe* was trying to dig itself out from under yet another editorial catastrophe.

The headline on their about-face, 180-degree-turn editorial was, "Foul-Mouthed, Sexist Trooper Puts the Spotlight on State Police."

Well, better late than never, I guess. Too bad nobody at the *Globe* had even bothered to follow the Karen Read case, because they would have known that Proctor's texts were already on the record, months ago.

Like most people, as soon as I saw how moronic Paul was, I'd immediately assumed he must be a legacy. MSP is full of these below-average losers, like the guy who was arrested in Westfield after he pushed his wife's head into an unflushed toilet. As a reward, in 2020, he was assigned to fire the combat veteran–Sunday school teacher who refused to get the Fauci jab. His uncle was a captain, so the domestic abuser was golden.

How Proctor is it?

The MSP is a lot like the Archdiocese of Boston used to be. Just ask Father Geoghan. That pederast priest's uncle was a monsignor. He always got his nephew out of every jam, until he no longer could.

Sunday afternoon I emailed the state cop flacks, asking them if Conehead #4 was related to Trooper David Paul, who made $306,000 last year. I didn't expect a response, but within hours I had one.

Shockingly, the answer was no, Paul the Lesser and Paul the Least are not related.

The MSP also denied rumors on social media that Trooper Proctor, also known as Conehead #2, was once on Maura Healey's security detail.

That story didn't seem very likely, for any number of reasons, but the state cops hadn't bothered to respond to my earlier inquiries.

So the MSP seems to be trying to do at least a bit better with the civilians.

But then Conehead #4 returned to the witness stand yesterday.

Here he is on his "accident reconstruction," such as it was:

"When you look at the roadway I think it's spun around kinda clockwise. It's possibility that the curb is there and any blunt force object on the ground as the ground is pretty blunt."

So the blunt force object could have been the ground because the ground is pretty blunt? May we quote you on that, Mr. Conehead #4?

Jackson asked him at another point how John O'Keefe's cell phone happened to land under his body? Isn't it natural, if you're hit by a 6,000-pound vehicle, to not be able to keep control of whatever you're holding in your hand?

In Conehead #4's theory, as O'Keefe was spinning through the air, he retained both his cell phone and his cocktail glass in his hand. Mr. Conehead #4, Jackson asked, how did that happen?

"It just did."

"Somehow," Jackson said, "as he landed he 'tucked' the cell phone under his body?"

"It just did," Conehead #4 replied. "That's the evidence at the scene. I didn't put the evidence there so—"

"Well," said Jackson, taking advantage of the obvious opening, "YOU didn't—"

It's safe to say that Conehead #4 will never testify in court again. Nor will Trooper Proctor nor Sgt. Bukhenik—Coneheads #2 and #3. (Bukhenik did, and it was disastrous, as you will see later.)

One more very ethical state trooper is scheduled as a prosecution witness, Nicholas Guarino. He made $190,000 last year. I wonder if Guarino is another Lex Luthor lookalike. (He wasn't, but he did blurt out, "Just kill me!" into an open mike. How Proctor is that?)

It's the Conehead Farewell Tour of 2024, coming soon to a state courtroom near you, to be followed in short order by a curtain call in front of the feds.

It's just Proctors being Proctors.

## "Seventeen Years of College Down the Drain"

*May 21, 2025*

In the movie *Animal House*, John Belushi's character Bluto had only gone to Faber College for seven years.

Turns out, Bluto was a world-class scholar compared to the prosecution's latest "expert" witness in the Karen Read murder trial in Dedham.

Meet Shanon Burgess, who although he's claimed on multiple occasions to have a bachelor's degree, doesn't have anything close to a BS, although he's currently full of it. BS, that is.

Under cross-examination Monday from defense attorney Robert Alessi, Burgess was grilled about his fabricated academic credentials.

> ALESSI [on Monday]: "If I do the math correctly, sir, you have been pursuing a bachelor of science degree for seventeen years. Correct?"
>
> BURGESS [in his Alabama cracker accent]: "Thass correct."
>
> ALESSI: "And you have not obtained it as you sit here today?"
>
> BURGESS: "Thass correct."
>
> ALESSI: "And yet there are various documents that we've seen that state that you obtained the bachelor of science, correct?"
>
> BURGESS. "Again, with errors or misinterpretations."

Shanon Burgess, Trooper Paul's replacement at the 2025 trial.

Whose errors? Whose misinterpretations?

This preposterous peckerwood was brought in to try to clean up after some of the disastrous testimony of earlier prosecution witnesses. Burgess claims to be an "expert" on technical matters.

The problem is that the prosecution's conflicting technical narratives are providing reasonable doubt about whether Karen Read actually struck her boyfriend with her car. The dilemma, the prosecution contends, is "clock drift."

But once Shanon began stammering in his backwoods drawl, it became clear the prosecution's problem was "truth drift."

He works for a company called Aperture, which rhymes with *departure*, which will probably be Burgess's next career move with the company.

The only question is, Hos long until he's fired?

To a battle of wits, Shanon comes unarmed. As embarrassing as his sworn testimony about his college career was Monday, Burgess doubled down on redirect. He was being questioned by Mob attorney Hank Brennan, now serving as "special prosecutor" for corrupt DA Meatball Morrissey.

Brennan asked him why he had claimed on his most recent résumés that he was still seeking a bachelor's degree.

"Because I am currently pursuing a bachelor's degree," he repeated.

In this trial, he was filling the technical role played in the first trial by Trooper Joseph Paul, also known as Conehead #4. He was the guy who claimed, "The crime scene spoke to me."

Paul was painfully stupid. But now Shanon Burgess makes him look like Albert Einstein. And with his traditional MSP chrome-dome look, Paul cut a slightly less ridiculous figure than the follically challenged redneck.

He purports to be an expert. But his only post–high school diploma is an associate's degree from world-renowned Wallace State Community College of Hanceville, Alabama, formerly known as the George Corley Wallace Trade School of Cullman County.

Bet it's a great school if you want to learn how to butcher hogs. Or, in Burgess's case, butcher "expert" testimony.

He confused *bytes* and *bits*, which is something any expert would know, or so you would think.

He repeatedly said he extracted data from the cell phone of "Mrs. Read." That would be Karen Read's mother because Karen is not married.

On cross-examination, he told Alessi how important it was to synchronize timelines on cell phones "down to the second."

Then Alessi pointed out that every date on his "expert" report was off by twenty-four hours. He had listed the wrong date, January 30 instead of January 29.

In other words, this hillbilly wasn't off by one or two seconds, he was off by a whole day—86,400 seconds.

"Parlance!" Burgess howled as his incompetence was shown.

Parlance? He knows what that word means, but when he was asked the previous day by Alessi if he knew the definition of the word *mendacity*, he drew a blank.

As a graduate of the George Corley Wallace Trade School of Cullman County, I'm guessing there are a lot of other words Burgess doesn't know the meaning of.

Speaking of mendacity, it is Burgess's contention that he volunteered his new report, mid-trial, to Brennan, totally unsolicited by Whitey Bulger's longtime mouthpiece.

So Alessi handed his cover letter to Brennan, which begins: "Dear Mr. Brennan, pursuant to your request I have completed an additional analysis . . ."

> ALESSI: "This wasn't done on your own initiative. You put it in writing that you did it at the request of Mr. Brennan. Which is it?"
>
> BURGESS: "Uh, so that was on mah own initiative. This is a, uh, a holdover, so a copy-and-paste from mah original ree-port."

Brennan has had this problem with witnesses in earlier trials. I've told you about how he used a drunk ex-FBI agent named Robert Fitzpatrick in the Whitey Bulger trial. That G-man lied himself into a six-count perjury indictment.

Obviously, Brennan is not real good at doing witness background checks.

Burgess's veracity problems didn't rise to the perjury level—he's just a fork-tongued cracker clown. But Brennan did try to dig him out from under his torrent of résumé lies.

Brennan tried to point out all the successful Americans without college degrees: Oprah Winfrey (who does have one), Steve Jobs, Bill Gates, etc.

Of course, none of them ever felt the need to lie for decades about their academic credentials, nor do, or did, they hold themselves out to be technical "experts."

Brennan asked Burgess about when one of his fraudulent résumés had been written.

"It would have been mebbe tin years ago."

He asked who had filled out the phony-baloney résumé.

"I don't particularly remember filling it out, but obviously I did."

Well, that must have certainly helped rehabilitate your witness with the jury, Hank.

And now Burgess slinks back in humiliation to his new home in Texas. Today in court he was wearing the same suit and tie he had on

Monday. Obviously Hank hadn't given him a heads-up on the multiday beating everyone else knew was coming his way from Karen Read's defense team.

How can Burgess ever testify as an "expert" again, on anything?

In the movie *Animal House*, when Bluto is on the ropes at Faber, he whines, "Seven years of college down the drain!"

When Burgess gets his Aperture departure, he'll have his own sad song to sing:

"Seventeen years of college down the drain!"

## Welcher by Name, Welcher by Nature

*May 28, 2025*

As a taxpayer of Norfolk County, I am hereby demanding a refund of my property taxes from District Attorney Michael "Meatball" Morrissey.

Even if my neighbors and I were in favor of framing an innocent woman for a murder she didn't commit, which we are not, I would argue that we are being overcharged.

Massively overcharged.

In the Karen Read trial in Dedham, an "expert" witness testified that his lackluster company has been paid about $400,000 for their, uh, analysis of the murder of John O'Keefe.

Also, Norfolk County will be charged for the Lexus SUV these "experts" bought to do a Blippi-like reconstruction of the accident, which will probably set us back another $80,000. The new car was used in the clownish stunt that involved the "expert" splashing himself with enough blue paint to make himself look like a Smurf.

But there's more money being squandered. Don't forget the "special prosecutor," Mob mouthpiece Hank Brennan, who is billing $566,000 for his very special services.

And then there are the other two "special counsels" involved in a different, related railroading—that of Aidan "Turtleboy" Kearney, who has broken most of the stories about this law enforcement scandal. One of them is a retired judge who is already collecting two pensions from us, to the tune of $203,000 a year.

Now, I understand that the Norfolk County District Attorney's Office is actually a line item in the state budget. But still, this national embarrassment of a trial still falls upon the residents of the benighted twenty-eight communities of Norfolk County.

As a taxpayer (if no longer a voter) in Norfolk County, I think I speak for all the non-hacks in the shire when I say that we do not object to spending whatever it takes to put the bad guys away.

What we do object to is the exorbitant cost of framing innocent parties.

I know the district attorney's office is trying to make cutbacks here and there, to provide more funds for their job one, which is frame-ups. For instance, exactly a year before John O'Keefe's death in Canton, a pregnant twenty-three-year-old woman was murdered, allegedly by her pedophile cop boyfriend from Stoughton, the town next door (see Chapter 13).

To reduce expenses, Meatball's crack sleuths immediately ruled that obvious murder was a suicide because . . . professional courtesy.

Cops don't arrest cops, even murdering cops. Not in Norfolk County anyway. They don't even investigate cops. Remember when disgraced ex-trooper Michael Proctor was asked by one of his high school buddies if the guy whose front lawn BPD Officer John O'Keefe's body was found on would get jammed up in the investigation?

"Nope," said the crooked, gift-soliciting conehead clown, "homeowner is a Boston cop."

The lesson here seems to be, as expensive as it is to convict a guilty party, it costs even more to frame somebody for a crime they didn't commit.

As Meatball Morrissey noted in an email on October 3 when he hired Aperture: "This is something we're gonna have to pay for out of forfeiture. I know it's going to be expensive."

That was an understatement. So far they've been paid almost a half-million to re-create the fatal accident—or, the fantasy of what the fatal accident could have been, had Karen Read in fact struck John O'Keefe, which she didn't.

The slogan on Aperture's home page is "We exist to shine a light on truth."

Surely they meant to say, "We exist to put a shine on a sneaker."

And not a very good shine either. Last week, Aperture had a prevaricating peckerwood witness named Shanon Burgess disemboweled by Karen Read's attorneys.

Now that extra from *Deliverance* has been replaced by someone named Judson Welcher. He gets $750 an hour—three times Hank Brennan's rate. When Welcher flew from California to Boston, he charged for four hours' time, at $750 an hour.

Three thousand bucks, just to fly in to make a fool of himself on the witness stand.

Welcher by name, Welcher by nature.

How much of a disaster was Welcher on Wednesday? The bumbling judge, Beverly Cannone, got confused and called him "Dr. Burgess" at one point. That is not a compliment.

Welcher was very polite when being questioned on direct by Whitey Bulger's lawyer, Hank Brennan.

Maybe it's because they have so much in common—Welcher's pocketing that $400,000 from the taxpayers, and Brennan's grabbing $566,000.

Welcher and Brennan are laughing all the way to the bank, as Liberace used to say. Laughing as they try to put Karen Read in prison for the rest of her life.

Welcher said he doesn't "have a dog in the fight." But he admitted that his presentation changes from day to day, hour to hour actually, depending on what Brennan orders him to do.

He says weird things, repeating words like "totality" over and over again. He puts air quotes around random statements, like "received an assignment."

On Tuesday he informed the jury, "You know, modern cars have what's called a VIN number."

Modern cars? VIN numbers have been around since at least 1954.

Interestingly, the first payoff to Aperture from Meatball Morrissey came last year. They got the big payoff last month, almost like, well, pay to play.

When he hired "Dr." Welcher, Meatball Morrissey emailed prosecutor Adam Lally what he was hoping for.

"(Let's) see whether he can provide an opinion that might help us out with the case."

Sorry, Meatball, another disappointment. It was more great entertainment on TV, but it was very, very expensive for the taxpayers.

I want my money back.

# Something's Afoot in the Karen Read Case

*May 8, 2025*

Back in 1971, in a courtroom scene from his movie *Bananas*, Woody Allen perfectly summed up what would be going on fifty-four years later in this ongoing second Karen Read murder trial.

"This trial is a travesty," Allen's character yelled at the judge. "It is a travesty of a mockery of a sham of a mockery of two mockeries of a sham. I move for a mistrial!"

C'mon down, MSP Sgt. Yuriy Bukhenik, chief of the elite Rubber Ducky Detail in Norfolk County, and also a member of the district attorney's so-called homicide unit.

Bukhenik is a naturalized US citizen from Ukraine, where he lived until he was nine. His grasp of his second (or third) language, English, tends to fail him under pressure. He also can't do simple math. Last year he forfeited five days of vacation for his unspeakable behavior in this very same murder investigation.

In short, Bukhenik is a knucklehead's knucklehead. But he has figured out what he has to do to keep his phony-baloney job that pays $211,080, which is a lot more than he ever made in his other jobs with the Veterans Administration police and then the Attleboro Police.

His boss is the bloated district attorney Meatball Morrissey, and Bukhenik has eight hundred connections to Meatball—all of which have George Washington's portrait on them.

You scratch Meatball's back, he scratches yours.

In 2021, Bukhenik's homicide unit deduced that, despite overwhelming evidence to the contrary, a twenty-three-year-old pregnant woman, Sandra Birchmore, had committed suicide in Canton. The feds thought otherwise. They arrested Matthew Farwell, Bukhenik's fellow cop and Stoughton High graduate. Farwell, no longer employed by the Stoughton Police Department, is now in federal custody.

When Farwell was arrested, Meatball Morrissey was stunned. He saw him on TV being lugged off his garbage truck in Revere by the feds, and immediately emailed his minions in shock:

"Is there any truth to this?"

Apparently, Meatball still believes what his "detectives" tell him. Nobody else does.

But Bukhenik is a crack sleuth. He didn't rest on the laurels of his suicide finding in the alleged murder of the pregnant woman by his fellow cop and neighbor from Stoughton High. He wasn't baffled. He knew what had happened to John O'Keefe, the Boston cop.

"At dat point," he stammered, "our theory has had evolved to a vehicle strike and I was suspectin' dat he was hit out of his shoes."

His shoes? Oddly, O'Keefe's sneakers became another bone of contention Thursday, when at one point Bukhenik introduced the wrong shoes into evidence. To suspicious minds, it might appear that something was . . . afoot. Were the cops . . . sneaking around?

Sgt. Yuriuy Bukhenik: Mixing up the shoes.

To paraphrase O.J. Simpson's lawyer, "If the shoe ain't right, the case ain't airtight."

Bukhenik and his fellow "detectives" from the district attorney's office had to step into the murder probe because of the fact that a bunch of local cops were involved in one way or another in the murder of the Boston cop O'Keefe.

I'll let Bukhenik give you the ESL explanation of why the Canton Police Department gumshoes checked out.

"We had learned that there was a loose familiarial (sic) connection through town channels the address and the possibility of a Canton police officer or detective out of overwhelming precaution of impropriety not that there was one decided to step away from any interview investigation assistance with us."

By the way, he did say "familiarial."

The Canton Police Department wasn't worried about being removed from the frame-up, er investigation. Because if the MSP's homicide unit could allegedly cover up the Sandra Birchmore murder during a snowstorm, it could just as easily broom the O'Keefe murder in a blizzard exactly one year later.

Bukhenik knew what he had to do.

"I would have to pick up the slack," he said in his garbled English. "I'm a team player. I always want to assist in any which way I can to make others' life easier."

It's important to get to the scene of the crime as soon as possible.

"Timing is essential," he explained to the jury. "We have to make sure we get to any and every location that could possibly have evidence and prevent that evidence from being destroyed, altered, or concealed."

For the record, John O'Keefe was murdered on January 29. Bukhenik made his first visit to the crime scene, 34 Fairview, on February 3.

Many questions were left unasked on direct examination. Bukhenik mentioned that he lives "in the real world." I beg to differ.

"Sgt. Bukhenik," he could have been asked, "in the real world, don't you think most cops really try to find out the identities of the real murderers, even if they're your pals? Don't you think most cops maintain a chain of custody, even with the shoes of the murder victims . . ."

Bukhenik seems much more comfortable on the Rubber Ducky Detail. Last July, he tracked down a young mother of two, who was suspected of dropping a rubber ducky toy on a bench in front of a restaurant owned by one of the McAlberts, a jailbird selectman named Chris Albert.

On the bottom of the rubber ducky was scrawled: "Free Karen Read."

This will not stand—not in Norfolk County! Not when Yuriy Bukhenik is on the beat.

He took off in his cruiser and tracked her down, and began yelling at the woman in front of her children: "I just wanna get it from you where the ducks come from . . . Where did you get these little ducks… You see how that looks?"

The young mother couldn't believe some guy was giving the third degree in pidgin English. What did rubber duckies have to do with these unsolved murders in Canton that this hulking moron was supposed to be investigating?

He answered her question: "We investigate homicides and this being relative to the homicide investigation . . . Did you purchase these ducks, uh, uh, for a certain reason? Why—what's the reason you purchased these tiny little ducks?"

That's Yuriy Bukhenik. He's dumber than a box of rocks, but one thing he's figured out: It's better being in Norfolk County and getting paid big money for doing nothing than it is going back to his own country and fighting the Russians.

Like Woody Allen, I move for a mistrial!

## Get Karen Read "Detective" a Good Translator

*May 10, 2025*

Is it too late to find a translator for MSP Sgt. Yuriy Bukhenik before he resumes his testimony in the Karen Read murder trial Monday?

On Friday, the thuggish $211,080-a-year MSP "detective" finally revealed the reason for his abysmal performance, both on the witness stand and as a crack sleuth on the MSP's elite Rubber Ducky Detail.

Under oath, the Ukrainian drifter admitted that English is not his second, but his third language. Bukhenik hails from the old Soviet Union, lived there until the age of nine. Apparently his assimilation into civilized society has been somewhat less than complete.

You can take the boy out of the USSR, but you can't take the USSR out of the boy.

Am I right, Comrade Bukhenik?

The reformed Red made this confession Friday morning. In his customary pidgin English, he had been telling defense attorney Alan Jackson about his "theories" of the Read persecution, er prosecution.

Bukhenik had mentioned his "theories" at least twice, so Jackson didn't think it was a stretch to ask Bukhenik a simple question:

"You know what the word *theory* means?"

To which Yuriy replied: "I'm sorry, English is like a third language for me. So if you can bring up the *Webster's Dictionary* I can read it out."

Jackson did a double take.

"You want me to pull up *Webster's Dictionary* to define a word you used in an answer about forty seconds ago? 'We were working off a theory.' Quote unquote. You said it, not me!"

For the record, here is a transcript of how Comrade Bukhenik had used the word in his testimony, less than a minute before his tenuous grasp of the English language failed him yet again.

All dialogue guaranteed verbatim: "Utilizin' dat information wit' de evidence at dat point dat we had was a broken cocktail glass so the theory would be why is the cocktail glass broken? Because it came into contact wit' da victim—"

So far it's been a catastrophic cross-examination for Bukhenik. And Jackson hasn't even started asking him yet about the worst miscarriages of justice in the Commonwealth's ongoing frame-up.

But someone must serve as the fall guy for DA Meatball Morrissey's calamitous overreach. Bukhenik drew the short straw this time, following in the footsteps of his ex-partner, Trooper Michael Proctor.

After the first trial, Proctor was fired from MSP. For his own despicable deeds with Proctor, so far Bukhenik has only forfeited five vacation days. Perhaps playing the role of patsy this time around is part of the deal for him to keep his six-figure job.

Bukhenik's difficulties with the English language may explain at least in part MSP's staggering incompetence. Do you remember how in the first trial, yet another low-IQ statie, one Joseph Paul, explained how he reached his deductions about who did what to whom.

"It was told to me by the crime scene," Paul testified, haltingly.

I mention this only because Bukhenik had a very similar experience as Paul at the crime scene, or so he testified on Friday.

It's all part of what Jackson calls the "paranormal" goings on in Canton—inexplicable, impossible deletions of incriminating Google searches, eerie butt-dials from cell phones that aren't in anybody's possession, etc.

On Friday, Bukhenik was trying to explain, once again, "de evidence."

"I wasn't assumin' anything," he told Jackson. "De evidence was speakin' to us."

De evidence was speakin' to him? Of course it was! It's Norfolk County. If only Jackson had asked Bukhenik the obvious follow-up question: "Trooper, what language was the evidence speaking to you in at 34 Fairview? Your first, second, or third language?"

Maybe when he goes to any future crime scenes, Bukhenik should take with him a translator app on his phone. That way the app could convert the deductions of "de evidence" into Ukrainian, or Russian, or both.

A translator app would also come in handy when he's back on the MSP's Rubber Ducky Detail. He loves speeding around Norfolk County like Sheriff Buford T. Justice, jumping ugly with housewives who've had the temerity to leave a tiny rubber ducky on a public bench in Canton or posting Free Karen Read messages on social media.

Yuriy will go full KGB or Stasi on some suburban mom, especially when he's packing a sidearm on his fifty-inch waist. Once last summer, he tracked down a woman who'd had the temerity to make a Facebook comment about the Karen Read trial.

"I was cooking a pork chop," she later told me, when Bukhenik began banging on her front door. As she came out of the kitchen,

Bukhenik began channeling his inner Lavrentiy Beria, fantasizing himself a member of Stalin's secret police as he gave her the third degree.

The woman, who was born in America, not the USSR, was having none of Bukhenik's Warsaw Pact bullying. She chased the knuckle-dragging moron back to his taxpayer-funded cruiser, yelling words that perhaps he could not comprehend.

"You're going to jail!" she screamed at the Slavic slob.

If only he'd had that translation app on his cell phone, maybe Bukhenik could have listened to her admonitions in words more understandable for a native-born Communist: "You're going to the gulag!"

One final caveat for Yuriy "Red" Bukhenik: Comrade, you are a naturalized US citizen. You are here at our sufferance. If you commit any one of a certain number of crimes (think perjury), you can be stripped of your US citizenship and deported back to the Eastern Front.

Do you understand? Or as your countrymen would say: "Ty rozumiyesh?"

Consider that before you're tempted to, uh, embellish your sworn testimony on Monday. You know, about issues like the inverted video at the Canton Police Department that you . . . misidentified . . . at the first trial.

Beware, Bukhenik. You could end up in a trench on the front lines, cannon fodder for Zelensky.

Before you speak, heed these words, which I'm sure you will understand better if I put it in your native tongue: "Ty mayesh pravo movchaty." You have the right to remain silent . . .

## From Semper Fi to Semper Lie

*May 13, 2025*

Sgt. Yuriy Bukhenik became a US Marine after fleeing his Communist homeland, and the motto of the USMC is "Semper Fidelis."

Semper Fi—not Semper Lie.

But Monday, as his catastrophic cross-examination in the second Karen Read murder trial continued, Bukhenik did not appear to be especially truthful, to put it mildly.

The $211,080-a-year ex-Red was shown the text messages sent to him and some American-born crooked state troopers by since-fired disgraced Trooper Michael Proctor. In one message the dim-bulb Proctor bragged that he was going through the cell phone of Karen Read, whom he described as "retarded."

He leeringly texted to his knuckle-dragging buddies that he had found "no nudes so far."

Alan Jackson, the defense attorney asked Bukhenik: 'What do you think he was looking for when he wrote that phrase?"

"I don't know what he was looking for." Semper lie.

Jackson then asked, "What would be a responsible explanation of what he was looking for when he wrote 'no nudes so far'?"

"I don't know what he was looking for." Semper lie.

"You certainly did nothing, you took no action to stop him, from potentially looking for naked pictures of my client?"

"That's correct." Bukhenik told the truth! For once.

Then Jackson asked him about his statement on Friday under oath that Michael Proctor had conducted his investigation with "integrity and honor." Proctor's actions included the solicitation of a, er gift, from the McAlberts after his arrest of the innocent woman Karen Read. He cautioned them to make sure they sent the "gift" to his wife rather than himself.

Like Sgt. Schultz, Bukhenik claimed he knew nothing about the text. That's his story and he's sticking to it.

"Do you stand by your statement that Michael Proctor conducted this investigation with integrity?"

"Yes I do." Semper lie.

"Did you think that (no nudes so far) text was appropriate?"

"I don't remember reading that text." Semper lie.

Bukhenik was Proctor's supervisor. He had to write his quarterly evaluations. Jackson read back to him his own words, his overall evaluation of the gift-seeking, drunk-driving, misogynistic Proctor.

This is Proctor, in Bukhenik's own words: "(He) displays professional demeanor, composure, dignity, and respect during the performance of his duties and especially during his interactions with the public. This is seen during interviews with witnesses, suspects, as well as with victims and their families."

Bukhenik wrote this after Proctor described Karen Read as "retarded" and with "no ass"—among other slurs—in text discussions with the sergeant and his other buddies. And after he sought out that "gift" in return for arresting the innocent woman.

Rating: Four stars out of five.

Jackson finished reading and asked Bukhenik: "Was that statement in your evaluation true or false?"

Bukhenik: "It was true."

Bukhenik admitted Friday that his grasp of the English language often fails him. He grew up in the old Soviet Union, so English is his third language. That's what he said, under oath. It's his fallback, whenever he really gets jammed up on the witness stand by Jackson.

"You knew Michael Proctor's proclivities," Jackson asked him after reading the first evaluation. "Obviously. He told them to you."

Bukhenik interrupted.

"Da term, 'proclivities,'" he said. "What does dat mean?"

So then Jackson continued reading the Proctor evaluation. And remember what Jackson said in his opening statement to the jury: "Do you know how much it takes to get fired from the State Police?"

There are dozens of retired state cops who've committed every sort of imaginable crime, and they're relaxing in Florida with six-figure pensions, even if they did a month or two in prison for, say, embezzlement of federal funds while assigned to the now-disbanded Troop E.

Nobody on Troop E ever got fired, but Proctor did. Yet this is what his superior, a naturalized US citizen named Bukhenik, wrote about him: "Trooper Proctor has had a high-profile caseload with a lot of pressure from external sources from the first day of the investigation. He handled himself in all the cases with utmost professionalism and competence. He is able to investigate his cases thoroughly and with strict integrity."

Rating: five stars out of five.

"'With strict integrity,'" Jackson repeated. "Did it show 'strict integrity' when he called Miss Read 'retarded'?"

"I believe," Bukhenik said, "that as a US citizen he has the right to comment. That's his First Amendment right. We uphold the Constitution . . . He might have been voicing his frustration."

About what? Did he not get his, you know, "gift" from the McAlberts for railroading Karen Read?

Remember, Bukhenik's duties at the Norfolk County District Attorney's Office included running the elite Rubber Ducky Detail. If anyone in the county made any remarks that Kamala Harris delegate Meatball Morrissey considered an affront to him, Bukhenik would be dispatched to try to intimidate them.

But now, he's all into the First Amendment. Freedom of speech.

Semper Fi? More like Semper Lie.

Jackson returned to how Bukhenik, tormentor of pro–Karen Read women across the county, "liked" the message that his boy Michael Proctor was searching her phone for nudes.

"The fact is, sergeant, he put that in writing and you liked it, correct?"

"I acknowledged the text message," Bukhenik testified. "I never saw the vile term."

Semper Lie.

## Trooper Proctor, MIA

*June 7, 2025*

Where the hell is Trooper Michael Proctor, the lead cop in the Karen Read murder investigation?

Is the knucklehead cop still searching for nude photos of Read on her cell phone—as he leeringly told his fellow semiliterate high-school buddies from Can-UHN?

Proctor is the under-investigation cop who isn't there at the trial in Dedham. His name comes up about once every thirty seconds. But Proctor himself is MIA, and apparently none of the parties are allowed to mention his whereabouts.

Did he spend yesterday at a disciplinary hearing at MSP headquarters in Framingham? The jury hasn't been told that he's under investigation by the MSP's Internal Affairs unit because . . . hackerama.

Yesterday, Read's defense lawyer Alan Jackson finally got a chance to cross-examine Sgt. Bukhenik. But Jackson's mind was on a different bent trooper.

> JACKSON: "Trooper Proctor, you were notified—"
> BUKHENIK: "I am not Trooper Proctor."
> JACKSON: "I'm sorry. No you're not. Uh, Sgt. Buke-nik—"
> BUKHENIK: "Sgt. Bu-ken-ik."
> JACKSON: "How is it—?"
> BUKHENIK: "Bu-ken-ik."
> JACKSON: "Bu-ken-ik? Is that better?"
> BUKHENIK: "Yes. That's better. Thank you."

Actually, it wasn't much better. Bukhenik is on the spot. He can't answer like an honest man would because, well, you know.

The prosecution has videotape, apparently with multiple jump cuts, from the Canton Police Department garage where Read's vehicle was stored after O'Keefe's death. The "evidence" against Read, such as it is, involves pieces of a broken taillight—even though the cop from Dighton, who originally saw the SUV, said the taillight was intact. Yet all the "evidence," some of which didn't appear until weeks later, came from the vehicle that the cops claim Read drove to kill her BPD boyfriend.

So Jackson stopped the CPD garage video at the point when someone in a black hat (appropriately enough) is lurking around the taillight.

Guess who was wearing a black hat? The aforementioned Proctor. Jackson asked the sergeant if he could identify the black hat as Michael Proctor.

"I can't," Proctor, er Bukhenik began, "I don't want to be locked into a statement where later on, you show me it's somebody else, magically. I can't testify to that."

Magically? You mean, like by producing some real evidence, as opposed to concocting it out of thin air to frame somebody?

You know what would really be magical? The MSP doing something right, or telling the truth.

The crime scene in this case was the lawn outside a house at 34 Fairview Road. It was owned by another BPD officer.

Jackson asked Proctor-Bukhenik, did the state cops "secure" the inside of the other cop's house at 34 Fairview?

"We did not secure the home."

Did you secure the outside of the home?

"I did not, no."

But he said the staties did arrive for an on-scene search on the day of O'Keefe's death, January 29, 2022. The "search" by those crack Keystone Kops began at 5:41 p.m. Sunset that day was at 4:55 p.m.

"I was not present," Bukhenik said.

But the cops found a lot of "fragments" of taillight in the days ahead. Usually when something breaks, whatever it is, you find the biggest pieces first, then the smaller ones.

But at 34 Fairview Road, as the days went by, they found ever larger pieces of taillight. Very, very important evidence, the prosecutors have said. They made a really big score on February 10. They found six pieces of broken taillight.

It was such important evidence that none of these clownish hack cops bothered to even log the evidence in until . . . March 14.

> JACKSON: "There is no log, is there?"
>
> BUKHENIK: "I do not know."

Even though the state cops never went inside 34 Fairview, or to the police station, they did visit the home of Jennifer McCabe, a menopausal housewife with bad teeth whose phone records indicate that at 2:27 a.m. she googled: "Hos (sic) long to die in cold?"

Hey, that's the one the troopers needed to talk to. Jen McCabe, star of *Real Housewives of Canton*.

Even at the absolute top of his game, Bukhenik presents as someone with the IQ of a soft-boiled egg. That's why he wears cuff links. Cool guys wear cuff links.

But when he's questioned by a fellow payroll patriot like prosecutor Adam Lally, he can at least speak in complete, if incomprehensible sentences, as he did on Wednesday when talking about his distance from defendant Karen Read's parents' house in Dighton.

"She was sittin' on the couch. I don't recall if there was a coffee table, but if there was a coffee table, we would standing on the opposite side of that coffee table if there was one present I do not remember if there was one present."

But when he gets flustered, his English fails him. He goes all *demsdese-dose*. Yesterday, he was asked about the incredible coincidence of running into the chief of police in Canton, another townie Barney Fife named Ken Berkowitz, at the crime scene.

Bukhenik said he drove by the house every morning in case more taillight fragments appeared. He did this, he said, "on da way to day office just to see if any more items would reveal demselves."

One morning he drove by and guess who he also saw prospecting that claim at 34 Fairview? Chief Berkowitz. Considering that the Canton Police Department had been removed from the probe because of its, uh, conflicts, wasn't the chief's lurking at the scene a little suspicious?

"I did not find it suspicious at all," Bukhenik said. "He's da chief of da police in da where he works and drivin' down the street, I mean that's not suspicious."

Unlike Inspector Clouseau, Inspector Bukhenik suspects no one. He will leave no stone unturned, except the one the guilty party is hiding under.

But where is Trooper Proctor? Why isn't he testifying in this kangaroo court? After a half day yesterday, Jackson told reporters he will be testifying. My first question would be, Did you ever find those nude photos of Karen Read?

No court today, because it's Friday. It's the hackerama.

## Bulger, Read, Birchmore Befuddlement on Display in Meatball's Case

*May 14, 2025*

Bad cops all look alike.

That's the lesson from Hammered Hank Brennan's very telling confusion late Monday, when he mixed up incompetent state trooper Nicholas Guarino with corrupt ex-FBI agent Nick Gianturco.

Trooper Nicholas Guarino with prosecutor Hank Brennan.

It happened late Monday afternoon. Brennan was trying to clean up the disastrous testimony of the moronic trooper Yuriy Bukhenik when he suddenly blurted out: "Are you familiar with the name Nick Gianturco?"

Bukhenik looked even more lost than usual. "Uh—"

"Guarino!" Brennan quickly said, correcting himself. "Sorry."

Don't tell us you're sorry, Hank. We know how sorry you are.

FBI agent Nick Gianturco.

But you can understand Brennan's befuddlement. Gianturco, Guarino. Once you've seen one bent badge, you've seen 'em all.

First you have Nick Gianturco, known to his paymaster and pal Whitey Bulger as "Doc." Bulger and his serial-killing partner Stevie

Flemmi gave Doc thousands in cash payoffs, according to Flemmi's testimony in multiple federal trials.

Doc Gianturco was so crooked that he was the master of ceremonies for the 1990 farewell dinner for John "Zip" Connolly, a Boston FBI agent who moonlighted as a hitman for the Mob.

Gianturco was so close to Whitey that in addition to the cash, Whitey once gave him a belt buckle from Alcatraz. Maybe it was a Christmas present. After all, Christmas is for cops and kids, as Whitey would say.

Doc succeeded Zip as director of security for Boston Edison. His brother Charlie was the first FBI agent Stevie Flemmi demanded to see when he was lugged in 1995. Then the G-men put Charlie in charge of the so-called worldwide manhunt for Whitey.

So you can understand why Hank Brennan had such a big man crush on Gianturco. Whitey must have told him what a manly man Doc Gianturco was.

Then there's Nick Guarino. He was the state cop in charge of investigating the texts between the pregnant twenty-three-year-old Sandra Birchmore and the cop from Bukhenik's hometown and high school, who is in jail, charged with murdering her in Canton in 2021.

The lovebirds exchanged 32,000 texts. Investigating their cell phones afterward, Trooper Guarino missed all 32,000 of the texts. He didn't find a single one.

DA Meatball Morrissey ruled the murder-by-cop a suicide. Professional courtesy.

You may ask yourself, what's the difference between cops taking payoffs from mass murderers or just being so incompetent that they let the killer walk free?

Interesting question, which Hank Brennan raised during the Whitey Bulger trial in 2013. He was cross-examining another of Whitey's corrupted FBI agents, John "Vino" Morris.

After Morris described himself on the witness stand as "compromised," Brennan asked him: "Is there a difference between *compromised* and *corrupt*, or did you mean the same thing when you said you were 'compromised'?"

"Same thing," Vino Morris said.

One problem with Brennan's representation in both the Bulger and the Read trials is that he doesn't prepare his witnesses very well. I've told you about Robert Fitzpatrick, his ex-FBI agent who was going to be his star witness in Bulger's defense.

In that same trial, Stevie Flemmi tried to explain the facts of life to Brennan on cross-examination.

For instance, he told him how to cover up a murder, which is something that Brennan really needs to have some understanding of, considering what really happened in the Karen Read case.

And who better to tell Brennan how to cover up a murder than Flemmi, who has admitted to having been involved in fifty to sixty of them (after a while, you lose count, I guess).

"When you commit a murder," Flemmi explained to the future persecutor of Karen Read, "you cover up on it, you don't admit it to people. I don't know if you're aware of that, you should be, you're an attorney . . . You don't know what's going on in the world. I'm giving you the real world."

The real world now is 34 Fairview Road, Canton.

Ironically, in 2013, Brennan bitterly blamed his idol Whitey's downfall on corrupt cops. Now he's defending corrupt cops. Oh sure, he's technically a "prosecutor," but he has no more chance of getting a murder conviction on Karen Read than he did of getting an acquittal for Whitey.

In his closing in federal court in Boston, Brennan complained to the jury about what the feds had just done to his witness, the soon-to-be-convicted-of-perjury FBI agent Fitzpatrick.

"They'll crush you," he said. "You saw what they did to Mr. Fitzpatrick. They bully him, they berate him, they crush him. That's what happens when you're not with them, you're either with them or you're against them."

Now, Brennan is one of "them." He's out to crush Karen Read—"the defendant," as he calls her at every opportunity he gets. Brennan bullies her, he berates her, he crushes her. And unlike Whitey, or even Fitzpatrick, Karen Read hasn't even done anything.

Anything for a buck, though, right Hank? You lose as a defense lawyer, you lose as a prosecutor. But the important thing is running up those billable hours, and the taxpayers pick up the tab as it runs into seven figures, combined.

Billable hours über alles.

Brennan's confusion over two terrible cops named Nick is just par for the course. He is not very smart, and he certainly doesn't work very hard. Look at his witnesses, all of them, in every trial.

The judge in the Whitey trial was Denise Casper. One day in the Bulger trial, Brennan was doing his usual piss-poor imitation of a lawyer.

"Objection!" he yelled. "Blah, blah, blah."

That's what he said. "Blah, blah, blah."

Fred Wyshak, the lead prosecutor, couldn't believe it.

"Was that even a legal argument?" he asked the judge. "I mean, did this guy even go to law school?"

"Mr. Wyshak," Judge Casper said, "that's enough."

Maybe, Judge, but it was a good question. And still is.

## Karen Read Jury Has Easy Out ... Reasonable Doubt!

*June 12, 2025*

The second Karen Read murder trial has basically come down to an IQ test.

She didn't kill her boyfriend, BPD Officer John O'Keefe. She didn't hit him with her SUV, period. So if Karen Read didn't strike him, obviously she couldn't have done it deliberately.

If there was no car accident, it was neither murder nor manslaughter. Not by Karen Read, anyway.

Not guilty.

The only way you can believe that Karen Read actually killed him is if you are either very stupid, very corrupt, or haven't been paying attention.

Of course defense attorney Alan Jackson won't say that to the jury this morning in his closing. But he doesn't need to. There are only two words that the jury needs to consider: *Reasonable doubt*.

That's not to say that the potbellied courthouse stooges of Norfolk County can't rig this case. They did it last year, after all. Just to cite one example, remember those verdict slips that had no box for the jurors to check off *Not Guilty*?

Rest assured that the hacks have been keeping close tabs on which jurors' facial expressions indicate that they aren't buying the persecution's kangaroo-court bait and switches.

Those jurors will be dismissed first thing this morning. They're all going to be alternates, count on it. Just the luck of the draw, the bouncing balls, and thanks for your services, suckers . . .

Karen Read's lawyers could object, but they know better. We're not in America, we're in Norfolk County.

Still, though, I think that this time, DA Meatball Morrissey's necktie party is not going to pan out for him.

Despite the claims of the preposterous Baghdad Bobs on TV (at least one of whom is pocketing a hack state judge's pension of $156,281 a year), the persecution produced no real evidence.

Other than those forty-six pieces of broken taillight—*wink wink, nudge nudge*.

So what if the cop who "found" most of them was busted for soliciting bribes, I mean gifts, from some of his fellow local townies.

This is not to say that you can't frame somebody for murder in Massachusetts. It's been done before, in Chelsea, by the FBI. Four innocent guys railroaded, two sent to death row. Two died in prison after thirty years. One of them wasn't even in the state when the murder was committed (see Chapter 21).

There was an even more recent murder frame-up in Norfolk County. The cops did it as a favor for Whitey Bulger, the serial killer who was represented at his own trial by Hank Brennan, the petulant fraud now trying to railroad Karen Read (see Chapter 22).

But now it seems even Hank Brennan, as rotten a human being as he is, knows that he's lost this one. You could see it Wednesday, with the last defense witness, Dr. Andrew Rentschler. Rentschler is a real scientist, originally hired by the FBI and offered as a witness to the prosecution, but they didn't want him.

They preferred to frame Karen Read. They needed a patsy, to protect their pals.

So DA Meatball Morrissey went out and hired his own "expert," a guy who's spent seventeen years trying to get a bachelor's degree, and lying about already having one. It cost the taxpayers $400,000, on top of Brennan's $566,000.

Brennan had nothing to shake Dr. Rentschler's testimony, so he started asking him about an earlier visit he'd made to Massachusetts, and what he'd had for lunch.

"I had a ham sandwich."

Brennan let that stunning fact sink in for a moment or two before zeroing in. This was his Perry Mason moment.

"When you sat at the table and ate, did you just eat your ham sandwich or did more go on?"

Did more go on? You know, like a soft drink or coffee? Or maybe potato chips—regular or barbecue? Did you order the ham on white, whole wheat, or rye?

"How long," Brennan continued, "were you at the table eating your ham sandwich?"

"How long's it take you to eat a ham sandwich?" the FBI witness replied. "Ten minutes?"

Brennan was having none of it.

"And after you finished your"—pause—"ham sandwich, and you told us you stood and in the corner, you got a ride back to the airport."

Well, there it is. Book him, Danno.

A few minutes later, Brennan announced that he'd changed his plans and wouldn't be calling any rebuttal witnesses. It was like Roberto Durán moaning, "No mas!" He was throwing in the towel.

Yesterday morning, Brennan couldn't even bring himself to handle the back-and-forth with the defense and the judges over the jury charges. Instead, he left it to his minion, Adam Lally, the chain-smoking sad sack prosecutor who handled the first miscarriage of justice last summer.

Lally makes $149,350 a year. He keeps his job the old-fashioned way. Since 2010, he's given cash to his boss Meatball Morrissey on sixteen separate occasions, for a total of $1,750.

Lally's job yesterday was to shut off any mentions of the vicious dog Chloe/Cora. The McAlberts' now-missing German shepherd figured significantly in testimony about the "animal bites" on the victim's arm that Brennan unconvincingly insists were made by those mysterious pieces of taillight.

Despite riding the pine all these weeks, Lally came off the bench in mid-season form. All dialogue guaranteed verbatim: "I would remind the court that there is absolutely no evidence, none, uh, not even a scintilla of evidence of a dog. There is no evidence of an absence of a dog. You have Ms. McCabe testifying that she didn't see it in the morning, which does not equate to there being an absence of a dog there."

May we quote you on that, Mr. Lally?

Please God, don't let the hackerama fix the jury again. After she's acquitted, we can all enjoy a celebratory dinner.

Ham sandwiches all around!

## Karen Read Case a Jihad Against Justice!

*June 18, 2025*

The lynch mob has been routed in Dedham. For once the hacks of Norfolk County did not get away from framing an innocent person.

And now it's time for retribution.

First, District Attorney Michael "Meatball" Morrissey must be defeated next year, should he dare run for reelection. How long will this obese, quadruple-chinned Kamala Harris delegate be allowed to continue perverting justice in Norfolk County?

Asking for Sandra Birchmore . . .

Meatball's got to go. After the verdict, I spoke to Bill Read, Karen's father, about what must be done to rid the county of the stench of Morrissey.

"We need to take back our government," he said.

So many despicable, dishonorable mountebanks who conspired together to frame an innocent woman.

Judge Auntie Bev Cannone deserves to be impeached, removed from office and stripped of her pension. Won't happen, of course, but a Norfolk County taxpayer can dream, can't he?

Hammered Hank Brennan, the sleazy Mob mouthpiece turned sleazy special persecutor, deserves to be shunned by every decent citizen, not to mention all the despicable criminals he's become fabulously wealthy representing (almost always unsuccessfully).

Meatball Morrissey's entire "detective" unit of MSP deserves to be sent packing, their offices fumigated and then sown with salt. Those bent badges should be exiled as far away as possible from the county they've both shamed and terrorized—to the Lee barracks.

I suggested that on the air yesterday and a western Mass listener texted back at me: "Keep your crooked cops down there! We have enough problems out here already."

For a while yesterday, it looked like the Norfolk County fix was in again. Around two o'clock, it was announced they had a verdict. Then they said they didn't have a verdict—even though they had delivered a signed verdict slip in an envelope.

Call it the "butt-dial verdict."

But whatever the Barney Fife Industrial Complex was conniving, the scheme quickly fell apart. The *not guiltys* started coming in and the crowds outside in the so-called buffer zone started cheering so loudly you could hear it in the courtroom.

Down on the street, everyone was wearing pink, and they were chanting, bringing back memories of some of the trial's top characters, even including the McAlberts' mysteriously vanished dog, Chloe.

"Where's Chloe?" they yelled.

And, "Lock up Jen! Lock up Jen!"

And of course, "Free Turtleboy!" referring to Aidan Kearney, the blogger who is collateral damage in Meatball's jihad against justice, doing two months in the Norfolk County lockup for... another frame job.

The hackerama, though, has learned nothing from their humiliation. Like the Bourbons, they forget nothing and learn nothing. So the McAlberts, on whose front lawn the body of Karen Read's boyfriend was found, immediately issued a press release.

"This prosecution was infected by lies and conspiracy theories spread by Karen Read, her defense team, and some in the media."

I read that statement to Turtleboy last night and he started laughing.

"Nice!" he said. "I got a shout-out!"

He's still looking at multiple counts of witness intimidation and God only knows what else. Meatball has hired two special prosecutors to railroad him, including one low-IQ retired judge who's grabbing not one, but two state pensions, worth $203,000 a year. Plus whatever he's pocketing from his fellow lifelong hack.

They have no shame, none of them, from Meatball on down. Michael Proctor is the disgraced, fired state trooper, who had the chutzpah to book an interview on fake news ABC last night, to claim that he's the one who was framed.

He was too dirty to be called as a witness even by Meatball, and now he goes on the sleazy network that just paid Donald Trump $15 million for defamation and fired Terry Moran.

That McAlbert statement denouncing the "lies," by the way, signed by a real cross-section of them—a witness who changed her story from one grand jury to another, another one who lied twice to the FBI in her first interview (including giving a false name), the woman who offered that "gift" to Proctor, a Canton cop who was suspended for getting so drunk with Proctor while on duty that he left his badge in the car, a Canton selectman who did six months for a hit-and-run manslaughter, and a Boston cop who destroyed his cell phone one day ahead of a preservation order from the court . . .

The McAlberts also said that they "may have more to say in the future."

Perhaps they're planning to write a book. Maybe they could call it, *If We Did It*.

Last night the Free Karen Read crowd was cruising Washington Street in Canton. They were crestfallen at the Waterfall, but the pink-clad supporters were honking their horns and waving pink pom-poms out the window.

They were planning watch parties for last night's Proctor interview. Fireballs all around!

This not-guilty verdict is devastating to law enforcement in Norfolk County. Three departments will now be disbanding their elite Rubber Ducky Details – the Canton and Stoughton PDs as well as the detective unit in DA Meatball Morrissey's office.

Think about it: The only thing they cared about after the murder of a BPD officer was pinning it "on the girl." But when citizens began protesting the lynching by dropping off rubber duckies, the law put out a county-wide dragnet to find out who was ordering them from Amazon.

It's the end of a golden age, of overtime if not justice. After the verdict, two of Meatball's local trooper thugs, Brian Tully and Yuriy Bukhenik, were seen lurking outside the courthouse.

Like Chloe the dog, Tully has already been "rehomed" out of the county. As for Bukhenik—have you ever visited the Cheshire barracks, Comrade?

Peru is quite scenic on the overnight shift, I'm told.

Next step: Get the kangaroo-court charges against Turtleboy dropped.

By then, it will be time for Meatball Morrissey's annual August fundraiser. You'll know a lot by who shows up for that Quincy circle-bleep. I hope somebody is outside taking pictures.

FBI, this means you.

## CHAPTER FOUR

# Calling All Canton Coneheads

Disgraced MSP Trooper Michael Proctor before his firing.

Canton selectman Jailbird Chris Albert.

Ex-BPD Sgt. Brian Albert, the Dark Conehead, trying to stare down Karen Read.

Plow driver Lucky Loughran, the Good Conehead.

MSP Trooper Joseph Paul: The crime scene "spoke" to him.

Canton Police Department Officer Steve Saraf.

MSP Det. Lt. Brian Tully, longtime enforcer for Meatball Morrissey, disciplined and transferred after the 2024 trial.

Canton firefighter/paramedic Daniel Whitley.

New colonel of the MSP, Geoffrey Noble: The tradition continues.

CHAPTER FIVE

# Trooper Michael Proctor, Badge Number 3863

## Male Chauvinists, the Massachusetts State Police Want You!

Proctor, old nickname "Chip." New nickname: "Porky."

*June 12, 2024*

Could you use a good job at a good wage?

Have you ever considered signing up for the MSP?

The troopers are looking for a few good male chauvinist pigs.

If you think you despise women enough, give the MSP a call.

The MSP is not for everyone. If your IQ is above ninety, forget about it. You won't fit in.

But if you move your lips when you read, and you're an embittered, low-rent townie from some wretched backwater burg, you may soon be wearing a Smokey Bear hat and stealing hot stoves with the best of 'em, and then coming back for the smoke.

"To Protect and Steal"—that's the motto of the MSP.

But the most important question for any MSP aspirant to answer is this: Are you fed up with these uppity broads who don't want to be railroaded into prison for crimes they didn't commit?

If so, the MSP could be your ticket—no heavy lifting, and all you do is sit around the barracks all day long picking your nose and waiting for the latest vile, misogynist texts from skinhead Trooper Michael "Chip" Proctor to land on your phone.

Do you like to grab some chick's cell phone and start scrolling through it for naked pictures? Be sure to keep all your knucklehead trooper pals in the loop about how the search is coming along—"so far no nudes."

And if Trooper Proctor sends you a comment that's rotten enough, text him back with a big smile emoji. How dare any broad object to being framed!

Do you enjoy endlessly slurring female defendants with the c-word and the r-word? Then you can chuckle to yourself as Trooper Proctor makes sport of a woman's disease, her accent, her derriere, and calls her a whack job.

Do you have the right stuff to become a Massachusetts state trooper?

Thanks to the FBI's investigation of the corruption in the Norfolk County District Attorney's Office, we've known for a while just how much Proctor loathes women, or at least the one woman he was looking so forward to arresting . . . and then collecting the "tip" for his fine services to the McAlbert clan in his hillbilly hometown of Canton.

What we didn't know until Monday was how many other state troopers were in on his disgusting text chats about Karen Read.

On cross-examination, Proctor listed which of his fellow MSP millionaires he had shared his obsessive hatred of women with.

From the witness stand, Proctor was directed to read the list of state cops to whom he'd been spewing his hate speech. Below are their names, rank, and how much money Proctor's pals made last year. The number is a total of their salary, overtime, and what's listed as "other" on the state comptroller's payroll.

These were the bent cops receiving texts from Proctor, who himself made $146,050 last year:

Lt. John Fanning, $230,960 a year.

Sgt. Yuriy Bukhenik, $211,080.

Trooper Chris Moore, $142,110.

Trooper Jeff Kotkowski, $142,980.

Trooper Dave Dicicco, $155,560.

The head of the MSP detective unit in the Norfolk County District Attorney's Office is Lt. Brian Tully, expected to be a witness today in Dedham after Chip's demolition is complete.

Tully made $214,640 last year.

Here's the thing about the Fab Five (and Tully). Proctor was asked if he'd ever been reprimanded, or anything, by anyone in MSP for any of his vile texts.

"Not that I can recall," he said.

Apparently none of the cops thought there was anything wrong with Proctor's sexist screeds. They were just hoping Proctor would get lucky after he texted them the sad news about Karen Read's cell phone—"so far no nudes."

Proctor will be back on the witness stand Wednesday morning, as his cross-examination by defense attorney Alan Jackson continues.

As devastating as Monday's testimony by Proctor was for the prosecution, it's likely going to get even worse today.

One thing we know from the opening arguments is that Proctor also texted his sister that he hoped that Karen Read would kill herself.

Think about that. Suicide was exactly what J. Edgar Hoover recommended that Martin Luther King Jr. do back in the 1960s. The FBI bugged King's hotel rooms. Then Hoover anonymously sent King audiotapes of his extramarital dalliances and suggested that the only way out was . . . to kill himself.

Another of Proctor's investigative techniques he's sure to be asked today about is the trick of misspelling the names of all the witnesses, most of whom have slithered out of the same inbred alcoholic cesspool of Canton.

If you're employed by the defense, your searches into the prior public records of witnesses don't get very far if the cops give you fake names.

You know who else was into that misspelling racket? Everyone who worked for Anthony Fauci. They misspelled everything to foil those pesky Freedom of Information Act (FOIA) demands for documents relating to the Red Chinese-engineered panic of 2020.

One last point: Guess who's a delegate to the Democrat National Convention in Chicago in August?

None other than the employer of Proctor, Bukhenik, et al. That's right, the grotesquely bloated district attorney of Norfolk County, Michael "Meatball" Morrissey, the ex-officio head of the Courthouse He-Man Woman-Hating Club.

He's in the same delegation with such noted feminists as Ayanna Pressley, Maura Healey, and the Fake Indian. Wonder if they appreciate his employment of a guy who uses the c-word to describe an innocent woman he's trying to railroad into prison?

I tweeted out the story about Meatball's impending junket and the reaction was instantaneous.

"How does he even fit on a plane?" one tweeted back at me.

"Of course he's going," said another. "They have free buffets at conventions."

Back in the old days, whenever Billy Bulger ran into a rotund hack who was all jammed up, he had a standard line for them.

"It's so nice to see," Bulger would say, "that you're not letting your travails affect your appetite in the slightest."

With his pal Proctor back on cross-examination, this could be a long morning for Meatball Morrissey—at least three, maybe even five crullers.

## Trooper Proctor's Epic Canton Collapse

*July 26, 2024*

You're Michael Proctor, just another corrupt conehead cop from Canton, and you're wondering why you and so far only you have been singled out to be the patsy, the fall guy in the failed Karen Read frame-up.

Of all the jammed-up Keystone Kops in Norfolk County, how come you're the only one who is not getting paid?

You weren't even at the death house at 34 Fairview Road that morning. You just tried to do your fellow cop thugs a solid by looking the other way, and this is what happens to you.

Suspended . . . without pay.

You're Michael Proctor, and your bent bosses in the Norfolk County District Attorney's Office are both under investigation by the Internal Affairs unit of the MSP . . . but they're still happily slurping at the trough.

The district attorney they "work" for, Meatball Morrissey, even just got a pay raise, from $191,000 to $223,000.

You're Michael Proctor, and when you got knee-walking drunk with fat Canton Police Department detective Kevin Albert and drove around shitfaced in your MSP cruiser, it wasn't you who lost his gun and badge—it was Kevin Albert.

So now Kevin Albert is suspended, but he's still getting paid—$176,388 last year.

In Canton, they don't even call it a suspension, it's "paid administrative leave," key word: *paid*.

Then there's Kevin Albert's brother, thug Boston cop Brian Albert, on whose front lawn the body was found.

Proctor gave Brian Albert a good leaving alone, didn't even go inside his house, misspelled everybody's names in the reports, didn't inquire about their missing vicious dog, refused to interview any witness who might dispute the narrative—all to cover for Albert and the rest of the McAlberts.

Brian was allowed to retire from the BPD, and is now pocketing a kiss in the mail of $101,797.32 a year.

Then there's Brian Higgins, the drunkard ATF agent—so shady he had to testify at the trial with his criminal lawyer standing beside him.

Like the other Brian, Higgins destroyed his cell phone the day before the court issued a preservation order. Higgins is riding the pine at ATF, but he's . . . still . . . getting . . . paid.

You're Michael Proctor, and as a trained sleuth, you begin to notice a pattern here.

You've been set up, railroaded, hung out to dry like you're Karen bleepin' Read or somebody.

Now you're sweltering in your crappy little ranch house in Canton.

Your dumpy wife Lizzie is giving you the evil eye because the money's running out and even Jill Daniels and her elderly boyfriend are still flush enough to be guzzling doubles down in Falmouth, singing their favorite Elton John song, "Saturday Night's Alright for Fighting."

Kevin Albert, Canton Police Department: Lost badge while drunk with Proctor, not fired.

You're Michael Proctor, and it all leaves a bad taste in your mouth, like you've just had two slices of mushroom pizza from Jailbird Chris Albert's D&E Pizza.

You're wondering if your old boss, Meatball Morrissey, is having his annual summer barbecue at the Adams Inn in North Quincy, and if so, why your invitation has been lost in the mail.

You're thinking about maybe catching up on your reading, starting with the novel *Pop. 1280* by Jim Thompson, about a crooked sheriff.

You open the book, and you get goose bumps as you lip-read this paragraph:

> *I had it made and it looked like I could go on having it made as long as I minded my own business and didn't arrest no one unless I just couldn't get out of it and they didn't amount to nothin'.*

You throw the book down because that's your life story the guy is writing.

You're Michael Proctor and you knew the rules in Norfolk County: Never, ever arrest anybody with any dough, especially if they come from Marina Bay.

And don't lug nobody from Wellesley, Brookline, or Milton either—at least not unless they live close to the Dairy Freeze or on the Mattapan line.

Damn it, you miscalculated that Karen Read didn't amount to nothin'—that's why you were measuring her for the frame.

But it turned out Karen Read had . . . gone to college. And not one of them Trooper Paul GED community colleges like you and everybody else in the MSP.

You're Michael Proctor, and no wonder you wanted Karen Read to kill herself, her with her weird Fall River accent and no ass.

And why did you ask the McAlberts for that bribe, er gift?

All the great trooper times you're missing this summer—you didn't get to go on the fun road trip with Sgt. Bukhenik to harass Free Karen Read women in Walpole and Woburn.

No more inverting videos for Michael Proctor.

No more searching Karen Read's phone for nudes.

Now you're watching Lizzie fix dinner, and you know it's going to be the same thing she's been dishing up to you every night.

Hot tongue and cold shoulder.

You're Michael Proctor, and maybe you should drive down to O'Reilly Auto Parts on Washington Street and buy some taillights.

Then take the taillights into the garage and smash them into forty-five or so pieces . . . at least then you'd feel like you were back doing something constructive again.

You keep asking yourself, Why do bad things keep happening to Proctors in Massachusetts?

John Proctor, hung as a witch in Salem in 1692; Capt. William Proctor of the MSP, outed for lying at the Sacco and Vanzetti trial in 1921 that ended with the Italians' execution at the state prison in Charlestown . . .

You're Michael Proctor, and you're wondering when your people are finally going to catch a break in Massachusetts.

You think back to all those other troopers he sent obscene text messages to, like David DiCicco, and how he texted back to you, "Bleep her bleep."

And yet Dicicco's still getting paid—he even went up to $181,210 in 2024.

You look around for something else to read, and you find what Cadillac Frank Salemme (another former Norfolk County thug) told Mob hangers-on who didn't pay attention and then ended up in the glue: "Don't play off like you're some kind of abused hero. Sure you got screwed, so has everybody, that's the life you chose. You want to be a gofer, that's the price you pay. That's the life, the proverbial street life . . ."

You're Michael Proctor, and you can't stop asking yourself the recurring question: Who have I got to trade up to the feds?

## Trooper Proctor Threw His Dismal Career Away

*March 19, 2025*

One corrupt conehead down, many, many more to go.

And so farewell, Michael Proctor, the overserved, undereducated "detective" for the MSP, finally fired this morning for his abysmal misbehavior as a crooked cop over the years, most spectacularly in the ongoing Karen Read miscarriage of justice.

So many lessons here from old songs, starting with, "Drinkin' doubles don't make a party."

What made Milwaukee famous has made a loser out of Trooper Proctor, written off by the new colonel in his dismissal order as "Mr. Proctor."

To paraphrase Dean Wormer from *Animal House*, "Bald, corrupt, and stupid is no way to go through life, Proctor."

This guy was a disgrace to Barney Fife. He was dumber than Sheriff Buford T. Justice's clueless son in *Smokey and the Bandit*.

Proctor was so crooked he needed a corkscrew to get into his jodhpurs in the morning. He threw his dismal career away like a handful of broken pieces of taillight tossed carelessly on a snow-covered crime scene in Canton.

"Proctor Trooper" was what one of the McAlbert shrews affectionately called the loyal stooge during the first Karen Read trial. He was just trying to be a good friend, in the way the term *good friend* is traditionally understood in Canton.

Friends help you move, good friends help you move bodies. Or at least look the other way, and give any witnesses who might create, you know, reasonable doubt, a good leaving alone. Just ask Lucky Loughran, the tow truck driver who didn't see any dead bodies on the lawn at 34 Fairview. No wonder Proctor, uh, forgot to interview him until the FBI found him first.

At the beginning, Proctor wasn't even in the middle of Canton's second cop-involved unsolved murder in as many years. He was just an extra, like his former MSP superiors in *The Departed*, a movie about an earlier generation of crooked cops.

Now, though, Proctor is the first to get two in the hat. That's how these mob movies always play out. Jack Nicholson doesn't get hit until the last reel.

Can you imagine how Proctor's firing must sit with his bride, Lizzie? She's married to a thuggish dolt with an IQ of ninety, tops, and yet he was still grabbing $146,050 in 2023, which now turns out to be his career year.

What about all of Proctor's obscene, misogynistic text messages? How did Col. Noble describe them in his you're-fired memo? "Derogatory, defamatory, disparaging and/or otherwise inappropriate text messages about a suspect in that investigation."

What did Proctor say about Karen Read? That she had a "leaky balloon knot?"

Now his wife Lizzie comes to the realization that she may have to go to work as a cocktail waitress, like Leigha Genduso? Is Scuttlebutts hiring? Funky Murphy's?

Lizzie's advice, counsels, and urgings are no doubt ringing in Michael Proctor's ears:

> *You got fired, you bleepin' idiot? Why didn't you go out on the Turnpike—how much money did those guys steal and they're all getting the kiss in the mail in Florida, even the ones who had to plead out. You bleepin' idiot!*
>
> *Brian Albert's still got his pension, your drunkard buddy Kevin Albert didn't get fired for leaving his gun and badge in your cruiser. Even that fat bleep Brian Higgins hasn't been fired from ATF! What the bleep is wrong with Elon Musk that he can't DOGE that big POS?*

How'd you like to be getting an earful of that, twenty-four seven? It would give a better man than Michael Proctor a leaky balloon knot, that's for sure.

Has Proctor's old boss, Norfolk County District Attorney Michael "Meatball" Morrissey, been reached for comment yet?

He was out last week for the St. Patrick's Day times, and he looked more dissipated and bloated than ever, "a pot-bellied courthouse stooge," to quote a perfect description of Meatball in a 1953 novel called *The Hot Spot*.

Maybe Meatball can loan Proctor his boat, the *Class Action*, for a three-hour cruise . . .

Now that he's got nothing to lose, maybe he'll flip. As everyone knows, a crooked cop never stands up. Never.

It's a sad day for Michael Proctor. But he should at least look on the bright side—spring is almost here, and you know what that means.

The landscaping industry is hiring. The cruiser, the badge, the gun, they're all gone.

But whatever else happens, Proctor, they can't take your rake and pruning shears away from you.

CHAPTER SIX

# Meet Hank Brennan

*I first encountered attorney Hank Brennan in 2013, when he was the second public defender for serial-killing gangster Whitey Bulger in his federal racketeering trial.*

Hank Brennan in 2013, when he was representing serial killer Whitey Bulger.

Whitey hated me and didn't want me covering his trial. Same with four Boston Globe *reporters*. So he ordered Hank to put all five of us on Whitey's witness list—I was number seven, "Howard Carr, Brighton MA."

If we were potential witnesses, we couldn't attend the trial. It might, you know, taint our own testimony.

It was a silly stunt. It actually just made the five of us look good—if Whitey hated us because of our reporting. In an odd way, being on that witness list became a badge of honor.

Judge Denise Casper saw through the ploy, and allowed us all in. But it showed me how in awe of Whitey that Hank had become, that he would do something that pointless at the mobster's behest.

Later, after Whitey's inevitable conviction, Brennan handled other matters for the Bulger family, including their "wrongful-death" lawsuit against the Bureau of Prisons after Whitey was beaten to death by New England wiseguys in a federal prison in West Virginia in 2018.

Having watched him flop so spectacularly at Whitey's trial, I wasn't expecting much from him in Dedham. But he was even worse than I'd anticipated.

He never learns from his mistakes. Before the second trial started, he put out the prosecution's witness list. On it was "Aidan Kearney, Holden, MA"—Turtleboy.

"Welcome to the club!" I told Turtleboy. Of course it didn't work. Hank never learns.

Here are some of my *Herald* columns from the trial about him.

# Ghost of Whitey Bulger in Karen Read Case

*September 20, 2024*

When he was representing Whitey Bulger at his 2013 murder trial, Hank Brennan had to tell the judge why the serial killer refused to speak before his sentencing.

"He believes the trial was a sham," Brennan told Judge Denise Casper.

A sham? You call the Whitey trial a sham, Hank? When it comes to sham trials, you ain't seen nothing yet.

Now, all these years later, Brennan returns to the limelight, not as a defense lawyer, but as a special prosecutor of Karen Read, who has already endured one sham trial and now faces a second one in the spring.

That trial is going to be Sham 2.0. And instead of decrying governmental overreach against Whitey, which he did (unconvincingly), this time Brennan will be tasked with trying to frame Karen Read.

Ironic, because in 2013, despite all evidence to the contrary in the Bulger case, Brennan seemed to believe that cops were capable of railroading people they don't like to protect their corrupt cronies.

In his closing in federal court, Brennan even brought up the fate of a crooked FBI agent from Boston who lied on the witness stand as a defense witness for Whitey.

"They'll crush you," Brennan said. "They bully him, they berate him, they crush him. That's what happens when you're not with them, you're either with them or you're against them."

Paging Karen Read . . .

Whitey had two lawyers—Brennan and Jay Carney, who was the lead guy, older and more jaded about his mobster client. Brennan, on the other hand, developed a massive man crush on Whitey. It was weird, how much he seemed to idolize the monster.

After Whitey was murdered, Brennan handled the lawsuits for the hack Bulger family against the feds. They were laughed out of court, naturally. Brennan also attended Whitey's funeral.

It's safe to say that when Whitey yelled, "Jump!" Brennan answered back, "How high?"

And now Brennan goes on the payroll of Meatball Morrissey, who was elected to the state Senate back in the days when it was run by . . . William M. Bulger, Whitey's younger brother.

When Billy Bulger yelled, "Jump!" Meatball likewise answered back, "How high?" Meatball was Billy Bulger's butler.

So you can understand why Meatball had his nationwide search for Hank. They're both in "the element," as they used to say.

Brennan appears to be at least the fourth special prosecutor that Meatball has hired to continue his twisted jihad of retribution and revenge against Karen Read et al.

Turtleboy, Karen Read's biggest supporter who was thrown into jail for two months, is now being chased by a couple of Meatball's special prosecutors.

They're all hacks too, just like Meatball himself and Brennan.

Consider Robert Cosgrove, a retired hack judge and another member of the Meatball Mafia. He was picked to go after Turtleboy in a ridiculous case, but maybe he needs the dough.

In addition to whatever Meatball has been paying him, Cosgrove currently gets two—count 'em, two—state pensions. As a former hack in the Norfolk County District Attorney's office, his kiss in the mail comes to $64,264 a year.

As a retired judge, Cosgrove collects a separate pension of $139,301 a year.

Total annual grab: $203,565.

Can't Meatball find anyone already on his payroll to try what he believes, however delusionally, is an important case? And don't even get me started on Meatball's detectives from the MSP, who by their own account spend much of their time searching for nude photos on female defendants' cell phones . . .

The question in this Karen Read case is whether she has been made the patsy for other corrupt bad actors who likely murdered her boyfriend. In the Whitey trial, Brennan was all in on the frame-up theory.

Whether it's in South Boston or in Canton, it's all about the cover-up, and what career criminals will do to avoid getting caught.

Stevie Flemmi was Whitey's partner in crime who became a prosecution witness against him. Brennan was assigned to cross-examine Flemmi. He questioned Flemmi at length about how he murdered Deb Hussey, his stepdaughter, after taking her shopping.

BRENNAN: "You didn't tell her you were going to murder her?"

FLEMMI: "Of course not."

BRENNAN: "You lied to her, yes?"

FLEMMI: "Is that a sensible question?"

BRENNAN: "And you dumped her body in an unmarked grave?"

FLEMMI: "It wouldn't make sense to mark the grave."

Then Brennan pointed out how, after Deb's body was secretly buried in the basement, Flemmi had tried to present himself as a victim, telling Deb's mother that he would hire a private investigator to find her.

FLEMMI: "Mr. Brennan, that's all part of the cover-up."

BRENNAN: "You wanted to assure them in the sense that you didn't know where Debbie was, isn't that true?"

FLEMMI: "It's all part of the cover-up, yes. When you commit a murder, you cover up on it, you don't admit to people. I don't know if you're aware of that, you should be. You're an attorney."

Talking about a different murder, Flemmi again mentioned how clueless Brennan seemed.

FLEMMI: "You don't understand the underworld at all, nothing.

You're an attorney. You don't know what's going on in the world. I'm giving you the real world."

I wonder if Brennan realized that Stevie Flemmi was just trying to educate him on how a cover-up must be run, in Boston or in Canton.

Probably not, because by taking on the job of prosecuting Karen Read, Hank Brennan will be trying to do to Karen Read exactly what he accused everybody else of doing to his hero, Whitey Bulger.

What a sham.

## Whitey Bulger's Pal Hank Brennan's Latest Humiliation

*June 14, 2025*

Do you suppose Stevie Flemmi watched any of his old nemesis Hank Brennan's latest courtroom humiliations in Dedham last week?

Probably not. The serial-killing partner of Hank's late client (and hero) Whitey Bulger is ninety-one now. Stevie is locked away for life in some secret federal prison reserved for treacherous rat bastards like both Flemmi and Bulger.

But let the record show that it was "the Rifleman" who at Bulger's 2013 trial was the first witness to make a complete ass of Hank Brennan during one of his trademark nonsensical cross-examinations.

Now Brennan is the $566,000 "special" persecutor in the second Karen Read murder trial in Norfolk Superior Court.

Traditionally, a prosecutor is supposed to be a white hat—a good guy or, failing that, at least honest and truthful.

It is a role for which Hammered Hank Brennan is spectacularly miscast. And so it was that he melted down at the end of the trial, first in another series of disastrous cross-examinations, and then in a bumblingly bad closing argument to the jury.

They're not making Mob mouthpieces like they used to. Nor are the traditional Norfolk County jury-intimidation tactics working anymore.

At Read's first trial last year, thug ex-Boston cop Brian Albert and his punk nephew, Colin Albert, showed up to glare at the jury during closings. Both Alberts were no-shows Friday. Instead, the jurors had to file by a different Keystone Kop, MSP Sgt. Yuriy Bukhenik.

Bukhenik is the as-yet unfired member of the "detective" unit that framed Karen Read back in 2022. He materialized at the courthouse Friday in a black suit with pants cuffs absurdly above his ankles.

The suit looked like something off the rack from KGB Haberdashery, to be worn only to a USSR commissar's funeral in Vladivostok in 1977.

Even more preposterous than Bukhenik's Sunday-go-to-meeting duds were his striped white socks.

Black suit and white socks. Seriously, it was a full Kyiv. He looked like one of the old Wild and Crazy Guys on *SNL*.

When Karen Read's lawyers spotted him lurking around the hall, glowering at the jury and channeling his sinister Iron Curtain vibes, they complained.

Finally, the hulking moron fled back into his boss DA Meatball Morrissey's lair. Maybe someone called 911 to report a suspicious rubber ducky sighting somewhere in Norfolk County, and he had to scramble to Milton with sirens blaring.

Or perhaps a housewife in Avon had posted something mean about Meatball Morrissey on Facebook and needed a good talking-to, in Bukhenik's broken English, about a witness-intimidation rap.

This is how Bukhenik earns the big bucks—$211,960 last year. He loves screaming at young rubber ducky–wielding moms almost as much as he relishes those $750-a-shift no-heavy-lifting F Troop details at the airport.

Despite fleeing his homeland, he now poses as a big Ukrainian patriot. Invincible in peace, invisible in war, that's Bukhenik.

He's big into the war effort, although oddly, he prefers banging on the hoods of double-parking motorists dropping off their kids at Terminal C to returning to the old USSR to toss grenades at Russian tanks.

Maybe that's why Bukhenik was roundly booed by Karen Read supporters outside the courthouse as he took it on the lam Friday afternoon. Or perhaps the crowd was just appalled by his unfortunate sartorial choices.

But getting back to Hank Brennan, I knew back in 2013 what a crappy lawyer he was when he got his head handed to him by Stevie Flemmi. The Rifleman was testifying against his partner in pedophilia and murder, Whitey Bulger.

On cross, Hammered Hank just kept yelling at Flemmi. The prosecutor finally complained to the judge that Brennan had no interest in questioning Flemmi and was merely trying to "embarrass, humiliate, demean and badger the witness over and over and over again."

Sound familiar? You can't teach an old Bulger hack new tricks.

During cross-examinations, Hank abandons himself to a bizarre obsession with food. Last week, with FBI witness Dr. Andrew Rentschler, he couldn't stop asking him about ham sandwiches. He returned to the subject again in his closing. Ham sandwiches.

In 2013, with Flemmi, Brennan became fixated about the alleged gourmet dining in WITSEC, the federal prison system for snitches.

BRENNAN: "It's like the Club Med of federal facilities?"

FLEMMI: "You really think so?"

BRENNAN: "You have a store at your prison that doubles as a delicatessen."

FLEMMI: "That is absolutely ridiculous."

BRENNAN: "Can you get rib-eye steak?"

FLEMMI: "If I gave some of that food to my dog, he'd bite me."

It was comic gold. And it wasn't like Flemmi couldn't have been dusted up.

In 2018, he was back in federal court in Boston as a witness in a different Mob murder case. On cross-examination, the first question Flemmi was asked was how many murders he'd participated in over the decades.

He had to think about it, add them all up in his head.

"Probably about fifty," Flemmi finally answered.

After that admission, how much more did the jury need to know?

Brennan could have come up with a decent question like that, or at least a less ridiculous one than jailhouse steaks. But that would have required some thought. And as everyone can now see, to a battle of wits, Hammered Hank Brennan comes unarmed.

On that fact, there can be no dis-poot.

One last question before the verdict, this one for Bukhenik: Comrade, how long do you have to wear those white socks to win the bet?

## Karen Read Prosecutor Hank Brennan's Mangled Vocabulary

*July 12, 2025*

For $566,000, the taxpayers might have expected a little more effort from Hammered Hank Brennan.

For that kind of money—for just nine months—couldn't he have worked a little more competently at trying to railroad Karen Read for a crime she obviously didn't commit?

Maybe he was overconfident. After all, the hack judge was totally in the satchel for the frame job, at one point sustaining forty-nine consecutive Brennan objections to the defense's questioning of a single witness.

Hank Brennan's ESL.

At trial kickoff, Hank was handed the home-field advantage and a three-touchdown lead. But he ended up getting absolutely blown out by halftime. It wasn't even close.

Brennan's courtroom performance was so dreadful that unlike last year, this time Judge Auntie Bev couldn't just summarily disregard the jury's acquittals and declare a mistrial.

This time the verdict was, as Donald Trump might say, TOO BIG TO RIG.

In memory of our wasted $566,000, let's look back at what Norfolk County taxpayers got for our money.

Here are some of Hank's greatest hits:

For starters, he kept calling the victim, John O'Keefe, "John Keefe." He also said he was a Canton native. (O'Keefe was from Braintree.)

One of his witnesses was Heather Maxon. He called her "Make-son."

Of course, it was nothing personal. In court filings, Brennan misspelled his own name as "Breenan."

One of the defense lawyers was Robert Alessi. Breenan insisted on calling him "Aleeci."

Breenan squandered another $400,000 in public funds on the cartoonish "experts" from Aperture, Shanon Burgess and Jud Welcher. Their buffoonery quickly became the butt of jokes, but Hank defended what's-their-names? to the hilt in his closing.

"As much as you want to make fun of him, Shanon Welcher found the key."

Can we quote you on that, Mr. Breenan?

He usually referred to Karen Read as "the defendant," but occasionally by name—"Ms. Wead," as he called her.

Here are two of my favorite Hank quotes:

"There is no constitutional right to ooo-surp the rules of evidence."

"The timeline is not in dis-poot."

After the verdict, defense attorney Alan Jackson said his team had gone to great lengths to understand the science, to make sure they weren't rolled by persecution "experts" like that composite Shanon Welcher guy.

Hank had no such concerns. He had the judge in his pocket, after all.

But Brennan should have at least . . . tried . . . to grasp the science. His complete lack of any prep work provided much of the trial's unintended mirth.

The TV crowd's favorite moment may have been when he referenced the occipital bone in the skull. Only he called it the "oxipital boner."

He thought a subdural hemorrhage was "subdermal."

He was corrected on that howler by former Rhode Island medical examiner Dr. Elizabeth Laposata. So then he asked her who was best qualified to determine a cause of death.

"The person who is best qualified is a physician," she answered.

"So," Breenan pounced, "a medical examiner wouldn't cut it in your opinion?"

"A medical examiner," Laposata responded with a sigh, "is a physician."

Watching Breenan mangle everything he touched, it was hard not to stifle a laugh, or as Hank would say, "Stiffle."

He pronounced *carotid* as "car-toy-ed." *Incisors* came out as "in-scissors." *Hematoma* became "he-ba-toba." He described a paramedic firefighter as a "parameric." *Glasgow Coma Scale* came out of his mouth as the "Goozma Scale."

His grasp of modern technology was just as tenuous. Over and over he called the Apple Health app something else, usually "Health Care Data." He fumbled the description of the software in Karen Read's Lexus.

It's *Techstream*. He kept saying it was "Telestream." He called thumb drives or flash drives "zip drives." *Hash values* became "hash tags."

It was like he was stuck in Bush 41. He occasionally flashed back to the glory days of his hero, cocaine-dealing serial killer Whitey Bulger. One day, Hank delved into the frostbite suffered by "John Keefe." Only he called the frostbite "freezer burn." You know, like some wayward wiseguys got in the movie *Goodfellas*.

Supposedly, Hank is a great lawyer. Or should I use his word—*supposably*?

The list of words mangled by Hank was endless. The defense team kept a running list for their own amusement.

*Anonymously* became "amonymously." *Nefarious* was "ne-fahh-hhh-rious." *Data* was "dater," *potatoes* "bodados." *Cache* was rendered "cash-ey." *Coup* was "coop." *Chamois* became "ka-mo-see." *Plethora* came out as "plithora." When he meant to say *eventually*, he would usually sputter "inevitably."

Same thing with legalese and cop lingo. You know, *laurenforcement*.

The debris field was in Hank's phrase the "dee-bwee fewld." An unattended death became "unintended." (Maybe it was.) He always liked to "co-wob-o-wate" the evidence. He complained about the lack of "we-sip-wo-cal" discovery. He called the plastic taillight on Karen's SUV "glass."

He thought the pavement on Fairview Road was concrete. (It was asphalt.)

One day he introduced himself to a witness with "Good afternoon." It was 11:45 a.m.

When talking about speed, most people use the word *quickly*. Hank prefers "fastly."

Here was another of Brennan's strangely worded questions to a witness: "Did you think of a way that you look below the top of the snow without unresting the scene?"

Despite his alleged erudition (to use yet another word he doesn't know the meaning of), Hank Breenan is not exactly cerebral, or as he pronounces it, "cerebri-uhl."

You know, chain-smoking career prosecutor Adam Lally could have handled this second trial too, and lost badly, just like he did the first time. And Lally would have saved the taxpayers a million bucks.

One final thought: Stay safe. Nobody needs a fractured oxipital boner.

CHAPTER SEVEN

# Welcome to Norfolk County

DA Michael "Meatball" Morrissey, a whale of a politician.

# Karen Read Trial Is a Corrupt Canton Townie Sideshow

*May 18, 2024*

Paul Revere used to summer every year in Canton, but he wouldn't recognize the place today.

One thing, though, hasn't changed since the 18th of April in '75—the locals still love their midnight rides, but with one big difference.

Paul Revere wasn't hammered out of his mind when he was on horseback, spreading the alarm to every Middlesex village and farm.

Through the first fourteen days of the Karen Read murder trial in Dedham, we have learned much about life in the Town of Canton, post–Paul Revere.

As you know, Read is accused of murdering her boyfriend, BPD cop John O'Keefe, by drunkenly running him over in a snowstorm in January 2022.

His body was found outside the home of another BPD officer, who has since sold the house, gotten rid of his phone and dog, and abruptly retired from the job, not that there's anything wrong with that.

How screwed up is this case? Well, the feds are all over it like white on rice.

Read's defense attorneys have said the G-men's accident-reconstruction experts have concluded that O'Keefe couldn't possibly have been killed by a car.

Then there are all those texts that haven't been "mistakenly" deleted . . .

The state's lead investigator is *thisclose* to the Hibernian hillbillies who are up to their eyeballs in this mess.

According to opening statements, MSP Trooper Michael Proctor's first thought when he was assigned the case was to text his Canton high-school buddies. He told them he was already searching online for nude photos of Karen Read.

Proctor is now under investigation by MSP Internal Affairs—if only because it's the feds who discovered his texts, rather than the corrupt staties themselves.

How will Proctor do on cross-examination? Do you remember an LAPD detective by the name of Mark Fuhrman?

Back on the stand Tuesday will be Jen McCabe. She's the one who's missing one of her front teeth.

Don't confuse Toothy McCabe with Julie Albert. Julie is the one who chews gum while testifying. Her father's name was Jack Daniels—coincidence?

Julie is married to Jailbird Chris Albert. He did a six-month state bid in 1995 after killing a Hungarian exchange student in a hit-and-run accident.

His public defender was one John Prescott, whose sister is the judge in the case—Beverly Cannone. She's a lifelong payroll patriot from Quincy, like the rotund district attorney, Meatball Mike Morrissey.

If you want to hide something real good, just stick it in one of Judge Cannone's law books.

From her courtroom rulings, Cannone seems to believe that the synonym for *exculpatory* is *excluded*, as in, if the evidence is exculpatory for Karen Read, it's excluded.

Chris Albert, by the way, is a Canton selectman. As the only jailbird in the fight, he was elected in a landslide. Forget it, Jake—it's Canton.

Even if you haven't been paying close attention, there are easy ways to figure out who's who. The townies—which is everyone except the defendant—all pronounce their hometown not as "Canton" but as "Can-UHN."

Here's how the examination begins after each witness is sworn in.

Where do you live? Can-UHN.

Where were you born? Can-UHN.

Where did you go to high school? Can-UHN High.

Have you ever been anywhere else? Yes, once I drove to a packy . . . in Stough-UHN.

Selectman Albert owns the local pizza parlor. On the night John O'Keefe died outside his brother's house, he closed his shop, then walked across the street to a local dive where he ordered "appetizers." That's how good his own restaurant is.

Welcome to Norfolk County | 77

Then, meeting up with the rest of the Can-UHN townies, the selectman ordered the usual—a round of Fireball. How Canton is it?

After last call, he offered to take the crapulous crew back to his pizzeria for some free eats. Everybody said . . . nah.

Almost all these people live, or did live, in the same houses they grew up in, bought by their parents fifty years ago as they fled Boston after the start of busing.

Lucky for them they inherited these tear-downs, because otherwise most of them would have already fled back to their kind's natural habitat—trailer parks.

See, Canton's on the commuter-rail line, so housing prices have been going up, up, and away. It's only a matter of time until all these low-rent losers are priced out.

So resentment is simmering among the old Can-UHN crowd. They don't like what's happening. Just last year, their favorite hangout, Big D's Neponset Grill, went out of business.

It was the last place in town where you could get a fried-baloney sandwich. Now that was some really fine Can-UHN cuisine.

What must the US attorney be thinking as he watches this legal lynching unfold in deepest, darkest Dedham? The defense has said in open court that the feds already have a proffer—a deal—with the only witness who didn't go to Can-UHN High.

The hack prosecutor did not dispute the statement.

Judge Cannone has instructed all the parties not to mention that federal grand jury, where at least three cops have apparently told conflicting stories from what they testified before Meatball's state grand jury.

But the other day, one of the younger witnesses was asked who's questioned him about O'Keefe's death.

"The feds," he blurted out in front of the jury.

Well, what could you expect? He went to Can-UHN High.

This trial is drawing a huge audience. Unlike Donald Trump's kangaroo-court case in New York, there are cameras in the Dedham courtroom. Live streaming coverage.

And the courtroom cameras like Karen Read. A lot.

Tensions are running high. There have been fights and restraining orders—and that's just among the reporters.

Aidan "Turtleboy" Kearney is the blogger who's made the case into a national story. He's been barred from the courtroom for certain witnesses—the "McAlberts," as he calls the Alberts and the McCabes.

The McAlbert witnesses begin weeping when they talk about Turtleboy. He makes them want to spit out their chewing gum and order another round of Fireballs.

How dare he call their hero Jailbird Chris Albert "Chicken Parm Charlie?"

I have Turtleboy on my radio show most afternoons. On Friday, he said Jen McCabe has a worse set of teeth than George Washington did.

The most appealing thing about this case is that you can watch it and feel better about your own hometown. In Holbrook, they listen to Chicken Parm Charlie and realize that he makes their ex-selectman Daniel Lee look like Daniel Webster.

In Methuen, they see Canton's Keystone Cops and think, you know, maybe Chief Solomon wasn't that bad after all . . .

If Paul Revere could only see what's become of Canton, he'd put the spurs to Brown Beauty and keep riding. Only instead of "The British are coming!" he'd be yelling something different: "The white trash are coming!"

## Plow Driver Only Honest Man in Karen Read Case

*June 22, 2024*

Finally, a Canton conehead whose testimony you can believe.

It took seven weeks, but yesterday, in the murder trial of Karen Read we finally got a chrome dome from Canton who was neither a jailbird nor a cop desperately trying to avoid becoming one after getting busted by the FBI soliciting a bribe in a text message.

Brian "Lucky" Loughran, the snowplow driver, was the first witness for the defense, and what a breath of fresh air.

He totally won over the jury when he began by describing the precautions he takes when he gets behind the wheel of his monster plow, Frankentruck, during a snowstorm.

"I am trying," he explained, "to be aware of any side traffic, any pedestrians and, God forbid, any animals."

How refreshing after all the prosecution's witnesses—sweaty, dissembling, mealy-mouthed cops, shady "experts" and full-blown drunkards, or all of the above.

Lucky Loughran, on the other hand, loves dogs.

"I am making sure," he elaborated, "that there are no animals, no pedestrians, no one coming out of their driveways."

Pedestrians are important, he said, and so are cars. But protecting animals—that's job one for Lucky Loughran.

Like most of the toothless hags and thugs who testified for the persecution, er prosecution, Lucky Loughran is a Canton townie. He went to grade school with Chris Albert, the ex-con selectman with the light-colored Ford Edge.

Lucky knew Chris Albert even before he hired Judge Cannone's brother to get him off with a six-month wrist slap after he killed a foreign exchange student in a hit-and-run accident.

Lucky's brother actually serves on the Canton board of selectmen with Jailbird Chris Albert.

Most significantly, Lucky is a cueball. You can't get any more Canton than that. He used to eat fried-baloney sandwiches at Big D's Neponset Grill.

In other words, Lucky would have every reason to dummy up—to observe Canton's version of omertà, which is to guzzle so many Fireball shots at the Waterfall that you pass out, usually behind the wheel of your MSP cruiser.

Losing your gun and badge while drunk—how Canton is it?

But Lucky is a stand-up guy, and he wasn't going to lie to protect the McAlberts. Instead, he demolished the state's attempt to frame Karen Read for the murder of her boyfriend, John O'Keefe.

The state's demented fantasy is that she ran him over at 12:32, or 12:46, or . . . sometime in there anyway, and left him to die in the snow.

Only one problem: Lucky Loughran was plowing the street in question, Fairview Road, and he didn't see any bodies in front of the Albert house that morning in January 2022.

He did, however, see a light-colored Ford Edge on the street. Normally, he would have called the police department to let them know that someone was violating the snow emergency. Rules is rules, after all. But Lucky gave the town DPW policy a good leaving alone.

"Out of consideration to the Alberts," he testified. To repeat, Lucky is a Canton townie. You can tell by how follically challenged he is.

The prosecutor, Adam Lally, is a complete disaster. But every year he gives just enough money to his boss, Meatball Morrissey, so that he's never been worried about ever being fired. Just like most of the state cops in Meatball's office.

Lally sneered at Lucky. The jury didn't like that. The jury likes Lucky a lot more than Lally.

Unlike all the dodgy, fork-tongued troopers, Lucky is a plain speaker. He doesn't "miscount" the number of pieces of broken taillight. He doesn't claim to be able to converse with crime scenes. He didn't say he only collects evidence "as it is able."

The prosecution was doomed before yesterday. But yesterday Karen Read and her lawyers were just nailing more nails into Meatball Morrissey's coffin.

The second witness for the defense was an emergency room physician who testified as to the cuts on the victim's arm. Dog bites, she said. The state police "expert" said they were made by pieces of taillight, none of which had blood on them. But hey, it's Canton.

The physician went to MIT.

So it was MIT vs. GED.

This next, final week will be mostly the defense shooting the wounded. I'm sure Meatball is already looking for scapegoats. It would behoove Lally, as well as Lt. Tully and Sgt. Bukhenik, to again do the right thing when the district attorney's annual birthday party invitations arrive, and this time it might be wise to max out.

You guys have embarrassed Meatball very, very badly.

It's time now to begin the recriminations for the greatest scandal in Norfolk County "justice" since Sacco and Vanzetti.

Who is going to be Meatball Morrissey's fall guy for this utter catastrophe, this failure to convict an innocent woman who had the temerity to challenge the cesspool that is Canton and Norfolk County? Will it be . . .

Turtleboy?

The breathtaking corruption of Trooper Michael Proctor?

The utter incompetence of the rest of the MSP?

Or the beyond-belief-bad prosecutor Adam Lally?

There is no wrong answer. Because this is what always happens, sooner or later, in a one-party state.

It's the hackerama.

By the way, when Hollywood starts casting this movie, one role has already been filled: Lucky Loughran, as himself.

## Canton Clashes Coming to a Bar Near You

Jill Daniels, sister-in-law of Jailbird Chris Albert

*August 2, 2024*

Does this look like someone who would go batshit crazy and suddenly start shoving the female manager of a nice Cape Cod bar while screaming unhinged obscenities at her and her young waitresses on a balmy summer Saturday evening?

Does this look like a woman who would hysterically yell "Old hag!" and the c-word at a fiftysomething woman, then start weeping hysterically and repeating herself while blaming it all on Turtleboy?

Meet Jill Daniels of, where else, Canton.

She is one of the McAlberts of Karen Read trial fame. Jillian A. Daniels is the sister-in-law of Jailbird Chris Albert. Her father was named Jack Daniels. Just sayin'...

Jailbird Chris is the brother of the former BPD officer on whose lawn the body of yet another BPD officer, John O'Keefe, was found under mysterious circumstances in January 2022.

Jack Daniels' daughter first went out of control in June on a Sunday night in Canton after which multiple police cruisers arrived. That evening, Jill was screaming at Aidan Kearney, aka Turtle Boy, whose cell phone she grabbed as he was minding his own business.

History repeated itself on July 20 in Falmouth, when the forty-three-year-old harridan and her sixty-year-old boyfriend arrived at the Shipwrecked bar and restaurant in Falmouth.

Her recorded insane rant in Canton has been seen by nearly everyone in Massachusetts. So it shouldn't have been a surprise that Daniels and her boyfriend Nick Marathas would be recognized when they strolled into Shipwrecked after a visit to Martha's Vineyard.

Say, wasn't there a cop on Martha's Vineyard a few years back named Jason Marathas who got a little jammed up . . . oh, never mind.

All that follows is from the Falmouth Police Department's incident report. No arrests, no property damage, but it still took them eleven days to come up with the narrative. It was well worth the wait, as it turns out.

Let us begin with Detective Ronald Carpenter's interview with Nick Marathas as to how the affray began. "An unknown male immediately screams out in a provocative manner, 'Jill Daniels is in the house!' The unknown male and members of his party also called Daniels 'white trash!'"

To which Marathas responded, in true Canton fashion, "What's your fuckin' problem?"

But the wrinkly Marathas was totally in control compared to his much-younger girlfriend, who in fact looks more like his mother, or maybe his grandmother.

The names of the victims are all redacted in the report, but the next account seems to come from the restaurant's manager. She had been trying to shoo the white trash out of her nice restaurant when Jill Daniels gave her the Canton salute: "She was shouting and being very animated by pumping her fist and pacing . . . She could not seem to get control of herself . . . I heard her say something like 'I bet you're for Karen Read' to me. She then shoved me with both hands on my back from behind."

A sucker punch! How Canton is it?

Nick got between the victim and his shrew, but by then Jill had gone full Canton on the poor woman.

"We made it outside. She stood on the ramp screaming at me. Saying things like 'old hag' and 'c***.' Some coworkers were there to support and she screamed similar things to them."

Nick, by the way, is described by the help at the Shipwrecked as a "regular." Of course he is! He's from Canton. He and all the rest of the McAlberts are regulars at every bar, everywhere.

There's a joke in Canton: How come none of the McAlberts are lawyers?

Because they couldn't pass the bar and there's one on the way home.

Nick tried to explain the Karen Read problem to the manager.

"He told me, 'You don't know the whole story.'"

After being tossed from the bar, the McAlberts fled next door to The Heights Hotel, where Officer David McGraw found them sitting dejectedly on the stairs. Jill Daniels was weeping buckets—"visibly upset with tears in her eyes."

"I asked her what had happened and she stated to me that there was a group of people who were targeting her, calling her names and taking pictures of her."

Why would they be doing that? Officer McGraw inquired.

"She stated to me that it was 'all about Turtleboy' and 'the fact that I am from Canton.' Daniels then stated to me that they were targeting her because of the 'Karen Read trial.' Daniels repeated herself several times and continually broke down in tears."

It would take a heart of stone not to laugh. What goes around, comes around.

"While Daniels was continually repeating herself, Marathas was sitting next to her and telling her to stop."

You know what really fries Jill's nose, as Mumbles Menino would say? The fact that if they were back in Canton, or anywhere in Norfolk County for that matter, the heat would be on those damn civilians. How'd they like to be arrested?

For witness intimidation. Maybe frisk 'em to see if they had any rubber duckies on their persons.

How'd they like to be charged with second-degree murder? And even when the jury found 'em not guilty, they'd still be retried. Double jeopardy? We don't have no stinkin' Fifth Amendment prohibitions against double jeopardy in Norfolk County!

There's an old line from Rudyard Kipling that seems appropriate here: "There comes a night/ When the best get tight."

The best? In Canton, there comes a night when everybody gets tight. It's called every night of the year.

You know, that same Saturday night those four Falmouth cruisers had to be called to the Shipwrecked to quell another McAlbert barroom brawl, I was dining in the North End, at Vinoteca di Monica on Richmond Street.

One of Karen Read's lawyers, David Yannetti, strolled in. We shook hands, exchanged pleasantries, and then went our separate ways. No shoves, no obscenities . . . in other words, no Canton.

There's another old saying in Canton: No McAlberts, no problems.

## Norfolk DA "Meatball" Morrissey Needs a Breather from Chasing His White Whales

*October 19, 2024*

You're Michael "Meatball" Morrissey, the seventy-year-old hack district attorney of Norfolk County. And on mornings like this, you sometimes dream of just heading down to Marina Bay and sailing away.

Except for parades, Meatball has mostly gone MIA from public events.

Captain Ahab had his *Pequod*, Captain Queeg had the *Caine*, and now you, Captain Meatball, pilot the *Class Action*.

Ahab was obsessed with Moby-Dick, Queeg with the missing strawberries, and now you are hunting the biggest game of all.

Karen Read and Turtleboy.

But as you obsessively track those public enemies, your scurvy crew is in full mutiny. You can't believe it. This never happened to the Skipper on the *Minnow*. Gilligan never even considered walking the plank.

You're Meatball Morrissey and Friday you lost the second conehead Keystone Kop on your MSP "detective" unit—Lt. Brian Tully.

Just because of that little Internal Affairs investigation by the MSP, and now this latest revelation that he was hacking, er, extracting data from Turtleboy's cell phone even though your prosecutors were claiming in court the phone was "pristine" and untouched by your crooked cops.

What did Turtleboy's lawyer call those statements?

"Patently false ... misleading ... false impressions ... clear violation of due process ..."

Tully could straighten a thing out. He put the first handcuffs on Turtleboy.

So what if he and the special prosecutor Ken Mello admitted under oath to a grand jury that they had been doing exactly what they repeatedly told judges they hadn't. So what? It's Norfolk County, and you're Meatball Morrissey.

Tully was even more valuable in the administration of your Norfolk County "just-us" than his fellow conehead Trooper Michael Proctor, now suspended without pay from the MSP.

Just because the FBI discovered that by his own text admissions, Proctor spent all his time scrolling through Karen Read's cell phone for nude photos, when he wasn't openly soliciting bribes for looking the other way in Canton murder cases.

First Proctor, now Tully. But then it got even worse for you on Friday. You lost your lifer hack flack, David Traub, who as a mark of his fealty had ponied up $2,225 to your "campaign."

You've also lost Lynn Beland, your loyal $201,000-a-year assistant, not just another pretty face. She's retiring at age sixty-eight to try out for a role in the new Netflix production, *Childless Cat Ladies*.

Good old Lynn Beland—at least she handed over $5,200 to your campaign account before she took it on the lam.

You're Meatball Morrissey, and you're worried now that you're gonna lose your last real go-to trooper—Sgt. Yuriy Bukhenik, that super sleuth who runs the elite Rubber Ducky Detail, mandated to stamping out the First Amendment in Norfolk County.

He's a thug's thug, that Bukhenik—like when he's one-finger typing a report, and he suddenly calls out to everybody in the office, in his broken English, "Do anybody here know, is dat word 'cat' spelled wit' one 't' or two?"

At least you've got yourself a new first mate—Hank Brennan, the $250-an-hour Mob mouthpiece who's been tasked with framing Karen Read in her double-jeopardy second-degree murder trial in January.

You're Meatball Morrissey and you bonded with Brennan as soon as you met him. He's a bargain at a mere $566,000 for the next trial.

You guys have so much in common—he was a stooge in court for serial killer Whitey Bulger and you were a stooge for Whitey's little brother Billy at the State House.

(Sure, you broke with Bulger a little bit at the end, but it was because you had to hang with your homeboy Sen. Bill Keating, because he was going to run for district attorney and then set you up for the job when he got into Congress after the previous district attorney who'd moved up to Congress himself . . .)

Sitting in Canton, you and Brennan can swap Bulger stories all day long. Brennan can say, "Hey, Meatball, do you remember what Whitey did to Donald Killeen?" And you chuckle and say, "What about what Billy did at the State House to Paul Harold?"

He says, "What about Brian Halloran?" You come back with, "Ever hear of Alan Sisitsky?"

And Brennan says, "How about how Whitey strangled Deb Hussey and pulled out all her teeth?" You say, "Let me tell you what Billy did to a court clerk named John E. Powers."

You're Meatball Morrissey and when you tell Brennan that you want him to do to Karen Read exactly what an earlier Norfolk district attorney did to a guy named Fred Weichel for Whitey Bulger, you don't have to draw Brennan a diagram.

Brennan's from the neighborhood. His task is putting Karen Read in prison for thirty-five years for a crime she didn't commit. Just like what Weichel got.

It's a Norfolk County tradition.

You're Meatball Morrissey, and sometimes you wonder, *Where are the ethical titans of yesteryear?* Like developer William O'Connell, or FBI agents like Zip Connolly, Vino Morris, and Paul Rico.

Those were the days!

At least you've still got the judges cowed. Turtleboy's lawyers somehow discovered that threatening note you sent to the two judges and the court administrators, demanding that they get rid of a lowly clerk in Stoughton who dared to give public documents to Turtleboy.

On your personal burner email account, you thundered at the judges: "These actions are completely unacceptable and must be resolved immediately."

By firing the clerk.

You typed those words and you felt like your old boss Billy Bulger turning the screws on Judge E. George Daher back in the day. And then when the *Herald* asked for a comment from the court system about your outrageous demand, the judges were so terrified all they had to say was this: "The Trial Court declines to comment."

You're Meatball Morrissey and you know why you can still get away with slapping the judges—because you're with House Speaker Ron Mariano, and if those bust-out failed lawyers ever want another pay raise, they better not bleep with the boys from Quincy.

The legislature controls the money, just like when you were worshipping at the feet of Billy Bulger. It's the same reason Diana DiZoglio will never get to audit the legislature's books, no matter how big she wins on the question 1 referendum next month.

If the Supreme Judicial Court rules in DiZoglio's favor, no judge in Massachusetts will ever get another pay raise.

(Update: The referendum to audit the legislature's books did pass, in November 2024, with 72 percent of the popular vote. At press time, as predicted, the auditor was still being stonewalled by the legislature and the courts.)

You're Meatball Morrissey, and you know how the system works. You need another million bucks to pay for Hank Brennan? You just write a letter to Speaker Mariano asking for the dough and voilà!

In that threatening note to the judges, somehow you misspelled the names of both Turtleboy and Karen Read—as "Aiden" Kearney and Karen "Reed."

Were you trying to make sure that if anybody ever got ahold of your emails and tried to run a name search, they'd come up empty? You know, the way cops like Michael Proctor do it in their reports.

Or were you just tired and emotional?

If that's what happened, it just reminds everybody of the four-car crash you had in Milton. You said you "blacked out."

Of course nobody believed your explanation, except for the part where you said that when you passed out on Centre Street, you were on your cell phone, ordering a large pizza to go.

That part of the story, everyone totally bought.

You're Meatball Morrissey and the only good thing about today is that the Pats are playing in London, so kickoff's at ten. And nobody will look askance at you if you sip a Captain n' cola or two a bit on the early side.

You're off to Marina Bay and the *Class Action* for a cruise around the harbor. And as always, your first mate will be Captain Morgan.

You're Meatball Morrissey, and you owe it to yourself.

## Karen Read and the Norfolk County Hackerama

*May 24, 2025*

It's almost halftime in the second Karen Read murder trial, and right now I'd have to say Meatball Morrissey and the Norfolk County hackerama are again behind on points.

That's not to say that the despicable Quincy crew won't eventually be able to lynch Read, or at least cheat their way to another "mistrial."

Maybe, as in the first trial, Judge Bev Cannone will give the jurors voting slips without the option to vote not guilty.

When she was called on her kangaroo-court forms last year, she shrugged and said, "That's the way we've always done it here."

Just ask Sacco and Vanzetti. They were framed in the same courthouse in Dedham, in 1921, at least in part on the false testimony of a corrupt state trooper named Proctor.

History does indeed repeat itself, or tries to anyway.

If she can't pass out the fake jury slips this time, perhaps the judge will again try to ignore any unanimous not-guilty verdicts, the way she did with two of the three counts the first jury returned against Read last summer.

In school, children are taught that double jeopardy is unconstitutional in America.

But remember, kids, we're not in America. We're in Norfolk County.

Still, the hacks' grip on this rotten borough appears more tenuous than ever. They've lost control of the board of selectmen in Canton, the belly of the beast. Last year the Morrissey stooge lost by 200 votes, this year their thirty-year incumbent was crushed by a 2–1 margin.

The Meatball Mob couldn't oust a dissident county politician last year, even with a well-financed Quincy hack. Meatball's minion was crushed 72–28.

As you know, in the hackerama, Memorial Day is Memorial Week. Which is why the Read trial recessed at mid-afternoon Wednesday, until next Tuesday. But there was another reason why the pot-bellied courthouse stooges took an early slide Wednesday.

Over in Norwood, the Norfolk County Bar Association was holding its annual bender, er, dinner. And the Person of the Year was Judge Beverly Cannone. Of course she was!

But wait, it gets better. Every phony-baloney banquet needs a keynote speaker. For their annual toot, the bar association selected the new $174,532-a-year county clerk of courts, Walter F. Timilty, who has succeeded his father, Walter F. Timilty.

Would you care to guess how many times the keynote speaker failed the bar exam? The over-under is five, and if you took the under, you lose.

The keynote speaker for the Norfolk County Bar Association dinner, who is also the county's clerk of courts, has failed the bar exam six times—once each in 1995, 1997, 2000, and 2001, and twice in 1996.

By the way, on his birth certificate his name was listed as Walter F. Timilty III. His father was Walter Timilty Jr., until Walter III needed his own hack job in the legislature. So on the ballot, *Jr.* became *Sr.*, and *III* became *Jr.*

Shouldn't running for office under false names be against the law? Oh, I forgot, it's Norfolk County.

(By the way, now that he's retired, Daddy Timilty's pension is $106,146 a year, not to mention the $16,664.97 he pocketed as "leave buyback" when he handed the hack job to his nitwit son.)

It's a very prestigious body, the Norfolk County Bar Association. The secretary is one Michael Barbadoro. Would you care to guess if Barbadoro works in the Dreaded Private Sector, or in the Norfolk County hackerama?

You are correct. He's "first assistant register" of probate in Norfolk County. Two diminutives in his job title—he's a hack for sure.

Perhaps this political incestuousness is why the hackerama is struggling so to frame Karen Read. It's one thing to be stupid, which they all are, but they're also inbred.

Welcome to Norfolk County | 91

I mean, why would anyone capable of earning an honest living want to associate with the dismal low-IQ likes of Meatball, Auntie Bev, Walter Timilty, or the first assistant?

Those who can, do. Those who can't, get hack jobs with Norfolk County.

Some become judges, others cut grass at Presidents Golf Course. The pay varies, but every last one of them is a hack job, and there's only one qualification. You must know somebody, preferably somebody named Meatball.

The talent pool in Norfolk County has gotten so shallow that Morrissey has had to hire three "special prosecutors" to try to railroad Karen Read and her supporter Aidan "Turtleboy" Kearney.

One of Turtleboy's persecutors is Robert "Triple Dip" Cosgrove, who is seventy-three years old and has never once raised his snout from the public trough. Currently he's pocketing a $64,264-a-year pension from Meatball's district attorney office, as well as a $139,301-a-year pension as a retired judge, and we all know what an ethical bunch Massachusetts judges are.

Just ask Bev Cannone.

And now on top of his $204,000 in state pensions, Triple Dip Cosgrove collects a third check for trying to throw Turtleboy in prison. His crime? He exercised his First Amendment rights to make a face in the window of a business owned by an ex-con selectman in Canton who was represented in his hit-and-run manslaughter case by Judge Bev's brother.

You see what I mean about the political inbreeding in Norfolk County?

And I haven't even mentioned Hank Brennan, another of Meatball Morrissey's special prosecutors, currently handling the Karen Read frame-up.

He was the lawyer for Whitey Bulger, Norfolk County's preeminent gangster and serial killer for decades (after moving from Southie to Quincy). In those days, Meatball was a state senator and Whitey's brother Billy was the president of the Senate, known as "the Corrupt Midget."

The Corrupt Midget would tell Morrissey, "Jump!" and Meatball would answer, "How high?"

(Bulger's pension, for the record, is now $274,149 a year. He's been collecting since 2003.)

Nothing ever really changes in Norfolk County, except the COLA increases in all their hack pensions. But if Karen Read is found not guilty, it will be the end of an era, or should I say error?

It's the hackerama.

## Norfolk County and Its White-Trash Grifter Leaders

*May 31, 2025*

For the Norfolk County hackerama, the worst thing about the Karen Read murder trial is that it has exposed to the entire world just how corrupt and rotten the entire enterprise is.

Nothing on the level, everything is a deal, and no deal too small.

It is the wealthiest, probably best-educated county in the state. But it's run by a crew of white-trash grifters from Quincy who operate like it's still 1958 and they're in Plaquemines Parish, Louisiana.

All the swells in places like Dover, Brookline, Cohasset, Needham, and Wellesley can't be bothered with doing anything about the festering, metastasizing kleptocracy that they're paying for with their tax dollars.

The Beautiful People don't need those hack county jobs at Presidents Golf Course. Hell, they've got way too much money to even think about playing a round there. That's for the plebeians.

Nobody outside Quincy or Braintree or Canton ever gave a second thought to Norfolk County government. And that's the way the local hacks wanted it. Out of sight, out of mind, and behind that comes the pension.

But now the local yokels have gone too far. They're trying to lynch an innocent woman. And they won't take no for an answer.

"This was a vindictive prosecution that should have never been brought," said Karen Read's attorney Alan Jackson. "They say they've done their best. Some would say they've done their worst."

Judge Beverly Cannone: Defined exculpatory as "excluded."

The hacko di tutti hacki is Meatball Morrissey, the bloated hack Democrat district attorney, a Kamala Harris delegate to the national convention last year. How much more do you need to know?

For his second attempt to railroad Karen Read, Morrissey has spent at least $566,000 hiring a defense lawyer named Hank Brennan as his special prosecutor.

Brennan used to work for serial killer Whitey Bulger. He's not exactly Perry Mason, but the hack judge, Bev Cannone, has been running cover for him.

At a pretrial hearing, she harrumphed that she had "grave concerns" about the defense spending $23,000 of their own money on travel expenses for their crash-reconstruction experts.

But then last week it was revealed that the prosecution has squandered $400,000 in public funds on their own shoddy "experts," one of whom has been futilely trying to get a bachelor's degree since 2007.

Yet the judge had no grave concerns about that $400,000 because . . . Norfolk County.

The other Tom Brady from Norfolk County.

On Thursday, when one of Read's attorneys asked a damning question of the prosecution "expert," Bev had to prod her BFF, Brennan, who apparently wasn't paying attention.

"Objection, Mr. Brennan?" she prompted her teammate. Could it be any clearer whose side she's on?

But it's not just the courts in Norfolk County that are rotten to the core. Last week, the former number-three guy at the county jail, Tom Brady, for that is indeed his name, was indicted by the feds for extortion.

They said he was shaking down his underlings for free work on his house in Norwood.

Here's the Brady backstory: He was always just another townie hack guard, working overnights. Then a Democrat named Pat McDermott decided to run for sheriff against the last Republican in Norfolk County, Jerry McDermott.

Between 2019 and 2022 Brady coughed up $3,200 to McDermott (D) who defeated McDermott (R). In the finest county tradition, Brady's pay doubled, from $70,000 to $138,000.

His wife, of course, has her own hack courthouse job, because . . . Norfolk County. Jennifer Brady makes $163,763 a year as chief

Welcome to Norfolk County | 95

probation officer at Hingham District Court. The chief justice in Hingham is one Heather Bradley, who got her $207,832-a-year job the old-fashioned way.

After a nationwide search.

Her husband was a state rep with Meatball Morrissey. He's since gotten jammed up with the Board of Bar Overseers over his own legal career. One judge castigated him for his "blatant falsehoods," but hey, he's a Democrat so no problem, right?

As for Brady, the little bit of power he was handed at the jail went straight to his empty head. Soon he was in trouble with the State Ethics Commission. As his attorney, he hired one Jonathan C. Rutley, who practices in, where else, Canton.

Rutley used to work in, of all places, the Norfolk County district attorney's office. He was a coat holder for Bill Keating, now a $174,000-a-year congressman while simultaneously pocketing a $111,879 pension from his county job.

Double-dipping—another Norfolk County tradition.

Rutley, meanwhile, has been collecting a mere $78,222 for his Norfolk County pension. He's been "retired" since 2011.

And yet Rutley still does the right thing by all the county Democrat bosses. He's handed Meatball $1,825 over the years, as well as $1,175 to Brady's boss, Sheriff McDermott (D).

I'm sure when Brady picked Rutley, he was looking for reasonable doubt at a reasonable price. But sometimes it pays to seriously lawyer up before, not after, you have to do the perp walk on Northern Avenue.

Maybe Brady should have consulted with his brother-in-law, Brian Walsh, who himself happens to be a judge in Norfolk County, at Stoughton District Court. Another nationwide search!

## Extra Helping for DA "Meatball" Morrissey

*August 7, 2024*

You only need to know one thing about the race for register of deeds in Norfolk County: The twenty-year incumbent, Bill O'Donnell, is being opposed by Norfolk County District Attorney Michael "Meatball" Morrissey.

Along with all his hack cronies, Meatball has been funneling cash to O'Donnell's opponent.

O'Donnell's opponent is Noel DiBona, who henceforward I'm going to call Noel DiBona-Morrissey, for that is what he is, a stooge for Morrissey and the rest of the Quincy Democrat hackerama.

You can't vote against Meatball Morrissey this year, but you can vote against his sock puppet.

Morrissey just turned seventy last Friday, but in his dotage he remains extremely busy, not apparently just trying to frame Karen Read in a second murder trial after her acquittal last month.

Among his other accomplishments, there's the ongoing scandal of the murder of twenty-three-year-old Sandra Birchmore who was allegedly pregnant by a married cop—another Canton miscarriage of justice now being investigated by the same FBI that's all over the Karen Read corruption.

And Meatball is still trying to keep the lid on the 2020 police killing of unarmed Juston Root in Brookline—shot thirty-one times in three seconds by assorted cops who got away with it because . . . Norfolk County.

Busy? Tubby Mike is also a delegate to the Democrat convention in Chicago because . . . free buffets and open bars! And he's got a time next week in Quincy to fatten up his $443,000 campaign war chest.

But with everything else on his heaping plate, Meatball still found time in June to send $100 to DiBona-Morrissey. And one of his in-laws has duked cash to DiBona more than a dozen times over the years.

It's the hackerama, baby! DiBona-Morrissey is a Quincy city councilor. It's Quincy being Quincy.

Calls were made yesterday to both Morrissey and his anointed payroll patriot, Noel DiBona-Morrissey. The calls were not returned.

The Norfolk hacks have picked DiBona-Morrissey to rid themselves of the incumbent register of deeds, Bill O'Donnell. They hate him because the registry makes a lot of money for Norfolk County, and he won't cut up the pot with them.

The commissioners want that cash for themselves to keep hiring and handing out obscene pay raises to their worthless families and friends.

O'Donnell has sued the Norfolk County commissioners twice, and won. That's verboten. The way things work in Norfolk, O'Donnell is just lucky the hacks haven't tried to frame him for a murder he didn't commit.

Just ask Karen Read.

Like Meatball Morrissey, two of the three county commissioners are all in with Di-Bona-Morrissey. So are all the county hacks and beneficiaries of Meatball "just-us"—like the O'Connells of Quincy. Google 'em if you want to find out even more about "just-us" in the Norfolk County annals of crime.

Meet Peter Collins, a $49,736-a-year part-time county commissioner since 1994. His father, James Collins, preceded him on the commission from 1964 to 1992. That late James Collins is not to be confused with the late former treasurer of Norfolk County, Jailbird James Collins, who went to prison for embezzling $100,000 in county funds.

Peter Collins runs a law firm, and one of his lawyers is Joseph Labadini. After Labadini joined Collins and Collins, a nationwide search took place, and his wife, Michelle Labadini, was hired as "county personnel director."

She started out at $83,436 and now makes $107,688. Does the county pay for her family's health insurance? That would probably save some dough for Commissioner Collins's law firm, eh?

By the way, the county owns Presidents Golf Course in Quincy. In 2022, there was another nationwide search, and Matthew J. Labadini was hired as a custodian, for $40,047 a year.

Presidents Golf Course is a real family affair for the Norfolk County hackerama. Commissioner Collins's brother-in-law is Steven Doyle, a groundskeeper at $50,080. Summer hires at the golf course in recent years have included yet another James Collins (not to be confused with either Grampy or Jailbird James Collins) as well as one Matthew Doyle.

A second county commissioner is Joe Shea. He makes $52,590 a year as chairman, and was a career hack at Quincy City Hall. His wife Josephine is on the Norfolk County Retirement Board. Would you care to guess where their daughter works?

You got it. The golf course. Her name is Amy Baker—$81,094 a year.

Shea gave DiBona-Morrissey $250 directly. Collins preferred to let his wife handle the contributions to DiBona-Morrissey—$1,000.

The incumbent register of deeds, O'Donnell, is a hack himself. He even used to be a county commissioner. But he's not from Quincy, which makes him a foreigner. He's from Norwood.

So they dip into his budget and deny him funds for technological upgrades. But if you've bought or sold property in Norfolk County (and I have), you appreciate a smoothly functioning Registry of Deeds, which is what we have now.

Morrissey, Collins, Shea et al. want to rid themselves of O'Donnell almost as much as they want to send Karen Read to prison for a crime she's already been acquitted of. They'd rather beat O'Donnell than keep the trigger-happy cops in the Birchmore and Root cases out of jail.

They desperately need that money from the Registry of Deeds. It's not just all for their families either. How about John Cronin, the "county director," hired at $122,000 three years ago and now up to $148,000. He was a defendant in one of the cases O'Donnell brought against the county commissioners.

Mrs. Cronin—Denise—handed $100 to DiBona-Morrissey.

The assistant "county director" is William Buckley, a hack from Walpole who used to work for Rep. Jolly John Rogers, who once compared convicted felon House Speaker Charlie Flaherty to Jesus Christ.

Buckley's pay has skyrocketed to $96,776.

By the way, Cronin and Buckley are also grabbing huge extra bucks for "administering" federal COVID relief money—the hacks used to get an extra ten large a year. Now it's up to thirty grand annually, and it continues, even though the Panic is long in the rearview mirror.

Between them, when it's all over, Cronin and Buckley will have pocketed $240,000 that could have gone to the cities and towns if county government had been abolished in Norfolk as it has been in most of the Commonwealth.

On his campaign site, DiBona-Morrissey says he is "no stranger to Norfolk County."

Norfolk County payrolls, anyway. He used to work in the county sheriff's department. It, uh, didn't work out. Then he went to, ahem, "work" for O'Donnell. Ditto.

On September 3, vote O'Donnell in the Democrat primary. Give Meatball another *L*. He's got it coming, big-time.

CHAPTER EIGHT

# Rubber Duckies Everywhere

Rubber Ducky, you're the one!

At a hearing before the first trial, Alan Jackson made a point about the evidence indicating that Karen Read could not have possibly hit her boyfriend John O'Keefe.

"If it walks like a duck," he said, "and it talks like a duck, it's a duck."

Ducks! As in rubber duckies. It caught on. Instantly, rubber duckies—and fake $100 bills—became a symbol of the Free Karen Read movement. Soon they were everywhere.

*The hackerama in Norfolk County went crazy! Rubber duckies—this will not stand. In a county with an unusually large number of "unsolved" murders, cops were suddenly put on the real crime problem roiling Norfolk County—rubber duckies.*

*I wrote columns on the assorted "probes" across the county.*

## Canton Cops Continue to Duck Responsibilities

*October 5, 2024*

The Town of Canton can rest easy this morning.

Pay no attention to those two still-unsolved murders involving corrupt local cops in one way or another.

The real menace to the law-abiding citizenry of Canton isn't murder, it's . . . rubber duckies.

And now the Canton Police Department can report a major breakthrough.

The kingpin of the sinister local rubber-ducky cartel has been brought to justice.

How do you plead, Richard L. Schiffer, Jr., age sixty-five?

At first glance, to the untrained eye, this Schiffer party may appear harmless enough—a grandfather, French-bulldog owner, longtime proprietor of a small business called Canton Fence.

But don't be fooled by his affable, avuncular pose. It is but a clever ruse.

In fact, Schiffer is Mr. Big, the godfather of an international conspiracy, to wit, throwing tiny rubber duckies and prop money onto the streets of Canton.

It's more fallout from the Karen Read murder case. The feds are crawling over this scandal, and their target is neither Schiffer nor Karen Read, who is facing a second trial even though she's already been acquitted of murder.

Please, don't ask me to explain how the local cops get around the double jeopardy prohibition in the Constitution. Suffice to say, we're not in America, we're in Norfolk County.

The G-men have already done 3,074 pages of reports on the local Keystone Kops' appalling misconduct in the Karen Read case.

In the other unsolved Canton murder, from 2021, those same feds just charged a depraved Stoughton cop with murdering his pregnant twenty-three-year-old girlfriend.

Per tradition, the Canton police had ruled that heinous crime by their fellow cop a suicide. Professional courtesy . . .

Sooner or later, though, when cops get this irredeemably corrupt, the population begins to take notice, even in Norfolk County.

Thus, Schiffer posted on his sign outside Canton Fence this large message: KAREN READ WAS FRAMED!

You may say that's freedom of speech, protected by the First Amendment. In Norfolk County, however, it's considered probable cause.

It's the truth, but Canton cops call it "propaganda." Really, they do.

After a six-month "investigation" by the Canton Police Department, Schiffer has now been summoned to Stoughton District Court October 23 to face the consequences of his monstrous conspiracy.

He has been charged with ten counts, six of which are . . . littering.

The Canton cops put a hundred times more time and effort into the rubber ducky caper than they did on both murders—combined.

The lead sleuth on the rubber ducky squad is Det. Tim Taylor, the Inspector Clouseau of Canton.

He is quite proud that he quacked the case. Mr. Big was acting with mallard aforethought. This is all about fowl play. And it is no yolk, er, joke, to the Canton Police Department.

Taylor has memorialized, as they say, his groundbreaking probe in a thirty-six-page, single-spaced report.

"It has included," he brags, "letters of preservation, the execution of search warrants, surveillance, which included my observation of several crimes committed, witness statements, some of whose identity (sic) is (sic) being withheld at this time due to fear of retribution, similar to that of what is further described throughout this report . . ."

Retribution? Complaining about murders and endemic police corruption is now considered "retribution?"

According to the CPD report, Schiffer has been the subject of at least five search warrants, in addition to the "preservation orders" to Facebook.

Twice, Taylor has read him his Miranda rights.

In paragraph 85, the cops list items seized from Schiffer, including "1 Rubber Duck."

Last May, DA Meatball Morrissey's "Digital Forensics Division" obtained a warrant to download information from Schiffer's truck. But in the finest tradition of Troopers Paul and Guarino, Meatball's minions were utterly defeated by even the simplest technological task.

Fat, drunk, and stupid may be no way to go through life, but if you work for Meatball or the Canton Police Department, it's a résumé enhancer.

Over and over, in his ESL prose, Det. Taylor accuses Schiffer of engaging in "propaganda," whatever that might be, and which in any event seems to be protected under the Bill of Rights. Except in Canton.

To bust this international crime ring (Schiffer sent some rubber duckies to the UK), the Canton Police Department pulled Ring camera videos from so many locations that I lost count.

On April 10, in a multiagency effort, Canton and Stoughton police converged on Schiffer's home in Stoughton and conducted a "trash pull."

"Prior to our arrival . . . the rear hopper was emptied. Upon arrival . . . there was a single trash barrel out front. The contents of the trash barrel were emptied into the rear of the trash truck by me, Detective Taylor. The contents of the barrel were 3 trash bags."

The Sherlocks of Stoughton and the Columbos of Canton were seeking evidence of the origins of the contraband—the rubber duckies and what Taylor describes as "counterfeit" currency, that is, prop or toy fake money.

"Items retrieved from the trash contents were an empty prescription medication bottle prescribed to Richard Schiffer, a white box, an Amazon package envelope . . ."

At this point, perhaps you are wondering what the significance of rubber duckies is in the Karen Read scandal. Well, Det. Taylor has developed a "theory of the crime." It must be very significant, because he puts it in italics over and over again.

In paragraph 223, Taylor blames the sinister conspiracy on that statement in January by Karen Read's lawyer Alan Jackson: "If it walks like a duck, talks like a duck, it's a duck."

He's so impressed with his duck theory that he repeats Jackson's quote, again in italics, on pages 34 and 35.

This is crazy. If you wrote this as a Hollywood script, the producer would throw it back and say that not even the dumbest cops can be this stupid or corrupt.

But in Norfolk County, they can and are.

Just ask MSP Sgt. Yuriy Bukhenik. Or disgraced Trooper Michael Proctor. Or . . .

In paragraph 164, on page 22, Det. Taylor ominously notes, "Behavior is escalating."

I fear he's correct. It's past time for the feds to intervene, and de-escalate the escalating behavior with a big roundup. One, two, many Matthew Farwells. Lug everybody with a Canton, Stoughton, or MSP badge and let a jury on Northern Avenue sort it all out.

One final question: Has the Canton Police Department ever investigated the reported horrific death of a certain adorable chocolate Lab puppy named Wilson that was abandoned by his idiot owner to be baked alive in a sweltering car back in the summer of 2023?

Why have no charges been filed in that atrocious animal-cruelty case?

Can Det. Taylor find time to do some sleuthing on that crime, even if it didn't involve a single rubber ducky?

## The Rubber Duckies Are Quacking "Free Karen Read" in Canton

*September 28, 2024*

If rubber duckies are outlawed, only outlaws will have rubber duckies.

But never fear. The Keystone Kops known as the MSP are on the case, and are determined to rid Norfolk County once and for all of the criminal scourge of . . . rubber duckies.

The MSP are about to get a new colonel, Geoffrey Noble. Job one for him should be figuring out the mysterious death of the poor cadet in a boxing ring at the academy in New Braintree, and why none of the current brass could be bothered to undertake even a half-hearted investigation for eleven days (see page 178).

After dealing with that squalid cover-up, Col. Klink, er Noble must confront the overriding obsession of the MSP, at least in Norfolk County.

Rubber duckies in Canton.

Forget all the MSP's endless other scandals—too numerous to chronicle here.

The troopers are on the job—and their only job appears to be the rubber ducky caper.

Sgt. Yuri Bukhenik is the lead sleuth in the MSP's elite Rubber Ducky Detail. He's fresh off losing five days' vacation for his vile, misogynistic behavior in the recent Karen Read frame-up—a résumé-enhancer in the MSP.

After Karen Read beat the murder rap, little rubber duckies began appearing in Canton, a spontaneous protest against the corruption of local police and prosecutors.

On the bottom of each tiny ducky was written, among other things—*FKR*, for "Free Karen Read," because even though she was acquitted by the jury, she must stand trial again next spring for the same crimes.

It's Norfolk County. The Bill of Rights no longer applies here.

This heinous rubber ducky crime wave convulsed Canton all summer. It's a little town where there have been two unsolved murders since 2021, both involving ethically challenged cops.

Naturally both of those homicide investigations involving cops were utterly botched by Bukhenik and his fellow Keystone Kops. Professional courtesy . . .

Murders? Who cares? The real problem is . . . rubber duckies.

Bukhenik et al. have been seeking a complaint in Stoughton District Court against a young mother of two. She is accused of dropping off one or two of the tiny Free Karen Read rubber duckies on a public bench in July.

That bench is near a crappy restaurant owned by a local ex-con who happens to be both an elected selectman and a pal of Bukhenik and the rest of the local townie cops.

Among the charges they're seeking against the young woman is witness intimidation—a felony! For leaving a rubber ducky or two on a public way.

The duckies turned up in July when the woman, who doesn't even live in Canton, made the mistake of having lunch in the rotten borough with her retired parents.

After the rubber duckies turned up outside the business of the ex-con (he killed a foreign exchange student in a hit-and-run and did six months), the jailbird pol hysterically texted his pal Bukhenik.

Instantly three MSP "detectives" were assigned to investigate the heinous crime of rubber ducky littering.

The hulking, simian-looking Bukhenik sped to the woman's home to begin an unhinged interrogation of her in front of her preschool son.

At the court, along with his application for a felony warrant for rubber-ducky littering, Bukhenik filed a transcript of his knucklehead interview with the young mother. The public transcript was first revealed by Aidan Kearney, known as Turtleboy.

Just the facts ma'am. All dialogue guaranteed verbatim from Stoughton District Court:

> BUKHENIK: "So I just wanna get it from you where the ducks come from... So, the ducks you had in your possession, where did they come from?... Where did you get these little ducks?... So you purchased them on Amazon? When did you purchase them?"

After that last question, the shocked woman replies, "I'm starting to feel, like, very uncomfortable."

This is what your undereducated, undertrained MSP are paid hundreds of thousands of dollars a year to do, when they're not embezzling millions in fraudulent OT, overdosing on contraband drugs, illegally selling guns or CDLs, drunkenly killing motorcyclists, brooming cases for junkie children of corrupt judges, or viciously beating up their wives and girlfriends.

> BUKHENIK: "Did you write the *FKR* on his, uh, on that duck?"
>
> WOMAN: "I'm not sure. I—I could have."
>
> BUKHENIK: "You could have? So you wrote the *FKR* on the, on the duck, and, uh, then you left it in front of his (the killer jailbird politician's) business. You see how that looks?"

It looks like the First Amendment to me. At worst, littering.

> BUKHENIK: "My superiors are gonna a—wanna know. The court would wanna know, so that's why I have to ask these questions."
>
> WOMAN: "The court? For ducks?"
>
> BUKHENIK: "Well, it's not just ducks. It's the message."

The message being: Karen Read was framed. Which is true, and that makes it even more proscribed to say.

> BUKHENIK: "Did you purchase these ducks, uh, uh, for a certain reason? Why—what's the reason why you purchased these tiny little ducks?"
>
> WOMAN: "I have children . . . We have crates of toys."
>
> BUKHENIK: "You still took it upon yourself to write a message, *FKR*, Free Karen Read, and leave it on a little duck . . . You did that! You still, at the very least, littered, you deposited, deposited rubbish in the street."
>
> WOMAN: "Charge me with littering . . . I don't know what else to tell you."
>
> BUKHENIK: "Did you leave any ducks anywhere else?"

Finally, the woman's husband arrived, to find his wife being stalked by this armed, menacing, crewcut fiend. The woman regained her composure enough to push back against his latest misogynistic bullying.

> WOMAN: "I've been thinking about, how is this a State Police matter and not a Canton Police matter?"

> BUKHENIK: "We investigate homicides and this being relative to the homicide investigation . . . ."
>
> WOMAN: "See, to me this feels like intimidation. I feel intimidated by you showing up at my house with a gun, and all of this for putting down a duck, instead of the Canton Police coming. You come to my house about a, a little duck that was put down."
>
> BUKHENIK: "We have to enforce the laws and maintain order and civil, civil order, uh, in our society 'cause if we don't, the next, the next episode of not—I'm not saying with this case, but the next episode that happens will be ten times worse because nothing was done right now! You know?"

In other words, if he doesn't charge a young mother with a felony for dropping a tiny seventy-nine-cent rubber ducky near a connected jailbird killer's business, pretty soon there will be . . . ten rubber duckies on that bench.

> BUKHENIK: "You left a duck with a clear and concise message of *FKR*, Free Karen Read, on the duck. So you have very, very small portion of this, but it's the totality of it . . ."

At the end, Bukhenik had the audacity to deliver a "Scared Straight" lecture to the young mother: "Hopefully you don't re-offend, or don't, you know, take action that would rise to the same level of, uh, intimidation or harassment."

Intimidation? Re-offend? With a rubber ducky? Finally, her husband stepped up and told off the unhinged thug: "You need to stop!"

Col. Noble, you need to stop this! You need to get rid of every one of these disgraced, bent troopers in Norfolk County and wherever else they're violating the civil rights of innocent citizens.

The next time some cop groupie tells you the MSP is getting a bum rap just because of a few hundred bad apples, remember two words: *Rubber duckies.*

## CHAPTER NINE

# Copland

It's gotten easier and easier to be a crooked cop in Massachusetts over the years.

It wasn't supposed to work out this way. Starting in the 1970s, the legislature began "reforming" law enforcement, supposedly to create better cops, more educated police.

In the old days, your average cop wasn't well educated, to put it mildly. Any police officer who'd gone beyond high school was dismissed as a "college boy." Most cops had grown up in the same neighborhoods as the criminals they were supposed to be policing.

They were underpaid. Opportunities abounded, of course, for cops to supplement their income. As early as 1943, in his book about the social structure of the North End of Boston, *Street Corner Society*, sociologist William A. Whyte devoted much attention to the BPD's role in the rackets. For a price, usually quite modest, the laws protected local wiseguys. If a new hood tried to muscle in, the cops were expected to take him down—it was the unspoken part of the deal, what they were paid for.

In blue-collar cities like Revere, Chelsea and Somerville, many cops were pretty much part of the Mob, if only casually and informally. In Somerville, a Metropolitan police officer named Russ Nicholson was actually involved in the hit that started the Irish Gang War in

1961. He drove the getaway car. Nicholson was later murdered by the McLaughlin crew out of Charlestown.

By that time he had been suspended by the Mets, charged with "being in the company of persons of ill repute, with whom he admitted being friendly."

But Nicholson's firing was the exception that proved the rule.

Perhaps the most corrupt Met of all time was Capt. Gerry Clemente, who went to prison after taking part in the $8-million Depositors Trust bank burglary in Medford in 1980, and who stole civil service exams and then sold them for $3,000 apiece.

In a remarkable 1987 book called *The Cops Are Robbers*, Clemente laid out the rules of the cop game in the 1960s, which have survived to a greater or lesser degree until now.

With an older officer on the overnight shift, Clemente answered a burglary alarm. When he got there, he saw another Medford cop with a lawn chair in his arms. The older cop let the other police officer go, and then told Clemente the facts of life.

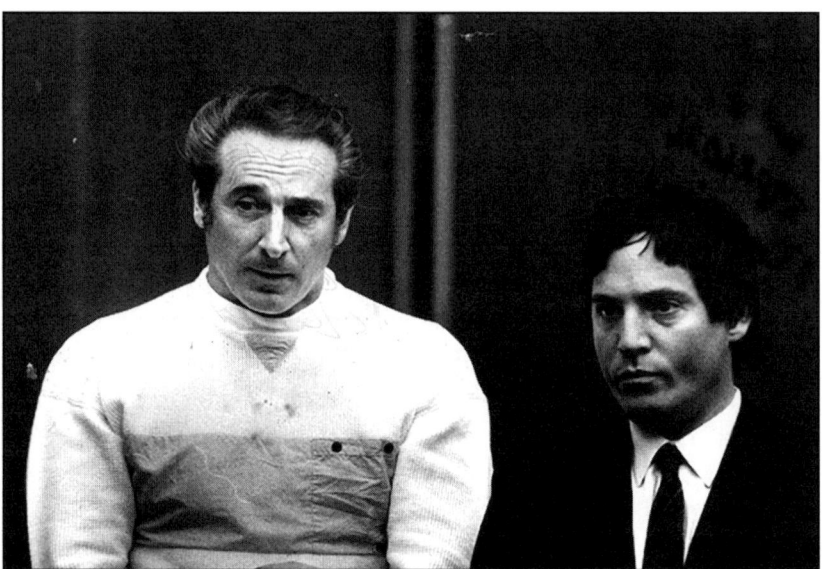

Capt. Gerry Clemente, the ultimate Met cop, in court in 1985 on bank robbery charges, with his lawyer, Marty Weinberg, who worked on Karen Read's appeal.

"Lesson number one, Gerry: You see another cop with a chair, a television, whatever, you keep your mouth shut. You say your hellos and you move on your way. Whatever he's doing is his business.

"Lesson number two: Don't play high and mighty. You want to be part of the club, you act like people in the club. You don't want to, hey, that's up to you—but don't expect people to trust you."

Theft was part of the job. So was taking payoffs.

"Stealing made you one of the guys, part of the club. If you didn't participate, you weren't trusted; it was as simple as that. The others had to have something on you so that they knew you wouldn't talk if you saw them transgress. And everybody, or almost everybody, transgressed. If you were dispatched to the scene of a break-in, you lifted a couple of items and stored them in the trunk of your cruiser while waiting for the owner to show up."

The legislators understood what was going on—a lot of them had close relatives on the job. They tried to do something about it, if only to keep their kinsmen from getting jammed up.

Or maybe they were just setting up a new, more white-collar grift for the boys in blue. Beacon Hill passed the "Quinn Bill," which provided bonuses to cops for additional education. Soon educational mills for cops were churning out thousands of bachelor's degrees. The cops were often taught by fellow cops. For a few nights, and a few hundred bucks, they set up themselves up to make thousands of dollars more in pay, every year, forever.

It was just another cop scam.

Police were allowed to retire earlier than other public servants, with full pensions at age fifty-five. They were in "Group 4." Soon other groups were adding riders to unrelated bills to put other bargaining units into Group 4, even district attorneys (see Chapter 22). And it became easier to go out on "disability." If you got jammed up, arrested, you could suddenly either "retire" or become disabled.

As a Merrimack Valley police chief told me once, more than thirty years ago:

*Anybody who wants to quit, all they have to do is come to me in the morning and say, "I had a dream last night that I put a gun in my mouth." He never has to work again. He goes out on 72 percent, tax-free, plus any increases negotiated by the union . . .*

MSP officers, on the other hand, were mandated by law to retire at age fifty, just like FBI agents. So they needed to figure out their next jobs. Eventually, a trooper sued, and that mandatory-retirement-at-age-fifty regulation went away. A new retirement age has never been approved in contract negotiations, so now at Logan Airport, F Troop, troopers continue working into their seventies.

So the cops have it both ways. If they're jammed up, they can check out early. If they're not, they can keep making the big bucks forever.

What a deal. But the pay increases were coming so fast and furious that some cops who'd gone out earlier on disability now realized how much they were missing out on. Some tried to be reclassified as able to perform their normal duties. In at least one case, a cop returned to duty, and on his first day back went to a police local firing range to train on the newer weapons.

He shot once, then fell backward, claiming he'd been knocked over by the new weapon's recoil. He refiled for disability . . . at the new higher rate of pay.

Until the 1970s, cops often learned a trade (Clemente was, appropriately enough, a locksmith) to supplement their meager incomes. Some even went to law school at night. But as almost all other states did away with using police to control traffic on construction or utility details, Massachusetts doubled down. Every crew had to have a cop on detail—by law.

The details—at least four hours, sometimes as many as eight, with supervision light, to say the least—became so lucrative that fewer cops bothered to learn any trades that they could use later for moonlighting or a post-retirement career. Same with court appearances after arrests—soon in many departments they were being brazenly abused.

The court overtime flimflam led directly to the later OT scandals with the BPD in the evidence warehouse and on the Turnpike with Troop E of the MSP. They were just expansions of already existing cop rackets.

More than ever, being a cop became a family affair. You saw it in Canton. The late Kenny Berkowitz, the corrupt chief during the Birchmore and Read murders, retired but his son continues on the job. Berky's replacement as chief, Helena Rafferty, is herself the daughter of a former chief.

Local departments provided plenty of opportunity for easy money, but the big money was still at the state police level. Ambitious cops were always looking to move up. Yuriy Bukhenik went from the Marine Corps to the Veterans Administration police to the Attleboro Police Department before he got on the MSP.

That's one of those jobs where they say somebody "died and went to heaven." As long as he kept handing cash to his boss, Michael Morrissey, at his annual birthday "time" every August, Bukhenik's pay kept skyrocketing.

Also in Morrissey's detectives unit was Nick Guarino. His family owns a bakery in Norwood, he went to Westfield State, then became a Norwood cop before graduating to the MSP. He's the one who couldn't find the 32,000 text messages between Sandra Birchmore and the Stoughton cop who is charged with murdering her in 2021.

The Stoughton Police Department is a good example of how little things have changed in Copland since the days of Gerry Clemente. He wrote about how cops liked to do things together. In the case of Sandra Birchmore, she was apparently groomed and then passed down, from Farwell to his twin brother.

The acting chief (one of the last cops-turned-lawyer) was also charged with abusing her, although he denies it. The former dog officer of Stoughton (who also got himself promoted to the regular police department in Abington) also admitted having sex with the troubled teenager.

The department that grooms together . . .

In 1975, the Stoughton police chief was convicted of knowingly receiving stolen electric heaters from an apartment building being constructed in Hyde Park. A patrol officer pleaded guilty to the thefts.

Eighteen years later, the new police chief of Stoughton was fired after allegations that, among other things, he illegally issued a firearms permit to a local millionaire. (The chief was reinstated after an appeal—an increasingly common occurrence these days, which Michael Proctor is now counting on.)

In 1997, another Stoughton detective was investigated for allegedly stealing from the Police Relief Fund. Recall, this is the exact same initial crime that eventually led to the Ponzo brothers' arrests for stealing $43 million from Mass Saves.

Canton was bad, but Stoughton's police department may have been even more corrupt. At one town meeting after some of the scandals came to light, one resident said: "They were like the Wild West doing their own thing in the Police Department. And they finally got caught."

One citizen was handcuffed until he agreed to pay a debt to a cop's friend. Another taxpayer was wrongfully arrested on kidnapping charges. A lieutenant cooperating with yet another Norfolk County special prosecutor investigating corruption was almost run down by a cop under investigation. Still another Stoughton cop resigned after he went to Club Alex's, a strip club, in uniform, to have his picture taken with "the world's smallest porn star."

In 2020, a few months before the Stoughton cop allegedly murdered Sandra Birchmore, a Stoughton sergeant was found not guilty of killing a seventy-four-year-old man by negligently operating a motor vehicle.

In 2018, Ralph Hawkins was in a neighbor's driveway when he was run over by a pickup truck driven by off-duty Sgt. Paul Wiliams. Williams told Meatball Morrissey's office that he had choked on a lemon seed in his iced tea and lost control of his truck before killing the elderly man.

Williams went on paid leave for two years after the accident. He has since returned to duty. Now his son has been hired by the department.

This is Copland.

The same types of crimes are committed over and over again, with no consequences. They drink together, sometimes in their cruisers, like Trooper Michael Proctor and Canton Police Department Detective Kevin Albert, brother of Brian Albert, on whose lawn John O'Keefe's body was found. On a "cold case" down on the Cape, Albert got so drunk with Proctor that he left his badge in Proctor's cruiser. He also misplaced his gun.

One thing they all understood: if in the extremely unlikely event they were ever arrested for drunk driving, they should demand not a jury trial, but a bench trial—in front of a judge, a friendly judge. If one wasn't immediately available, your lawyer (preferably an ex–state rep or governor's councilor, who vote on judgeships) should just ask for continuance after continuance until a friendly face could be found, after which charges can be dismissed or continued without a finding.

Mary Lyons was the chief of the Mattapoisett Police Department on the Cape. She was the first woman ever elected president of the Massachusetts Chiefs of Police Association in 2009.

But she really showed she was one of the boys in 2018, when she was arrested for drunk driving. Her lawyer demanded a bench trial, and she was acquitted and took immediate early retirement. She said she'd been planning to retire anyway.

Chief Mary Lyons, center: Not just another pretty face.

Once you start stealing, it's hard to stop. Especially if you're a cop who can get away with it. Nothing is too small. In 2025, a state cop named Zachariah Kent was charged with the theft of more than $1,000 worth of golf balls from Target stores in Worcester County.

In 2018, the former police chief of Hanson and his wife were charged with shoplifting $405 worth of clothing from Kohl's in Hingham. When stopped outside the store, the wife said she was returning to her car to get her purse. And her husband, the former cop, just happened to go with her.

He'd retired as chief six years earlier after facing what was described as "a raft of accusations."

They hired a state rep as their lawyer and the ancient clerk magistrate at Hingham District Court told him he was giving his pal, the legislator, a break, and not the cop and his wife. They were ordered to write letters of apology to the store, but never did.

Even if a cop does get indicted, he just judge-shops and walks. Doesn't matter how bad the crime is, at least in Norfolk County. Walter Schoener was a cop in Dedham, the county seat. In 2014, he lent his badge, gun, and holster to a local drug dealer. The dealer had two of his minions kidnap a local Avon man, who was taken to Canton and beaten to death. His body was thrown into the woods and not found for two years.

The cop finally went on trial five years later, in 2019, and was found guilty of being an accessory before the fact of kidnapping. The judge sentenced him to six to nine years, but then let him walk out of the courtroom a free man, pending his appeal.

The cop had four more years of freedom until the conviction was finally upheld. He went to prison in 2023, almost a decade after the betrayal of his oath.

The judge was Robert "Triple Dip" Cosgrove. He had no problems letting a crooked cop go free, but in 2024, after his retirement (with two state pensions), he was hired as special prosecutor to put Meatball Morrissey's nemesis, Turtleboy, in prison for ten years for the crime of "witness intimidation."

The witness intimidation by Turtleboy included making faces in the front window of a restaurant owned by Canton selectman Jailbird

Chris Albert. So as far as Triple Dip was concerned, a cop who facilitated a vicious murder could be allowed to walk free, but a blogger belonged behind bars.

The difference? Schoener was one of the boys. Turtleboy wasn't.

In Copland, even if you're not handing over your gun and badge to drug kingpins, you learn certain tricks.

For instance, if you don't want, say, private investigators running internet searches on your witnesses, you misspell their names by one or two letters. Makes it a lot harder to run background checks. When Michael Proctor was first investigating the murder of John O'Keefe and talking to witnesses who could dispute the official Karen-Read-did-it narrative, he misspelled five names in a single report. It was also an FBI trick during the Russiagate hoax—covering their tracks by misspelling names. As mentioned previously, Meatball Morrissey did the same thing, with "Karin" Read and "Aidan" Kearney.

Last summer, a city hall aide of Mayor Michelle Wu was accused of striking a neighbor of hers in the North End with a high-heeled shoe. The BPD investigated—and misspelled the first names of both Michelle Wu's aide and her two sisters. (Their mother, by the way, was on the payroll of Rep. Aaron Michlewitz, the chair of the House Ways and Means Committee. It doesn't pay to cross anyone who works for either Wu or Michlewitz.)

If, God forbid, they are ever pulled over for drunk driving, they all have the routine down. Refuse the breathalyzer. Refuse the sidewalk Olympics. When asked as required by law where you were last served, you always say, "Private residence."

And when asked how many drinks you have had, a cop always says, "A couple of beers."

No more, no less. Rarely are there any follow-up questions. In 2024, though, Canton drunkard cop Kevin "Fat" Albert was asked how many "IPAs" he'd had before he lost his badge in Trooper Michael Proctor's MSP cruiser.

"A couple," Albert responded, by rote.

The investigator asked how many drinks constituted "a couple."

He replied, "About two or three."

Even when they're not being arrested for drunk driving, cops learn to speak carefully, very carefully. Especially in court or a deposition.

If you get asked whether you broke off a high-speed chase that you apparently didn't, just say you did break it off. You were just following the vehicle. (This is what the Boston cops said after the three kids were killed in the high-speed accident on Morrissey Boulevard.)

The defense attorney asks, "Why didn't you read my client his Miranda rights?

Because, the cop says, "I wasn't arresting him, I was detaining him."

"Why did you search my client without a warrant?"

"It wasn't a search, it was a pat frisk. For security."

"You rummaged through the trunk of my client's car without a search warrant?"

"It was not a search, it was an inventory."

Most of these interrogations take place in semi-deserted courthouses, with no reporters, cameras, or in most cases, even bystanders watching. Out of sight, out of mind.

After the death of George Floyd, and the wave of looting, arson, and violence that followed it across the nation, the state set up yet another new bureaucracy to police the police, to guard the guards themselves.

It is known as the Massachusetts Peace Officer Standards Training (POST) Commission. Like most bureaucracies, it's staffed by lifers, unemployables, and shady connected types (a former leader of the Boston Police Patrolmen's Association is on the board, for example).

To give you an idea of its effectiveness, until a massive outpouring of public outrage online last spring, Michael Proctor remained "certified" as a police officer, even after his firing by the MSP.

He is now officially "restricted." Not decertified, just "restricted."

Overall, there are 19,415 certified peace officers in Massachusetts, and 56 decertified.

Sounds about right for Copland.

## CHAPTER TEN

# BPD

When the old Yankee political establishment in Boston began losing control to the new Irish majority more than a century ago, they used their fading clout in the legislature to make sure that the presumably enduring Republican majority at the state level could retain perpetual control over three levers of power in the city:

Municipal finances
Liquor licenses
BPD

The Boston Finance Commission had less and less influence over corrupt city appropriations as time went by. And the Boston Licensing Board proved just as corrupt under appointees of suburban Republican governors as under those picked by urban Democrats.

And despite all the safeguards the Yankees tried to impose, the BPD had its problems too, no matter who ran it. Always has, probably always will.

And the Karen Read case once again showed just how deeply flawed the department is. A Boston cop, John O'Keefe, was found dead under mysterious circumstances on the front lawn of another Boston cop, Brian Albert, who didn't bother to come outside after the body was found.

Two days later, Gregory Long, the acting superintendent-in-chief of the BPD, who like the other cops lived in Canton, cleared his neighbor Brian Albert of internal-affairs charges that had been hanging over his head for years.

And when the dead Boston cop's girlfriend was arrested two days later, Long issued a statement: "Today the Massachusetts State Police and the Norfolk County District Attorney's Office arrested the person responsible for John's death."

No, they didn't. They just pinned it on the girl because that was the easiest way out. And most likely Acting Superintendent Long knew it. But even if he truly believed that Karen Read was guilty, despite the overwhelming evidence that she wasn't, isn't it customary for law

In 2022, then top Boston PD cop Greg Long of Canton cleared his Canton neighbor Brian Albert of earlier departmental charges after the death of a third Boston cop from Canton. At left in photo is now prison-bound ex-Boston City Councilor Tania Fernandes Anderson. At right in photo is disgraced ex-US Attorney Rachael Rollins.

enforcement press releases about arrests, including those from the US Department of Justice, to note that all parties charged are innocent until proven guilty?

Except apparently in Norfolk County.

Perhaps significantly, Long's wife is a $207,855-a-year state judge, just like Beverly Cannone. With the exact same legal-career trajectory—zero time in the private sector.

But Long's good-old-boy treatment of his pal Brian Albert was nothing compared to what his successor, Michael Cox, did with a witness in the second trial, a young BPD officer named Kelly Dever.

Cox might have been expected to care a little bit more about a defendant's civil rights than he did. He knew hoaxes firsthand, and police cover-ups.

In 1989, a white couple, Carol and Chuck Stuart, were shot in Mission Hill. Carol, pregnant, was killed, but her husband survived and identified the shooter as a black man. Outrage ensued, and stop-and-frisks of black men took place all over the city.

Finally, police settled on a suspect—Willie Bennett. Chuck Stuart picked him out of a lineup as the shooter.

But by then, in January 1990, it was becoming clear that the real killer was Chuck Stuart. His brother had come clean to the cops. It was an insurance scheme. Finally, with police closing in, Chuck Stuart committed suicide by jumping off the Tobin Bridge.

That night, Boston Mayor Ray Flynn went to Bennett's home in Roxbury and apologized to his family. But just as years later Karen Read would have to be found guilty of something—anything—so would Willie Bennett. In October, he would

Willie Bennett was almost framed in Boston, then sent away for 11 years on a different crime . . . in Norfolk County.

be convicted—in Norfolk County—of robbery of a video store and three counts of assault with a deadly weapon.

Bennett did twelve years in prison for that robbery. Another Boston mayor, Michelle Wu, would issue a second formal apology to him in 2023, but by then he was suffering from dementia.

Commissioner Cox had his own problems with the BPD's racism and lack of due process. While still in training, he was mistaken for a suspect and beaten. Another time, he was pinned against a wall by a BPD cruiser driven by an officer who assumed he must be the guilty party.

In 1995, at the age of thirty, plainclothes Cox was involved in a high-speed chase of a suspect, with other officers from several departments. He eventually left his car and pursued the suspect on foot. Four white officers mistook Cox for the suspect and beat him senseless, leaving him on the sidewalk with brain injuries. When they realized he was a fellow officer, they fled the scene without calling for medical assistance.

Later, when he was recovering, Cox received anonymous calls threatening him if he pressed charges or filed a lawsuit. Eventually, three of the four white officers were fired, and he received $900,000 in damages. A book was even written about the case.

Fast-forward twenty-nine years, to 2024.

Kelly Dever had been a Canton police officer on the night John O'Keefe died. She was working as a dispatcher when Karen Read's SUV was brought back inside the sally port at the Canton Police Department. On the surveillance cameras, she watched with growing suspicion as she saw her boss, Police Chief Kenny Berkowitz, and his dear pal, ATF agent Brian Higgins, lurking around the back of the SUV.

In August 2023, as the FBI began investigating the murky circumstances of the cover-up, agents questioned her about how long Berkowitz and Higgins had been puttering around the taillights.

"A wildly long time," she told the agents. Remember, it is a crime to lie to federal agents, even though that seems to be standard operating procedure in Canton.

She was called as a witness in the second trial, by the defense. By now, she was on the BPD. And she told a totally different story than the one she had told FBI agents less than two years earlier (see page 129).

Canton Chief Kenny Berkowitz, left, with ex-Boston Commissioner Ed Davis.

Now, she said, she had given the FBI agents a "false memory."

As a rookie officer, she had been called into Commissioner Cox's office, and he had told her to "do the right thing."

Questioned about the importance of changing her story, she became defensive.

"My whole career depends on what I say here."

Immediately after her testimony, Dever went out on "family medical leave." At press time, she had not returned to duty.

At his next public appearance after her sworn recantation of her earlier statement, Cox was surrounded by reporters. They asked him his version of the "Do-the-right-thing" sit-down with Dever. There were no witnesses, so it became a he-said-she-said situation.

"I have nothing to do with Karen Read," he said, smiling nervously. "As a matter of fact, I didn't even know this person was associated with Karen Read . . . We support all our folks . . . I have no idea what they're talking about with Karen Read."

Did he tell Kelly Dever to do the right thing?

"I didn't know she was even associated with that case. I was struck like, 'What do I have to do with the Karen Read case?' I've never said those words together."

He mentioned that when the murder happened, he was in Ann Arbor—during a brief sojourn as police chief of that woke Michigan college town. But O'Keefe was a BPD officer who had served with Cox, and his murder remains unsolved. Cox didn't seem concerned.

"That case is over," he said. "We've got other stuff to talk about."

Is it really over? It's an unsolved murder, of a BPD officer. But the commissioner shrugs his shoulders and says, "Nothing to see here, move along."

That's the way it's always been in the BPD. They've always been convulsed by scandal and controversy. In 1919, the underpaid police officers went out on an unauthorized strike and were fired en masse by then-Gov. Calvin Coolidge.

He issued a famous statement: "There is no right to strike against the public safety by anybody, anywhere, any time."

Four years later, he was president of the United States. At least one of the fired officers was also successful—he became the top racketeer in South Boston, and always kept a framed photo of Calvin Coolidge on his desk, to remind him of his good fortune in being separated from the BPD. When he died of natural causes in 1946, the Boston papers described him as a "sportsman." (His brother became the state senator from South Boston, setting the precedent for the Bulger brothers a half-century later.)

With Republican governors mostly in control, the BPD avoided major scandals for a while. But when James Michael Curley was elected governor in 1934, he appointed James Timilty, a second-generation Boston politician, as his police commissioner. He was known as "Diamond Jim."

Timilty's career ended when a Republican attorney general got a search warrant for his safe-deposit box, and discovered $350,000 in cash—a fabulous fortune in 1943.

The BPD suffered the usual big-city corruption, payoffs from racketeers for protection, etc. There were other, lesser-known shakedowns, especially of the gay population. The BPD had a "Restroom Regiment" that patrolled the public latrines on the MTA.

According to the history of early Boston gay life, *Improper Bostonians*, these toilets provided ample shakedown opportunities when well-heeled "confirmed bachelors" from Beacon Hill wandered in for a little rough trade.

Similarly, the bars around Kerry Village (now known as Bay Village) were also target-rich environments. The cops particularly took advantage of the closeted lesbians, "the Boston spinsters." According to the book, raiding parties of cops would often drag out the lesbians into back alleys. Even if they were short on cash, other alternatives to an arrest could be arranged. Often, the women would return to the bar a few minutes later "looking sheepish."

The so-called Irish Gang War began in 1961, and soon not only the entire Boston underworld and much of law enforcement was embroiled in the years-long carnage. While the Boston FBI agents usually only set up hits for the wiseguys, the BPD featured at least one actual hitman.

Det. Bill Stuart often worked with FBI Agent H. Paul Rico. According to Stevie Flemmi's official DEA 6 confession (contained in my book *Rifleman*), Stuart personally brokered the alliance of the Wimpy Bennett/Stevie Flemmi crew in Roxbury with the Winter Hill Gang in Somerville.

In the summer of 1966, Republican Elliot Richardson was running for attorney general. He had a serious drinking problem and a decision was made by local politicians to eliminate him. The perfect location was determined to be the L Street Bathhouse in South Boston, where he sometimes worked out.

"Stuart had a hot car and his plan was to run down the inebriated Richardson as he exited the bathhouse," Flemmi's confession read.

BPD Det. Bill Stuart—hitman with a contract to kill Elliot Richardson.

It would be a hit-and-run. An autopsy would show Richardson's blood-alcohol level to be way above legally drunk, meaning he had stumbled onto Columbia Road. It seemed foolproof, until a heat wave arrived. Stuart's car was hot in more ways than one, and he "found it difficult to sit in the hot car."

Plus, L Street was popular with Stuart's fellow cops. Too many of them recognized him. The hit was called off.

The next year, the Flemmi crew botched a hit in Mattapan and Stuart had to be called to run interference for them. Then one of the hit squad flipped and implicated Stuart. He was indicted in state court for being an accessory after the fact. He beat the rap in a sensational trial in 1970, was demoted and retired.

But Stuart continued doing contract hits. In 1976, he took out a failing businessman named George Hamilton, who had taken out two massive life-insurance policies, one of which was about to expire. Stuart knocked on his door on a Sunday morning and then shot him five times when he answered the front door.

The hit, like so many others, took place in Canton. William Delahunt, the same Norfolk County district attorney whose office framed Fred Weichel for the convenience of Whitey Bulger, never arrested Stuart or anyone else for the hit.

It's still on the books as yet another unsolved murder in Canton.

Stevie Flemmi's connections with the BPD were impeccable. One brother was a hitman, the other was a BPD officer. When the British Navy stopped a ship carrying contraband weapons from Boston to the Irish Republican Army in 1984, they discovered a bulletproof vest from the BPD.

It was Michael Flemmi's.

Michael Flemmi would later go to federal prison for assorted crimes, including moving his

Ex-BPD Officer Michael Flemmi, released from prison, 2011.

126 | Mass Corruption Volume 1: The Cops

brother's arsenal of illegal weapons, and selling some of his cache of stolen jewelry.

The same year Flemmi's bulletproof vest was discovered in an IRA weapons cache, the BPD was almost taken over by organized crime. The new mayor, Ray Flynn, was from South Boston, as was Whitey Bulger's younger brother Billy, the Senate president.

As Senate president, Bulger controlled the flow of much legislation affecting the City of Boston. He told the new mayor that he could have whatever he wanted from the state, and all Bulger asked in return was one favor.

He wanted FBI agent John "Zip" Connolly appointed police commissioner. Zip Connolly, who had already taken part in at least one Mob hit for which he would be convicted years later in Florida. Zip Connolly, who would receive a quarter of a million dollars in blood money from Bulger and his partner Flemmi over the decades.

Flynn refused. The *Boston Globe* may have been printing slobbering puff pieces about "decorated agent" Connolly on an almost daily basis, but Flynn knew better. Turning the BPD over to Connolly would have meant handing the largest law enforcement department in New England over to organized crime.

Instead, Flynn appointed as his commissioner Francis "Mickey" Roache. This was another slap in the face of Billy Bulger. Mickey Roache's brother Buddy had been shot and paralyzed by Whitey Bulger in a gangland shooting in 1969. A brother-in-law of Roache's had his nose bitten off in a drunken brawl during the same gang war.

This was how the BPD operated. There was civil service, like every other police department, but it was more political than most. Mayor Kevin White would appoint "provisional" deputy superintendents. If you stepped out of line, you went back to uniform.

After the FBI bugged Mafia boss Jerry Angiulo's North End headquarters in 1981, between thirty and forty Boston cops were quietly transferred when their names turned up on the bugs. The police commissioner, an alcoholic named Joe Jordan, owed "big favors" to Angiulo—again, Flemmi's words in his DEA confession.

The department has been hit with one scandal after another, its officers in those revolving doors at the federal courthouse in South Boston. In the early 2000s, several detectives were arrested in a drug deal in Miami. They also operated an after-hours club in Mattapan called the Boom-Boom Room.

There was an MSP-like scandal involving overtime in an evidence room in Hyde Park.

Patrick Rose, the head of the Boston Police Patrolmen's Association (BPPA), pled guilty to twenty-one counts of child rape and sexual assault over a twenty-seven-year period when he was mostly a police officer and often a union official.

The first criminal charges against him were filed in 1995, but dismissed in 1996. Internal Affairs then sustained the charges against him, but he was allowed to remain on the job for another twenty years as he rose to take over the union.

As head of the union, Rose never spoke out forcefully against the brass or the mayor. For obvious reasons. He isn't the only recent union leader to get jammed up with potential disciplinary charges. Negotiations go more smoothly that way.

The BPD seems to have two separate offices for discipline, or lack thereof. One is Internal Affairs. The other is the lesser-known Anti-Corruption Division, also run by the BPD, which handles all infractions involving city employees.

Patrick Rose, BPD union official and pedophile.

Once something is referred to Anti-Corruption, the city has something hanging over an employee, law enforcement or otherwise. And since the charges ostensibly involve "corruption," the city feels it can get away with stonewalling any and all media inquiries. It's a municipal version of what the Deep State used for years to block all attempts at investigating the Russian collusion hoax against President Trump.

"The investigation continues," or "Sources and methods must not be compromised."

At least one city councilor was involved in a post-midnight incident with another city employee. The incident went to Anti-Corruption. The city councilor has never spoken ill of the mayor or the administration since.

Punishments can be capricious, or not (see page 132). After January 6, one Boston officer was fired for sending pro-Trump tweets. Not for attending the protests in DC, but for texting about them.

"Conduct unbecoming."

Same thing for some of the BPD cops who refused to get the COVID vaccine. At least if they weren't on the team.

This is the BPD, where it pays to do the right thing.

## More "False Memory"

*June 2, 2025*

Is a "false memory" anything like a lie?

Asking for a friend . . . a friend in the FBI.

Did it ever occur to anybody in the town of Canton to ever, you know, tell the truth? Especially to the FBI, if maybe only because it's a crime to lie to them.

First, it was Jen McTooth, er McCabe. Her first thought when the G-men asked her name was to lie. Then she ran upstairs and called some of her co-conspirators, I mean friends, and when the FBI asked how many calls she'd made, she lied to the G-men again.

Didn't you always assume that it was a crime to lie to the feds anywhere, anytime?

Except in Canton, we now learn.

BPD Officer Kelly Dever: "False memory."

BPB Commissioner Michael Cox: "Do the right thing."

C'mon down Kelly Diva, I mean Dever, of the BPD, formerly of the Canton Police Department.

She was testifying Monday at the murder retrial of Karen Read. Despite her years on two rather troubled police departments, she doesn't seem to know how to testify properly, that is, how to frame, shall we say, her testimony, in order to frame . . . oh never mind.

First, you never let the jury see you sweat, Officer Diva. Nobody is expecting the truth, the whole truth, and nothing but the truth from a cop, especially a cop from Canton.

"I'm on the stand to tell the truth," she stammered, her voice cracking. "That's my livelihood."

Except, apparently, when she talks to the FBI.

She was on duty as a dispatcher on the day John O'Keefe was murdered. She told the feds she saw two of the shadiest cops in Canton—Police Chief Kenny Berkowitz, now deceased, and ATF agent Brian Higgins—loitering around the alleged death vehicle.

"For a wildly long time," defense attorney Alan Jackson pointed out.

A wildly long time. This is important because there are multiple questions about the taillight pieces from Read's car that mysteriously appeared at the death scene days—and weeks—later, but not in the immediate hours after O'Keefe's death.

The more time that elapsed after the crash, the more these pieces appeared. And they got larger and larger and larger, for three weeks. It's Canton, baby.

So it's important to know who was doing what to Karen Read's car, and when.

Her testimony, which she viewed on the surveillance camera, would have been devastating to the persecution, er prosecution.

So she had to change it. She, uh, mis-remembered. With great specificity, but these things happen. In Norfolk County anyway. And the recantations always, always benefit the crooked cops.

Defense attorney Alan Jackson asked Officer Diva the obvious question about her sudden change of memory.

"Have you ever heard of something called the blue wall of silence?" he asked. There was an objection by Mob mouthpiece Hank

Brennan, and it was of course sustained by Judge Cannone because . . . Norfolk County.

Officer Diva reeks of DEI. She says she's only testified in about a dozen cases. She claims that when she told the defense she was changing her recollection, they told her they would charge her with "perjury."

"Have you ever seen any defense attorney," Jackson calmly asked her, "charge anyone with a crime, ever?"

"Personally, no."

Because they can't. Not even in Norfolk County.

Potential witnesses are supposed to avoid watching trial coverage, so that their testimony is not influenced by what other testimony is offered. It's called a sequestration order. Jackson asked the sworn officer if she knew what a sequestration order is.

"No," she said.

First she testified that Karen Read's defense team said they'd tear her a new you-know-what. Then she said they told her they'd "eat her alive."

After she saw, and then didn't see, the two shady cops in the sally port, she was suddenly hired by the BPD. Another nationwide search!

Sometimes, it's just better to forget.

Back when John Gotti was the Mafia boss of New York, a concerned citizen saw him basically killing a guy. First the witness testified truthfully, then he came down with one of those Canton-like cases of "false memory."

The headline in the *New York Post* the next day was: "I Forgotti."

Yesterday was Kelly Dever's "I Forgotti" moment.

Good job, Kelly! You took one for the team, like in *Goodfellas*.

"Never rat on your friends and always keep your mouth shut."

My prediction is that she will be promoted to BPD Det. DEI "I Forgotti" Diva in three . . . two . . . one.

# Gunning for Just the Facts with the BPD

*April 18, 2025*

Months before two BPD officers went against orders and undertook a high-speed chase on Morrissey Boulevard that ended in the deaths of three teenagers, one of the cops involved improperly discharged a BPD firearm in his Hyde Park apartment, narrowly missing a sleeping neighbor.

Yet the politically connected officer, Triston Champagnie, remained on the job. And he seems to have thus far avoided being disciplined for the shooting, after a meeting between Internal Affairs cops and Police Commissioner Michael Cox, a contemporary of his father, Det. Sgt. Patrick Champagnie.

A notation in official BPD records says that last October, months after the deaths of the three teenagers, disciplinary action for the earlier shooting incident was placed "on hold": "Per GF (green folder) Mtg w/ Commissioner Cox, this case discipline is still on hold."

It also notes, "Discipline Pending Green Folder Mtg. Oct. 10, 2024. Days/hrs suspended: 0."

A department spokesperson said the phrase "green folder" refers to preliminary findings in an IA investigation.

Six months after Champagnie improperly discharged his departmental firearm, as the investigation dragged on, the three teenagers died following a chase by Champagnie and fellow Officer Matthew Farley on January 4, 2024.

According to a report in the *Boston Globe*, the cops were ordered to break off the dangerous pursuit. A supervisor radioed them, "Okay, just to confirm, we have nobody pursuing that motor vehicle. Is that correct?"

"Correct," Champagnie said. "No pursuing."

But the transmissions from Champagnie continued, monitoring the youths' vehicle until it crashed, after having attained speeds of up to 106 mph, according to the MSP.

Thrown from the vehicle and killed were Troy Winslow, age fifteen, Immanuel A. Brooks, fourteen, and Kevin Lenes-Davila, seventeen.

The BPD Internal Affairs investigation into the three deaths remains open. The gun violations against Champagnie have been "sustained" by what is called the Firearm Discharge Investigative Team. That finding triggered an IA investigation, which seems to have resulted in no disciplinary action.

The shooting occurred at Champagnie's apartment on Dana Avenue in Hyde Park on June 14, 2023. Another BPD officer, identified as Eric MacPherson, was also present although "he was in the shower at the time of the discharge."

So as his pal was taking a shower, Champagnie was for some reason handling his buddy's gun—a loaded Glock 43X.

"Officer Champagnie accidentally discharged one round, which went through the wall and into the neighboring apartment. The round traveled through the headboard where (neighbor) Ryan Kluska was sleeping, through the comforter, and another wall before striking the stove and stopping."

So did Officer Champagnie then follow BPD procedure and notify an Operations Division supervisor? He did not.

"Instead (he) notified his father, Sgt. Det. Champagnie, who notified District 18, who notified Operations."

Daddy Champagnie is a big shot in the BPD. He made $368,222.47 last year, according to city payroll records.

Triston, despite his checkered career, including at least two disputed traffic stops in addition to the shooting in Hyde Park and the triple fatality in Dorchester, was paid $111,387.05 last year.

One brother, also named Patrick, is also on the job, collecting $231,979.64 last year. Another brother, Preston, made $70,560.16 from the BPD last year.

The IA report on the Hyde Park firearms discharge was produced by a different sergeant detective, Daniel Conway. He made $333,069.33 last year.

By coincidence, there are as many Conways on the BPD payroll as Champagnies. In addition to crack sleuth Dan, Officer John A. Conway made $352,667 last year working in "headquarters dispatch." A John D. Conway grabbed $310,560,41 in "mobile operations." And Police Officer Kendra Conway made $165,687.34 in 2024.

The incident involving the firearm and the fellow officer in the shower occurred in June 2023. Yet the incident report is numbered IAD2024-0015, indicating the probe wasn't officially opened until early last year, probably after the three teenagers were killed on Morrissey Boulevard.

On Wednesday, I asked the BPD about the apparent six-month delay in officially opening an investigation. A BPD spokesman said that the 2023 Firearms Discharge Investigative Team had to first "sustain" the charges, before the IA investigation could begin in 2024.

In the interim between the two investigations, Champagnie's probationary period as a police officer ended, which meant that he had much greater civil-service and union protection from being fired. How convenient.

I also formally inquired if Commissioner Cox is a "personal friend of Champagnie's father."

There was no answer.

Doesn't the City of Boston now have a civilian review board of some kind? Surely this is the sort of matter that should rise to the level of their attention?

What about the Boston City Council? Do they still have a Public Safety Committee? At one time, I believe the chairman was Tania Fernandes Anderson.

Does she have time to probe this matter before May 5, when she is scheduled to plead guilty to multiple felonies committed in city hall?

On Monday, a lawyer for one of the aggrieved civilians seeking BPD internal-affairs documents on Triston Champagnie expressed his frustration about the Boston cops' reluctance to comply with court orders (not to mention public-records demands).

"They flat-out refused to comply with the court's orders," the lawyer said. "If we don't (follow) court orders, we get held in contempt."

Forget it Jake, it's the BPD.

In my official inquiry to the BPD, I had one final question: "Does the commissioner regret not taking action against Champagnie in 2023 that might have kept him off Morrissey Boulevard on the night when the three youths were killed? Would he like to issue a public statement of apology to the families of the dead youths for his apparent lapse in judgment?"

No answer.

It's enough to make you want to take a shower. But not in Officer Champagnie's apartment. That would be almost as dangerous as driving around on Morrissey Boulevard.

(Post script: In August Triston Champagnie "resigned" from the BPD with what the department described as "charges pending.")

CHAPTER ELEVEN

# BPD Hall of Shame

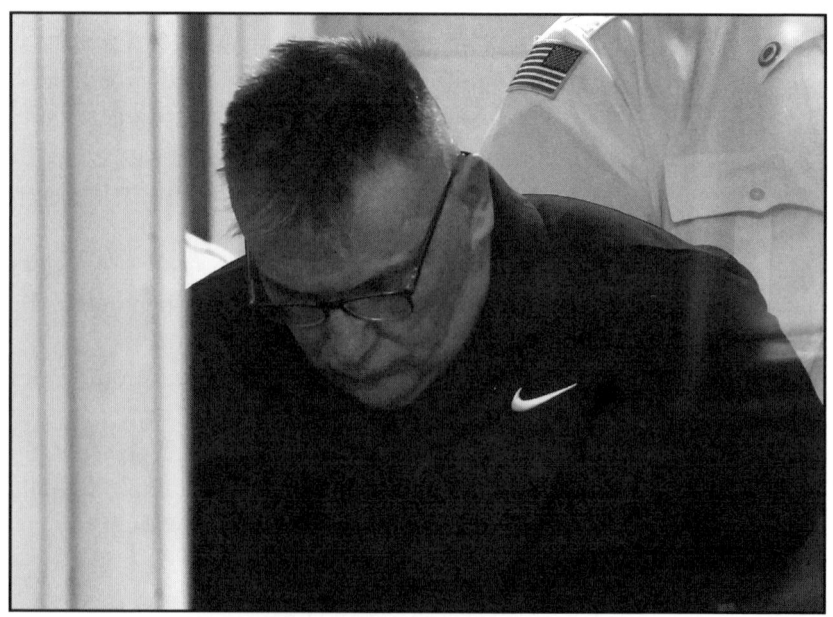

Paul Downey, thirty-year BPD officer, accused of rape of a fourteen-year-old boy, 2025.

Officer Ronald Nelson, charged with overtime fraud, charges dismissed after his death in 2022.

Detective Brian Smigielski, convicted of tipping off gang members to police activity, 2016.

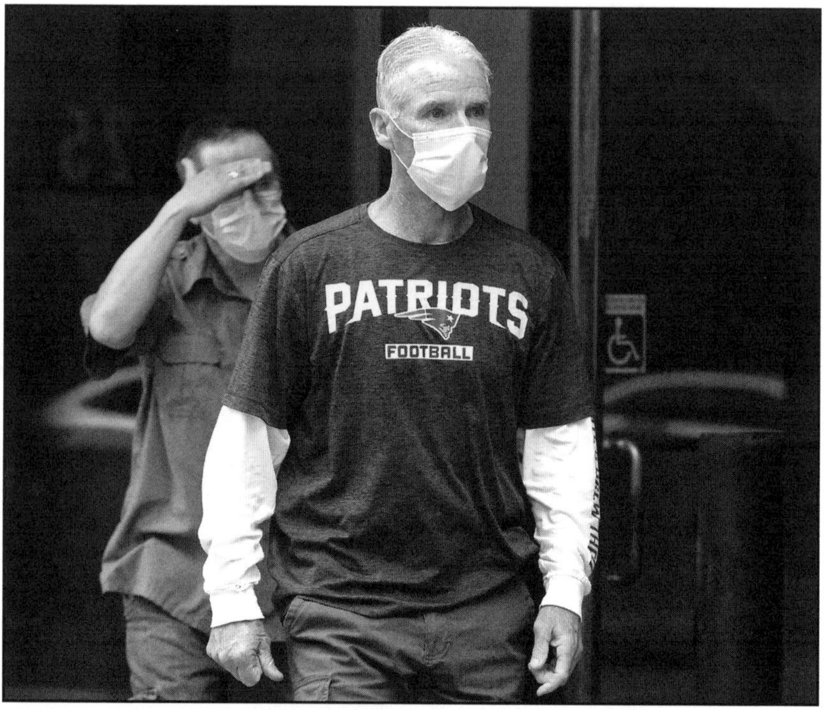

Off. Gerard O'Brien (in Pats jersey), convicted of OT fraud, 2021. In rear is Off. Henry Doherty, acquitted in 2023.

BPD motorcycle Off. Roberto Pulido, sentenced to twenty-six years in prison for conspiring to protect cocaine shipments into the city. Proprietor of the Boom-Boom Room in Hyde Park.

The Boom-Boom Room was a notorious after-hours club on Factory Street (just down the street from a frequently burglarized BPD drug storage warehouse) operated by and for the BPD, some on duty, where cocaine and hookers were available.

BPD Off. Nelson Carrasquillo, sentenced to eighteen years in prison in the same conspiracy with Pulido.

Off. Tim Torigian, charged with OT theft, acquitted 2023.

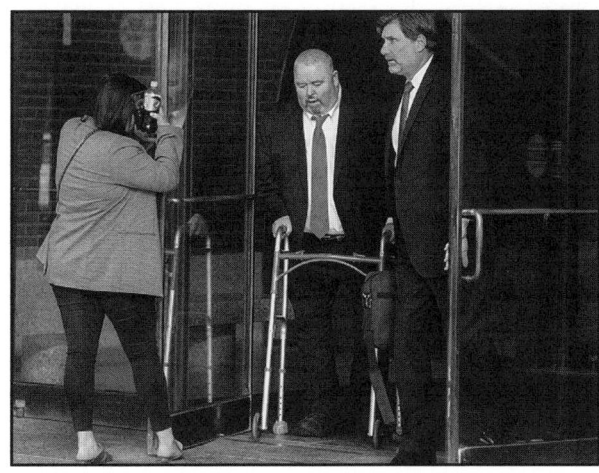

Off. Robert Twitchell, charged with OT theft, once featured in the TV documentary *Boston Finest*, acquitted 2023.

# CHAPTER TWELVE

# Jameson and Ginger

## Is Brian Higgins "Hot?"

*May 24, 2024*

Almost all these Canton townies that we've seen so far have one thing in common: They need to get themselves into a good twelve-step program.

And they must realize that they should never text when they could phone.

The theme song for the testimony yesterday in the Karen Read murder trial was, "Third Rate Romance, Low Rent Rendezvous."

Any number of embarrassing texts were read into the record Friday. But perhaps the most humiliating had to have been Karen Read's to Brian "Butt-Dial" Higgins, the three-hundred-pound boozebag from, where else, Can-UHN.

"You're hot," she texted him.

Higgins, dumb as a rock, at least looks in the mirror once in a while. He texted back: "Are you serious or messing with me?"

Brian Higgins is, or was, an ATF agent. ATF as in, Alcohol, Tobacco, Firearms and Explosives. From his testimony, and his dissipated face, Higgins has obviously been putting the "A" back into "ATF."

ATF agent Brian Higgins: How "hot" is he?

Defense attorney Alan Jackson tried to ask Higgins what his assignment is now. He nervously mumbled something about "Division Operations," and Jackson asked, "You were taken out of the field?"

"Objection," said the hack prosecutor.

"Sustained," said the hack judge for about the millionth time.

None of the cringeworthy texts between the Beauty and the Beast means that Karen Read killed her boyfriend. But for sure, Karen Read was a very unhappy woman, in an inbred backwater.

As somebody noted online, "Canton, Massachusetts, is like Appalachia. Apologies to Appalachia."

When those texts kept unfurling on screen in the courtroom, I wanted to cue up a sad Moe Bandy song from 1974: "It was always so easy to find an unhappy woman, 'til I started lookin' for mine."

From the texts, Karen doesn't seem to be a stupid woman. But she knew that living in Can-UHN, as the townies call it, is a dead end, at least if you live and hang out with nothing but born-and-bred Can-UHN hillbillies.

How sad was Karen Read's life? She had a nickname for one of her bars, the Hillside. She called it "the Hilly."

Jameson and Ginger | 141

When Tons o' Fun Higgins told her that she was the best-looking gal in the Hilly, she replied: "Thanks for saying that ☺ But low comps at Hillside."

Higgins texts her: "I thought you were in this happy relationship."

Karen: "Everyone is happy at the Hillside!"

Please, now I want to cue up Merle Haggard's "Swingin' Doors": "I've got everything I need to drive me crazy/I've got everything I need to lose my mind."

Karen Read was obviously mortified when these texts were shared with the world. Brian Higgins is not exactly Mr. Universe. He's a stumble bum, and again, apologies to stumble bums.

By his own admission, on the night John O'Keefe died, Higgins had started out at the Hillside for three or four drinks—"Jameson and gin-jah," he said, more than once. Then he staggered over to the Waterfall and had several more—he couldn't put a number on it.

Then after the Waterfall band quit for the night, the very sober Higgins went over to the death house. But he left because they didn't have any booze and "I'm not a beer drinker."

He then drove home to West Roxbury, had some more food, and admitted, "I might have had another couple of drinks."

Then he "laid" down on the couch and, uh, fell asleep. He has a way with words—getting them wrong. He described how O'Keefe and Read "had initially went," not gone, *went*. He says, "I may have drunk." When she says in one text, "Carpe diem," he reads it on the witness stand as, "Carp diem."

But then he throws in legalese like "pendancy" and "sum and substance." He took notes at the academy. Like Brian Albert, his drinking buddy from the BPD, he kept calling Karen Read "the defendant."

He knows cop lingo a lot better than he seems to know the streets, unless he's plowing them with his truck during a snowstorm. He doesn't seem to ever have done much work as an ATF agent. He drove around and planned out the night's boozing, when he wasn't going to funerals and memorial services for real cops.

He'd rather be grievin' than sleuthin'. You can get an earlier start on the day's drinking that way.

Despite the "low comps" of most of the Can-UHN townies, male and female alike, they do like to keep tabs on one another's sex lives. Early on, Karen tells Higgins that "I know you date girls who don't lock the door behind them. And are private."

Last Call Lucys, in other words.

Then Karen tells Higgins that O'Keefe "hooked up w/another girl on vacation."

"Did he bang her?" Higgins asks.

Because . . . when you're livin' here, lovin' there, and lyin' in between, it's always good to know first of all, who's available for you to hit on, and second, who might be planning to snake you.

Can someone play some Johnny Taylor for me right now: "Who's makin' love to your old lady, while you are out makin' love?"

Higgins said she came into the Waterfall that evening with a glass that was from a different bar. He apparently is an expert on the glassware of every licensed establishment in Can-UHN, and probably Stow-UHN as well. She was carrying what we used to call at J.J. Foley's "a foreign load."

At another point, Karen Read, the unhappy woman, texts Higgins: "What do you want ideally?"

"The real deal," Higgins says, because that's what you always say, when you're trying to bed your next Last Call Lucy.

"The real deal," he said.

"Doesn't exist," she told him.

Not at the Hilly, anyway. Not at 34 Fairview Road either. And certainly not in Can-UHN, period.

But after seventeen days of this trial, there is one thing we have learned beyond a reasonable doubt: If you're a cop, even a "cop" like Brian Higgins, you can drive drunk.

At least in Can-UHN.

## Fat, Drunk, and Stupid

*May 22, 2024*

Maybe Dean Wormer in *Animal House* got it wrong. Maybe fat, drunk, and stupid is a good way to go through life.

Just ask Brian "Butt-Dial" Higgins, the ATF agent who was a very dear friend of dead BPD Officer John O'Keefe, even though he couldn't be bothered to attend his funeral, despite the fact that he flies around the country for other funerals of cops he never met.

Yesterday, after a very bad day under cross-examination Friday, Higgins waddled back onto the witness stand. He looked like he'd spent the weekend swilling his favorite—"Jameson and gin-jah"—and brushing up on his favorite self-help book: *Testifying Under Cross-Examination for Dummies*.

Karen Read's lawyer asked him about how he (among others) just happened to decide to trash his phone almost simultaneously with getting a preservation order for it from the court.

Being the very high-class citizen that he is, Higgins had no trash service when he was squatting on the Cape. So he would drive to the nearby military base, Otis, now officially known as Joint Base Cape Cod, and surreptitiously drop his trash into a dumpster there.

I guess Otis doesn't have those warning signs like most places do, saying something to the effect that this dumpster is to be used by tenants or residents only—don't even think about using it as your own personal trash can, Agent Higgins!

So Higgins takes his incriminating, er, "beat-up" cell phone, removes the SIM card, destroys it, and then tosses it into his Hefty trash bag before making his weekly sneaky run to Otis. So much for getting that discount from the phone company for trading in your old phone!

Let's pick up Higgins's testimony with a question from defense attorney David Yannetti:

YANNETTI: "And you'll agree with me that you took that destroyed SIM card and put it in a trash bag, did you not?"

HIGGINS: "I believe it went in a trash bag, yes."

YANNETTI: "Well, you used the passive voice. 'It went in a trash bag.' Did it fly out of your hand unexpectedly into a trash bag, sir?"

HIGGINS: "No sir, it would have been disposed of with the phone."

YANNETTI: "No, I understand. But are you reluctant to say you put it in a trash bag?"

HIGGINS: "Objection!"

HACK JUDGE: "Can you answer that? Are you reluctant to answer that?"

HIGGINS: "No, Your Honor. I put it in a trash bag."

Then he went to Otis. Except that he didn't drive to it, he "cut through" the base. He said "cut through" twice.

I wonder where he was "cutting through" to. Probably to a place that served Jameson and gin-jahs.

As the days drag on, patterns are emerging among the prosecution witnesses. They have a tendency to destroy their cell phones as soon as the cops take an interest in grabbing them. Someone might almost think that these cops are getting tipped off by someone in the district attorney's office.

Another problem they have is that the cops make up stuff about them in their reports. Jen McCabe said two, maybe three cops have filed false reports about her.

Yesterday, it happened again. Defense attorney David Yannetti read into the record a report by "other people" (meaning the FBI, which he's not supposed to mention) saying that Higgins had told them he'd had a "factory reset" of the phone he later dumped into the DOD dumpster.

Yannetti had to hand him the FBI 302 to read. Higgins looked at it, but I don't think he actually read it, because his lips weren't moving. He finally looked over, a vacant look in his bloodshot eyes.

"I don't recall that. No, I don't recall making that statement."

When you're drinking double-digit Jamesons and gin-jahs every night, recollection can become hazy. So Higgins threw his fellow feds under the bus.

Oh, what a tangled web we weave, when first we practice to deceive.

On and on he stumbled. Beads of sweat appeared on his forehead. As they used to say of Brendan Behan, Butt-Dial Brian has a thirst so great that it would cast a shadow.

It was tough, being an ATF agent. Sometimes they ran out of gin-jah ale and he had to get a Jameson and Sprite. Once, he said with a shudder, a "tah-get" of an ATF probe got his phone "num-bah."

That was in July 2022. He had to get a new phone—two months later, just after he was told not to get rid of his old phone.

Yannetti asked Higgins if he'd ever discussed his text messages with Karen Read with anyone else.

HIGGINS: "Not to my knowledge, no."

Again, his memory is a bit cloudy. It must be the poteen talking.

YANNETTI: "Why not?"

HIGGINS: "To be honest with you, I mean I-I-I'm a personal on a personal level I-I kinda keep things to myself, um, I was a little embarrassed, um, wasn't really proud of 'em, uh, kind of maybe didn't show me in a good light with respects that I was John's friend."

He didn't say "with respect," he said, "with respects." To repeat, he respected John O'Keefe so much he was a no-show at his funeral, like all the rest of these low-rent losers.

He shifted nervously on the witness stand. It was 9:50 a.m. When does the Waterfall open?

But Higgins wanted everyone in the courtroom to know that, even though he couldn't be bothered even texting Karen Read back after she told him his close friend and brother-in-blue John O'Keefe was dead, he would have done something had he known, being in his "profession."

"If I had saw John O'Keefe on the side of the road, I woulda done somethin' to make a difference."

If he had saw him . . . not seen, but saw.

Not for the first time during this trial comes the recurring question: How the bleep does a fat, crapulous load like Higgins ever get to be a "cop?"

Maybe fat, drunk, and stupid is a good way to go through life—at least if you're a cop in Canton.

No more trial for the rest of the week—it's the hackerama.

# Jen McCabe, "Honestly"

*May 29, 2024*

Canton, Massachusetts, is the butt-dial capital of the world.

That's my first takeaway from the testimony yesterday in the Karen Read murder case.

Another takeaway is the more often you say "Honestly" or "To be honest," the more likely it is that you're not. Honest, that is.

It was not a good day for "Honest" Jen McCabe, the dentally challenged witness who faced the traditional "grueling" cross-examination from defense attorney Alan Jackson.

Jen, among others, is trying to railroad Karen Read into prison for allegedly running over her Boston cop boyfriend. And so Honest Jen somberly informed Jackson early in her testimony that after the body was found, she distinctly heard Karen Read say, "I hit him! I hit him! I hit him!"

Honest Jen McCabe not only recalls hearing those chilling words, but she added, "I can tell you today with one hundred percent clarity that she said it."

Which leads to another trial takeaway: If you remember any horrible statement "with one hundred percent clarity," perhaps it would behoove you to have mentioned it at least once during the first twelve times you were asked by cops and other assorted first responders what Karen Read said on the morning of January 29, 2022.

After McCabe repeated Karen Read's three alleged questions, attorney Jackson handed her the 223-page record of her (state, as opposed to federal) grand jury testimony.

On page 190, she quoted Read as asking her, "Did I hit him?"

On page 192, "Can I have hit him?"

On page 193, "Could I have hit him?"

On page 202, "What if I hit him and could I have hit him?"

On page 208, "Did I hit him? Could I have hit him?"

Jackson asked her if Karen Read had perhaps said it to a Canton cop. Maybe, she answered. And what was that cop's name? Sadly, she couldn't recall. Maybe it was a female EMT, she suggested. But no, that wasn't what she said to the female EMT either.

The butt-dials came up at the very end of the half day. Apparently she was calling the late John O'Keefe's phone immediately after he disappeared. She did so six times—six times!—in nineteen minutes.

"The phone was in my pocket," she said, glancing over at the jury—a tell for Honest Jen, the way when Biden says "Not a joke!" or "I'm not kidding!" you know he's pulling another Grandpa Simpson.

Butt-dialing seems to be quite the problem in what the townies call Can-UHN. Earlier, it was brought out that shortly after Jennifer McCabe's six butt-dials, two of the other McAlberts had been butt-dialing one another while they were asleep.

That was their testimony, anyway. Under oath.

Those were male McAlberts, as the townies are called. One had his phone on the nightstand when it mysteriously butt-dialed, and the other one had his in the bed while he was servicing his middle-aged wife after a full day of epic drinking.

When it comes to mysterious failings in the new technology, the town of Can-UHN is sort of a Bermuda Triangle, it seems.

In addition to the epidemic of butt-dialing, otherwise indisputable data about, say, GPS and phone-call completions are notoriously inaccurate.

As one tweeter put it yesterday: "Canton—where data lie but Jen McCabe doesn't."

Is there GPS data that contradicts the whereabouts of your daughter, whom you have just testified under oath was home at 12:30, when the data says she was cruising Canton an hour later, at 1:30 a.m.?

Who you gonna believe, a McAlbert or that lying GPS data?

Then there are the records that say Jen called her sister at 6:07 and 6:08 a.m., and that the phone calls were answered.

Surely some mistake, Jen McCabe testily testified.

Canton—where texts randomly delete themselves, over and over again. But it's just a coincidence.

"A lot of coincidence here," Jackson observed at one point.

When they aren't butt-dialing, the McAlberts are wildly deleting records of texts and cell phone calls. Or not.

Early yesterday, Jen McCabe testified, "I didn't delete any phone calls."

A few minutes later, that statement evolved into: "I don't recall deleting any phone calls."

When you're engaged in a conspiracy, everybody must stick to the same story. This is RICO 101. You must all hang together, or assuredly you will all hang separately. Truer today in Canton than when Ben Franklin said it in Philadelphia in 1776.

One of the leading characters is this tawdry tale is another Canton clown, Trooper Michael Proctor, currently under investigation by the Internal Affairs unit.

Jackson read from one of his reports, and she huffed that she didn't say that. Jackson asked, Did he get it wrong?

"You'd have to ask Proctor Trooper," she said. Not Trooper Proctor, but Proctor Trooper.

"I will," Jackson said.

Okay, we've learned a lot about Canton in these last few days. They get hammered all the time, with their kids no less, night after night. And then, when they're loaded, at a local dive bar called the Waterfall, the men grab each other's derrieres—"grab ass," as one witness described it.

The puzzled defense lawyer asked, "They grab each other's asses?"

"It's a figure of speech," Jennifer McCabe's husband elaborated.

A figure of speech—like butt-dials.

The cross-examination of Honest Jen McCabe resumes this morning. One obvious question for all these Canton witnesses is, "Were you lying then or are you lying now?"

But we all know what today's testimony will boil down to: "Ms. McCabe, what did you mean when asked the question, apparently at 2:27 a.m.: 'Hos (sic) long to die in cold?'"

I know, she must have butt-dialed it. It's a Canton thing.

CHAPTER THIRTEEN

# Sandra Birchmore: "Suicide" in Canton

Sometimes, cops don't have to clear a murder by framing an innocent person like Karen Read.

Occasionally, it can be simpler for law enforcement just to summarily declare the murder a suicide—especially if the murderer is also a police officer. No muss, no fuss. But such a course of action is possible only if the victim is on the fringes of society, with few connections—nobody to ask too many prying, embarrassing questions, in other words.

Sandra Birchmore was twenty-three years old and three months pregnant when she died shortly after receiving her final visitor, her married longtime boyfriend, Stoughton Police officer Matthew Farwell. She was found hanged in her apartment on February 4,

Sandra Birchmore: District attorney says suicide, FBI says murder.

2021. She had been dead several days before a wellness check was conducted.

The FBI had no doubts about what had happened to the expectant mother.

"MATTHEW FARWELL killed Sandra Birchmore," an agent wrote in support of a motion for detention after his arrest. "FARWELL committed this murder, at least part, to prevent Birchmore from disclosing to authorities his commission or possible commission of one or more crimes, including coercion and enticement . . . FARWELL's murder of Birchmore was the culmination of FARWELL's years-long pattern of abuse targeting Birchmore."

Stoughton Officer Matthew Farwell, charged with murder.

The Commonwealth of Massachusetts ruled her death a suicide. It was just easier that way. It wouldn't ruffle any feathers—any police feathers.

As scandalous as the prosecution of Karen Read was, the murder of Sandra Birchmore in Norfolk County may be an even more outrageous miscarriage of justice.

Sandra Birchmore was murdered in Canton, during a blizzard, almost exactly one year before John O'Keefe was also slain, in a snowstorm, in Canton. The same cops from Canton and the MSP detective unit from the Norfolk County District Attorney's Office investigated, with their customary carelessness, or worse.

Farwell had known Birchmore since she was twelve, and had joined the Stoughton Police Department's Explorer Program for young people. She never knew who her father was; her mother and her aunt died when she was a teenager. After grooming her for years, the highschool dropout Farwell began raping Birchmore when she was fifteen and he was twenty-seven.

All this was laid out in graphic detail in the 32,709 texts that they exchanged between December 2019 and February 2022. After her murder, the cell-phone extraction was handled by Trooper Nicholas Guarino, whose IT expertise consists of a handful of correspondence courses that begin with the words "Introduction to . . ."

Guarino was unable to locate a single one of the 32,709 text messages between the doomed lovers. You could call it a dry run for the Karen Read investigation, when he couldn't find the smoking-gun Google search by Jennifer McCabe at 2:27 a.m., a few hours before John O'Keefe's body was found in the snow: "Hos long to die in cold"

In the O'Keefe murder, the Canton and MSP didn't even bother to interview Brian Albert, the Boston cop on whose lawn O'Keefe's body was found.

As lead MSP investigator Michael Proctor explained to a friend on a text chain, he could expect no "shit" whatsoever because, "He's a Boston cop too."

At least they interviewed Matthew Farwell. Of course, he was on surveillance video at Birchmore's apartment building right before she died. But he told his fellow Norfolk County cops that although he'd been having sex with her, their relationship had only begun when she was twenty.

Then he asked if they had any more questions, because he had to rush to his wife's bedside. She was about to give birth to their third child, a son.

As always in any case involving a wayward police officer, Norfolk County DA Michael Morrissey couldn't exonerate the cop fast enough. The medical examiner ruled it a suicide. But there were questions. Even though Morrissey's MSP detectives rushed to say there was nothing of interest on either Birchmore's or Farwell's phone, the Stoughton Police were not reassured.

A few days earlier, on January 20, someone had called the Stoughton Police Department and told the dispatcher about Birchmore's pregnancy.

Farwell went on a rampage: "You're (sic) friend just called my fucking (department) to complain about me wtf."

Birchmore claimed ignorance, but Farwell didn't believe her.

"You also told me that no one knew about us yet she claimed we are fucking."

BIRCHMORE: "It's literally nothing."

FARWELL: "It's not nothing she called my job that's insane. Why would she call and drop my fucking name? Like what do I have to do with you not giving her something. Like you have no idea how bad what she did. I literally can't believe this is even real life like what else do I have to worry about now? Which other friend will do something tomorrow?"

Farwell's life had been spiraling out of control since December 20, when Birchmore had texted Farwell that she was pregnant. She included a photo of a poster celebrating her pregnancy.

Farwell responded: "I literally have nothing to say right now how could you express that in text when I said I didn't appreciate it."

She wanted Farwell's name on the birth certificate. As far back as October, she had sent a friend the draft of a text message she was thinking about sending to Farwell's wife, who was more than five months pregnant.

"I am just messaging you," she wrote, "to inform you that your husband Matthew has been out cheating on you since before you guys were even married . . ."

The FBI notes that there is no record that the message was ever sent. But there is little doubt that Birchmore was telling the truth. She and Farwell exchanged endless messages about sex, including, as the FBI noted in paragraph 24, "discussing role-playing during their next sexual encounter."

One time, Farwell "instructs Birchmore to act as if he were her older brother coming into her room at night to have sex with her."

On February 21, 2020, "FARWELL describes pinning Birchmore down during sex and asks her: 'Will you say Matt stop I'm 13 I'm not ready for this omfg please stop."

They had sex while Farwell was on duty—at Birchmore's former home in Stoughton, her new apartment in Canton, a Costco parking lot in Stoughton, a Five Guys parking lot in Canton. The FBI included a list of twenty-five assignations, with times, in 2020 and 2021.

Farwell didn't care about being on duty: "I'm going to sneak away from work quick," he wrote on April 10, 2020. On November 24: "Yes I will be on the clock."

Farwell made it clear he wanted her to act as if she were being raped. The FBI agent wrote: "His sexual fantasies were predominantly violent and included many references to choking and rape, and graphic details about their previous sexual encounters."

Nonetheless, she wanted to have his child. But she was promiscuous. The Stoughton Police Department report chronicled her "inappropriate" conduct with both Farwell and his twin brother Billy, another cop, a deputy chief, an Abington police officer, an animal-control officer, and a military recruiter in Quincy.

After she announced her pregnancy, Birchmore began to prepare for the new arrival. Ten days before her murder, she bought a baby stroller at Walmart. She asked a friend to be the child's godmother. She cut back on her coffee drinking. She talked about buying winter clothes for the infant. She texted Farwell, the FBI noted, about her due date, ultrasounds, genetic testing, gender reveals, and doctors' appointments.

Farwell did not respond. He often did not respond to Birchmore's happy texts. In the affidavit, Birchmore's friends are referred to by number.

"In January 2021, Birchmore called Person 2 and stated that, after telling FARWELL about the baby, FARWELL told her that 'he wished (she) just would die and he wants nothing to do with the baby.'"

It is a statement eerily similar to that made little more than a year later by Trooper Michael Proctor about Karen Read, another female victim of Norfolk County law enforcement.

"Hopefully," he texted his sister, "she kills herself."

Asked about the text on the witness stand, Proctor said it was "made in jest."

"It's just a figure of speech," he added. When they're busted, that's what they always say in Canton. It's a figure of speech. Right, Jennifer McCabe?

But Farwell apparently wasn't just fantasizing about getting rid of his female problems. About ten days before allegedly murdering

Sandra Birchmore, suddenly Farwell became tender, and interested in his girlfriend.

"I believe," wrote agent Chenee Castruita, "that FARWELL's shift in demeanor on or about this date was his attempt to appease Birchmore until he could kill her . . . Part of that plan included asking Birchmore to give him a key and keep it secret. Another part of that plan was inspecting various rooms of Birchmore's apartment, including the closet, to determine whether they contained items or presented options for how and when to kill Birchmore."

In October, he'd texted her that he didn't think it was a good idea for him to keep a key to her new apartment in Canton. Now he was asking not only for a key but for the passcode to get inside the front door of the building.

The FBI found that Birchmore drove to Walmart on January 24 and paid two dollars at 11:10 a.m. to buy the copy of the key that Farwell would use to enter her apartment to kill her a week later.

Birchmore's text to another friend—Person 9—outlined how Farwell was trying to ingratiate himself to her again. He brought her some ginger ale, she said. But then, as the FBI pointed out in its affidavit, Farwell's behavior took an ominous turn.

"Like last night he opened my closet door for something and then he went in my bathroom looking at my bathroom and then I have a dolly in my living room that he asked why I had it was just really odd he started looking around."

PERSON 9: "That's weird."

BIRCHMORE: "Yeah it was really weird."

On the last day of her life, February 1, 2021, Birchmore texted Farwell that she was being let out early from her job at the Sharon Public Schools because of the impending snowstorm. Later she texted Farwell that once she found out the sex of the baby, she wanted to purchase clothes in the right color for the child to wear home from the hospital.

She communicated with a photographer to book a newborn photo shoot. She asked a friend to obtain baby clothes for her. She performed a Google search for "Cubby Kids" furniture.

At 5:01 p.m., she accepted a DoorDash food order. As the snow starts to fall, she is seen on the apartment surveillance video going outside at 5:31 and 5:33 p.m., returning with a snowbrush.

The final time she was ever seen alive was at 5:33 p.m., with the snowbrush in her hands.

Do any of these actions sound like those of a person who is about to commit suicide?

Farwell arrived at her apartment at 9:14 p.m., "wearing street clothes, a hoodie with the hood up, and a (COVID) facemask."

"I have interviewed multiple witnesses who have each indicated that FARWELL resisted wearing a mask during the pandemic. One of these witnesses stated that FARWELL would only wear a mask when on duty and required by department policy to do so."

Farwell departed at 9:43 p.m. Her phone indicated that she made her final movements at 9:40 p.m.

When her family members arrived to clean her apartment, they noticed more indications that Birchmore had not been planning to commit suicide. There was a load of wet clothes in the washing machine and a second load in the dryer.

"Additionally, they observed a homemade sign saying, 'Congratulations, you're going to be a father.' That sign had an ultrasound photo on it and was sprinkled with glitter."

The family also saw a new baby stroller, still in its package. There were also onesies for the child "and other supplies."

"Birchmore had ordered items shortly before her death, and packages continued to arrive in the days following her death."

No one believed Birchmore had killed herself. No one except the Norfolk County District Attorney's Office, and the state medical examiner.

Soon the FBI retained an independent medical examiner, Dr. William Smock, who had more than forty years of experience in forensic medicine. His analysis "further confirmed that Birchmore's cause of death was homicide."

In addition to the broken bones and abrasions "commonly seen in cases of suffocation," he noted her beloved chain necklace, a thin gold chain with a flamingo pendant. The chain was broken, but not at the clasp.

"The cause of Ms. Birchmore's death," Dr. Smock determined, "is asphyxia and the manner of her death is homicide."

About thirteen hours after Farwell's last visit to Birchmore's apartment, his wife gave birth to their third child, a son, at Newton-Wellesley Hospital. An obscure local podcaster later discovered on social media a photo of Farwell holding his newborn child, while in the same clothes he had been wearing the night before at Birchmore's apartment when she was murdered.

Farwell was interviewed by his MSP friends two days after Birchmore's body was found. According to the FBI, he repeatedly lied. He said he only began having sex with her the previous year, although in his texts he and Birchmore agreed that he took her virginity in 2013, when she was fifteen and underage, and had wanted to do so a year earlier. He lied about the frequency of their sex, and the last time. He lied when he left the apartment. He said she had been "sectioned" (involuntarily hospitalized) multiple times, even though it was only once. He told Morrissey's sleuths that he had been trying to distance himself from Birchmore.

Farwell was quickly placed on administrative leave. He met "Person 4" at a local bar, where he expressed no remorse about Birchmore's death, only that he was "angry with MSP for looking into him."

That summer, Person 4 ran into Farwell at a party, and Farwell was joking about Birchmore being "hung on the door."

The FBI, after finding the texts that the MSP claimed didn't exist, chronicled at least twenty messages in which Farwell talked about choking Birchmore. Birchmore chronicled the sadistic sex favored by Farwell.

"According to her journal entries, FARWELL would engage in forceful oral, vaginal, and anal sex acts to punish her for her mistakes . . . (including) using certain sex acts to punish her for lying or being intimate with someone else."

On February 9, after giving his cell phone to the incompetent MSP detectives, he made and deleted two Google searches on his police phone.

One was: "Can deleted imessage be recovered by cellebrite."

Again, an eerie preview of the deleted searches on Jen McCabe's phone a year later—"Hos long to die in cold."

The other question he asked and then deleted: "Can you revoke consent in Massachusetts."

MSP didn't find any of those messages, from either phone. Maybe they didn't want to find them, just like they didn't want to delve too deeply into the cell phones of the McAlberts a year later.

Soon, both Farwell and his twin brother were gone from the Stoughton Police Department. Deputy Chief Robert Devine, who was also accused of having an "inappropriate" relationship with Birchmore, resigned in August 2022. The Abington police officer who admitted to having oral sex with her resigned and is a cooperating witness in the federal probe.

On August 27, 2024, Matthew Farwell was driving in Revere in his gravel truck, accompanied by his young son, when an armed FBI SWAT team surrounded his truck outside Sally Beauty Supply.

The agents read Farwell his Miranda rights as his young son sat on the street curb, his head in his hands. In the absence of any state charges, Farwell was charged with killing a witness or victim.

Farwell waived his detention hearing to remain in custody—jail. His wife has removed all traces of him from her social media. It appears he had no place to return to, even if he had been released from custody.

Meanwhile, as he awaits trial on the federal charges, the district of Norfolk County has apparently made no effort to indict him for murder.

Indeed, despite the overwhelming evidence against Farwell, Michael Morrissey seems to have little interest in bringing him before the bar of justice.

At a Democrat party event in his hometown of Quincy in late May, Morrissey was asked by a constituent what was going on in the Birchmore case.

"I still believe she killed herself," Morrissey said.

CHAPTER FOURTEEN

# Juston Root: 31 Shots in 3 Seconds

Juston Root, left, with a fake gun, being shot by a cop with a real gun, February 2021.

Almost exactly a year before Sandra Birchmore's murder, and two years before John O'Keefe's, the death of Juston Root followed the usual Norfolk County pattern.

The case involved the violent death of a vulnerable person, multiple police departments operating under suspicious circumstances, followed by a quick decision by District Attorney Michael Morrissey that nothing was amiss, followed by years of wrongful-death lawsuits and protests by outraged citizens about the cops' apparent cover-up.

Juston Root was a mentally disturbed forty-one-year-old when he was shot in Brookline either twenty-six or thirty-one times by Boston and State Police who had followed him down Route 9 from Brigham and Women's Hospital in Boston.

His mental-health clinic was next door to the hospital, and somehow he got into a dispute with one of the hospital security guards. He had occasional delusions of being a police officer. At some point, he pulled what appeared to be a weapon—it has been variously described as a "replica," a "clear plastic paintball gun," or just a "BB gun."

Whatever Root had on his person, it was not a functional firearm. A BPD officer on detail saw Root with the "weapon," and opened fire. Both Root and a security guard were hit. Root fled back to his double-parked car and took off west on Route 9 toward Brookline.

BPD officers followed him, at one point ramming his car, which is forbidden by BPD regulations. An MSP cruiser joined the chase. After crossing into Brookline, which is Norfolk County, Root crashed into another car in Chestnut Hill. He then abandoned his car and fled, with Boston and State Police in pursuit.

Wounded, he fell over. As he lay on the ground, a nearby EMT attempted to provide aid but was told to step away. Root was lying on the ground, but police ordered him to "get down."

According to the family's lawsuit, the police then opened fire. He was hit either twenty-six or thirty-one times. One BPD officer fired eight shots at the prone Root. That officer later claimed to investigators that his body cam was not on. But there was other video testimony to the contrary, as was pointed out by a federal appellate judge in her dissenting opinion when the appeal of the dismissed wrongful-death lawsuit was denied in 2024.

The dissenting judge cited evidence from the one body cam the six police officers claimed was functional that contradicted much of the officers' testimony. And even that camera, when turned over to authorities, was missing the five seconds immediately before the fatal shooting, just as so much video would disappear in the Karen Read trials a few years later.

After the shooting, police claimed that they found a "BB gun" under Root's body. They handcuffed the corpse and discussed the shooting among themselves, according to the body-cam footage cited in the federal lawsuit.

"Yeah, I killed that motherfucker," one of the cops bragged.

Another added, "I emptied my magazine on him."

According to the Root family's lawsuit, the conversation then turned to how to explain their actions.

Among the recorded comments: "You got a (union) rep coming?" And, "I won't talk." And, "I gotta get outta here."

The references to calling a union rep in the immediate aftermath of a suspicious death have become more commonplace in recent years. In January 2024, three youths were killed on Morrissey Boulevard when they lost control of their car while being chased at high speed by BPD officers who had been told to break off the pursuit.

One gory post-crash body-cam video posted on social media shows at least one dismembered arm on the pavement. Officers can be heard discussing whether a union rep has been called yet.

First things first.

Fortunately for the cops, Root was finally killed in Norfolk County. Less than two months later, District Attorney Michael Morrissey would formally absolve them of Root's death.

It is the Norfolk County way.

CHAPTER FIFTEEN

# Annie and Sonja

Leonardo Johnson did a year and a half in state prison for a crime he didn't commit, and he wasn't framed by a crooked cop or prosecutor. He was railroaded by a state drug-lab chemist named Annie Dookhan.

Johnson was one of more than 30,000 accused drug dealers whose cases were eventually thrown out, after it turned out that Trinidadian

Leonardo Johnson did eighteen months in prison for possession of a peanut.

immigrant Annie Dookhan, working out of the Hinton Lab in Jamaica Plain, and Sonja Farak, a chemist in Amherst, had been falsifying drug tests for years and years.

Dookhan just started making up results. Farak, on the other hand, was a drug addict. But no one noticed, or at least no one who mattered. When the scandal came to light, the state tried mightily to cover it up.

In the Farak case, the state attorney general (and future governor) Maura Healey filed a motion to suppress the evidence against Farak. Then Healey filed a motion to suppress the motion to suppress the motion to suppress.

In 2008, Leonardo Johnson was a crack cocaine addict when he was approached by an undercover cop in Boston looking to score. At a later civil trial in federal court, Johnson testified that when the undercover cop asked him for a "twenty"—twenty dollars' worth of crack cocaine—he saw a chance to make enough money to buy himself some crack.

The fact that he had no drugs was not a problem. He gave the cop what he described as a small peanut or some other kind of nut. He worried that the cop would realize he was being ripped off, but he didn't.

A few minutes later, Johnson was lugged by the BPD's drug unit, charged with distributing narcotics in a school zone.

Johnson had a few pinches for drug possession but none for dealing. In the usual course of justice, he would have accepted a rubber-stamp plea deal with no incarceration. But knowing that he hadn't sold any drugs, he refused to accept the prosecution's offer.

He went to trial and took the stand in his own defense in November 2009. But then Annie Dookhan, the forensic chemist in the state's public health department, appeared on the stand. She lied first about her educational credentials (she claimed a master's degree) and then lied about her drug "analysis."

Cocaine, she said.

Johnson couldn't believe it.

"I knew she was lying," he told the *Boston Globe* in 2017. "Ain't no way, no how a cashew can turn into crack."

But the jury believed her and came back with a quick guilty verdict. Johnson was sentenced to two years and one day. With time off for good behavior, he had long since completed his sentence when Annie Dookhan was finally charged with evidence tampering in 2012.

She pleaded guilty to all charges in 2013, served three years in prison, and was paroled in 2016. Johnson sued in both state and federal court. The state paid him $250,000 for wrongful imprisonment, and then in federal court he was awarded $2 million from Dookhan, although it appears he never got a cent in the settlement.

None of Dookhan's supervisors ever accepted any responsibility for her misdeeds. No one had ever bothered to check up on her background, about which she lied. She hadn't gone to Harvard, her parents weren't doctors. She wasn't an FBI "special agent of operations."

Apparently all they cared about was that she was clearing up the backlog. She married a fellow Trinidadian, became pregnant, and then miscarried. She said that working hard was her way of dealing with her grief, doubling the number of samples analyzed by the second-place chemist.

Of course, other lab workers noticed some problems. She used an uncalibrated scale, which meant she couldn't know how much

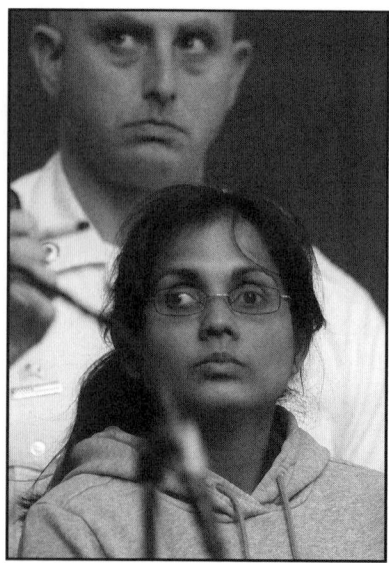

State lab chemist Annie Dookhan.

State lab chemist Sonja Farak.

contraband each defendant actually had, an important point, obviously, in determining the severity of a prison sentence.

She seldom used her microscope. She generated next to no trash, even though an on-the-level chemist should be using new glass sides for each test. She took drug samples out of the safe without bothering to check them out—a severe breach of chain-of-custody protocol, like Michael Proctor throwing John O'Keefe's clothes in the back of his car for months at a time. Hey, if somebody's guilty, what does it really matter?

She began forging her coworkers' signatures or initials on documents. At some point, she stopped doing most tests at all.

As a story in *Distillations* magazine noted, "If the cops said it was heroin, it was heroin, and that was that."

There was pro forma backup—two rounds of testing. If she went second, she just agreed with the legitimate analysis. If she tested first and the retest showed her guess was wrong, she had a backup plan.

"Dookhan would sometimes sneak off, find a pure sample of the drug she had initially claimed, and submit that for retesting. Presto, the second test now gave the 'correct' result. In other words, she started forging evidence to conceal her fraud."

Later, she tried to explain her behavior. She wanted to get criminals "off the street." She liked being the top chemist in the lab: "My colleagues call me 'superwoman.'"

"Eventually," *Distillations* reported, "a chemist reported Dookhan to his supervisor. To his frustration, the supervisor pooh-poohed him."

It's the Massachusetts way.

With the scandal starting to percolate, the lab was turned over to, of all agencies, the MSP. What could possibly go wrong?

Before it was over, 21,587 drug convictions had been overturned after lawyers began examining her 36,000 cases. The legislature had to budget $30 million to deal with the fallout, including notifying everyone convicted on her analyses, and later testimony in court, when she routinely perjured herself by claiming a fake master's degree.

(Again, a forerunner of the Karen Read case, and the Commonwealth's expert who claimed multiple college degrees, despite seventeen years of unsuccessfully seeking an undergraduate degree.)

Dookhan was arrested in late 2012. In January 2013, another state-lab forensic chemist from Amherst named Sonja Farak was appearing at a drug case in Springfield. After testifying all morning, Farak went out to her car at lunch and smoked crack cocaine.

As she returned to the courthouse, she was met by two state police detectives who took her to a conference room and began questioning her.

When the cops asked Farak why she had a crack pipe at her work station at the drug lab in Amherst, Farak answered, "I think I'm going to hold off talking and talk to my M.O.S.E.S. (union) representative, if that's all right."

Another recurring theme in all public-sector corruption: fall back on the union label. The union picks up the legal tab, at least at first.

Farak corresponded with Dookhan, it turned out. But unlike Dookhan, who just wanted to appear a "superwoman," Farak had a much more basic reason for tampering with the evidence. She was a stone-cold junkie. From 2004 until 2013, she worked continuously under the influence of drugs.

In a scathing 127-page ruling in 2017, Superior Court Judge Richard Carey laid out the evidence against Farak. "Farak's motive was simply to feed her own drug addiction," he wrote.

And if that meant evidence had to be falsified against defendants, most of them non-white, well, then, so be it. That was the attitude of the attorney general's office when the investigation began. Once again, Maura Healey, the future governor, turned a blind eye to the framing of hundreds of defendants.

In one 2012 case, Springfield police confiscated fifty-one real oxycodone pills—the gold standard of prescription opioids. They were turned over to Farak for analysis. When she returned them, the local cops discovered that instead of the original fifty-one oxies, she'd returned sixty-one pills with different colors and markings—some of them apparently vitamins.

The case of the missing oxies was discovered by an MSP detective named Joseph Ballou. He turned over his evidence to an assistant attorney general named Anne Kaczmarek, who according to the judge "dismissively replied in an email to Ballou, 'Please don't let this get more complicated than we thought. If she was suffering from back injury, maybe she took the oxies.'"

The judge continued: "When asked to explain that reply, Kaczmarek testified in 2016 that she feared that if Farak's drug tampering turned out to be more complicated than they had thought, 'an avalanche of work' would hit 'us.'"

The judge immediately threw out seven convictions that were based on Farak's testimony and "analysis."

One of the convicted was Rolando Penate, who went to prison for heroin distribution. Farak certified that she had tested his drugs on January 9, 2012. She kept a "worksheet" showing the drugs she ingested daily at the state lab, and on the day she supposedly tested Penate's stash, she recorded smoking crack in the morning. At lunch she took a dose of recently confiscated LSD.

"She later recalled," Judge Carey noted, "that the sensation of colors in the wind left her unable to function well at work, to drive her car, or to attend therapy . . . she did not recall running any tests that day (but) Farak endorsed certificates of analysis, including in the Penate case."

Penate was sentenced to five to seven years. When his lawyer tried to obtain the exculpatory evidence, he was met by "stonewalling," as the judge described it, "misconduct so egregious . . . (that it) qualifies as a fraud upon the court."

And what was future Governor Maura Healey's response to this scandal?

In 2016, she filed a "Motion to Impound Grand Jury Materials and Report" on the scandal involving her office.

Then her office filed a second motion to "impound its request for its Motion for Order of Non-Dissemination of Information."

Which means that she not only wanted to seal the shocking evidence, but to also seal her request to seal the evidence against her office.

Kaczmarek got a promotion, to assistant clerk magistrate in Suffolk County. The other assistant attorney general who worked with Kaczmarek was hired by Democrat State Treasurer Deb Goldberg.

The scandals got a good leaving-alone from most of the mainstream media. It would have made Maura Healey look bad. But the fact is, both drug-lab scandals followed the same pattern of most law enforcement corruption cases in Massachusetts:

First, next to no coverage by media.

Second, public-sector union support for the criminals.

Third, promotions for the perpetrators.

Fourth, no real relief for the victims.

Finally, in 2023, Kaczmarek was disbarred as an attorney. The other assistant attorney general, who had gotten a hack job at the State House, was suspended from the practice of law for a year and a day.

As for Leonardo Johnson, who won a $1.5-million judgment from Annie Dookhan for his unlawful eighteen months in prison for selling a cashew to an undercover cop, he has yet to receive a penny from the disgraced immigrant.

It's the Massachusetts way.

## CHAPTER SIXTEEN

# MSP: A Long Way from Norman Rockwell

In his opening argument to the jury in Karen Read's second trial, defense attorney Alan Jackson brought up the crooked cop who wasn't there—fired MSP Trooper Michael Proctor, the lead investigator in the case.

"A malignancy," Jackson said of Proctor, "a cancer that cannot be cut out, a cancer that cannot be cured. And that cancer has a name. His name is Michael Proctor."

Jackson looked at the jury, Norfolk County residents who knew how things worked.

"Do you know how hard it is to get fired by the State Police?"

They knew. It's almost impossible. And even if you do get fired, even if you serve a few weeks of prison time, you most likely get to keep the pension, the monthly kiss in the mail.

It is the MSP way.

But it wasn't always this way. The troopers weren't always a laughingstock, a punch line, a perennial source of headlines reinforcing everyone's worst prejudices about all law enforcement.

They were a police force out of a Norman Rockwell painting—literally. A state trooper made the cover of *The Saturday Evening*

*Post* magazine in 1958, in a Norman Rockwell painting of him at a Howard Johnson's in Pittsfield, with a young boy who was running away from home.

It became an iconic work beloved by many police departments, symbolizing the good works and compassion of law enforcement. The MSP were always the ones on the straight and narrow. They didn't do much work in Boston—that was left to the "Mets," the Metropolitan Police who patrolled most of the roads and parks around the city.

The troopers were seriously underpaid, especially considering that they were separated from their families for days at a time, living in the barracks. In the summer of 1978, I remember a budget debate on a Saturday afternoon at the State House, with angry MSP wives running through the halls, demanding pay raises for their husbands. Some said they were subsisting on food stamps. They denounced Governor Mike Dukakis for his penuriousness.

Shortly afterward, Dukakis was upset in the Democrat primary by Edward J. King, a law-and-order Democrat. Soon the MSP were getting pay raises. But their integrity was still unquestioned, at least compared to the Mets.

The Metropolitan Police were a legendarily corrupt force. The ultimate "Met" was Capt. Gerry Clemente, up from the ranks of the Medford Police Department (see Chapter 9). Along with two other local cops, as well as some organized-crime types, Clemente was the mastermind of the famous Depositors Trust bank burglary in Medford over the Memorial Day weekend of 1981.

Working three nights, the cops looted safe deposit boxes of millions of dollars in jewelry, gold, cash, and negotiable securities, as one of their uniformed Medford cops stood guard.

But the Depositors Trust heist wasn't the only racket Clemente was involved in. He had used his GI Bill benefits to take locksmithing courses, and he soon realized that state office buildings were the easiest of pickings, especially if he could work with the Capitol Police, another corrupt law enforcement agency.

Soon Clemente was breaking into the state civil service offices in the McCormack Building at the top of Beacon Hill. He began stealing promotional exams for police and firefighters, and then sold them to crooked first responders for $3,000 per copy. For an additional fee, he would break into the offices and change the grades of anyone who might have scored higher on the promotional exam than Clemente's fellow crooked-cop client.

By the time the Depositors Trust burglary and "Examscam" were solved in the late 1980s, the reputations of the Mets and the Capitol Police had been irredeemably ruined. Among the public, they were regarded with as much contempt as the MSP are today.

From prison, Clemente wrote a very instructive book called *The Cops Are Robbers*, discussed more fully in Chapter 9, "Copland." In the beginning, Clemente and his crew had been old-fashioned crooked cops, but like everybody else in the early 1980s, some of them had gotten deeply into cocaine. One of them shot another cop, one was arrested in a botched drug deal in Mississippi . . . it became a familiar tale in the 1980s. Cocaine changed everything.

In 1990, a Republican won the governorship for the first time in twenty years. William Weld was elected as a reformer. And one of his first reforms was to combine the pristine MSP with the three corrupt departments.

And that's what ruined the MSP.

It was then-Governor William Weld who destroyed the state police. That's what the old-timers still say.

As late as August 2025, former Mets were still going down. Calvin Butner was sentenced to three months in prison for his role in the CDL scandal. He joined the Mets in 1983—probably an affirmative-action hire under Governor Michael Dukakis.

He was arrested in January 2024 on a cruise ship about to hoist anchor in the Port of Miami. The feds handcuffed him. His wife looked on and then announced that she was remaining on board, to enjoy the cruise her crooked ex-Met cop husband had already paid for.

The Mets were susceptible to temptations that staties seldom encountered, living until the 1970s in the barracks, outside the big cities. It wasn't so much that they were that much more honest, it was that they had fewer opportunities, temptations. One trooper who was assigned to the State House was Richard Schneiderhan. Soon he was hanging out in the Combat Zone, where he was recruited by Winter

 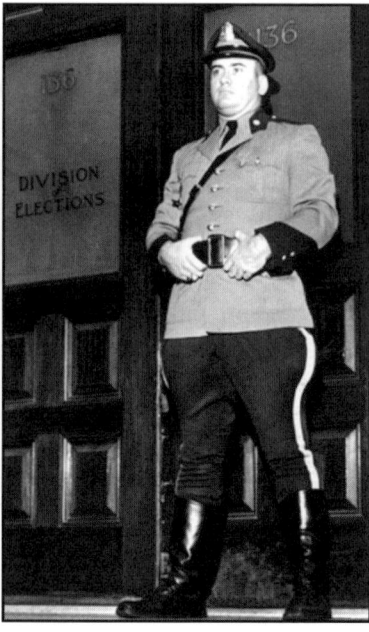

Felon trooper Calvin Butner: Time's up for the last Met.

Trooper Richard Schneiderhan, the first crooked statie, snitch for the Winter Hill Gang.

Hill hitman Johnny Martorano. He later went to prison for selling information to the Mob.

But Schneiderhan was an exception. Generally the staties were squeaky clean. In 1981, it was the MSP who bugged the West End garage that Whitey Bulger was using as his new headquarters. The FBI knew about it, but they were on Bulger's payroll. It was left to the MSP to set up the surveillance, including photographing most of the leading gangsters in Boston, both Winter Hill and Mafia, gathering for meetings. The FBI tipped off Whitey and then, in an act of revenge, a rider was "anonymously" inserted into the state budget to force the retirement of all the MSP brass who had approved the operation. (The rider was vetoed by then-Governor Ed King, although a later congressional investigation could not discover who had inserted the payback against the honest cops.)

But that's how good—and incorruptible—the MSP were. Until the merger.

Soon the MSP—many of them erstwhile Mets—were getting caught up in scandals. At first it was marijuana—the *Herald* began referring to "Pot Cops," with numbers to tell them apart.

It quickly got worse. In 2006, Sgt. Brian O'Hare was arrested after meeting what he thought was a fourteen-year-old boy for sex. It was an FBI agent.

He went to prison, but when he got out, O'Hare tried to get his pension back. He had no shame. As the state appeals court noted in turning down his attempt to regain his pension: "O'Hare's argument that his position of patrol supervisor and shift commander at the time of the offense meant that he was not responsible for policing crimes against children is not persuasive."

We were a long way from Norman Rockwell.

The money just kept flowing. Troop E on the Turnpike was the beneficiary of federal highway funds for extra patrols. Soon a system was worked out by which the troopers could cut short their extra shifts, if they worked them at all. To cover their asses, Troop E wrote fake tickets, and then mailed them out to unsuspecting motorists, most of whom hadn't even been on the Pike when their "tickets" were written.

When the feds began sniffing around, the Troop E payroll records were suddenly destroyed. In the end, dozens of state troopers were implicated in the embezzlement scheme. Many pleaded guilty, but were sentenced to only minimal sentences, if any time.

And practically none of them lost their pensions. They just made "restitution," took early retirement—sometimes on disability—and moved to Florida.

The MSP union is SPAM—State Police Association of Massachusetts. Like most public-sector unions in Massachusetts, it has wielded more and more clout at the State House as the years have gone by. Their seventh-floor office became one of the most popular watering holes on Beacon Hill. In addition to a well-stocked bar, MSP had a draft-beer tap for thirsty legislators.

The union boss was Dana Pullman, a state cop out of central casting (see page 192).

In the days before the merger with the Mets, the MSP had been somewhat short on clout. They didn't operate all that much in Boston, after all. But starting in the 1990s, the new, not-so-incorruptible MSP learned how to play the game.

Recently, their man at the State House was Ken Halloran. His uncle was Brian Halloran, the gangster gunned down by Whitey Bulger in 1981 (see page 229). Ken Halloran was an old-time cop—he went to law school at night and worked days at Quincy District Court—Norfolk County, in other words. He knew all the beer-bellied hacks in the district attorney's office. He parlayed his connections into an appointment as clerk magistrate of the Falmouth District Court, but soon resigned in the wake of sex and age discrimination charges.

Union boss Dana Pullman, now awaiting resentencing after a federal conviction.

As a trustee at Mass Maritime Academy, he was again accused, this time of conflict of interest charges. Back on the job, he was nowhere to be found while on a detail as another trooper was run over while trying to arrest the driver of a stolen car.

Halloran was found guilty of several payroll violations, but in the emerging tradition of the MSP, he was quickly promoted to detective lieutenant and then assigned to the State House as the MSP's liaison to the legislature.

In the meantime, Halloran hooked up with the sister of then-Attorney General Maura Healey. They are now described as "partners." In 2022, the year his girlfriend's sister was elected governor, Det. Lt. Halloran retired with a $79,667 pension and joined a lobbying firm headed by a former GOP state senator from Cape Cod who was once indicted on state corruption charges. (He beat the rap.)

As it became clearer and clearer that there were no repercussions for bad behavior by the MSP, their corruption grew ever more overt.

Lt. Col. Dan Risteen took up with a young woman named Leigha Genduso, formerly the live-in moll of a major drug dealer. Soon she was a dispatcher, then a cadet, then a trooper, and finally promoted to the coveted K-9 unit.

But then Genduso's past—as documented by her federal grand jury testimony against her ex-boyfriend—was turned up by a blogger from Holden named Aidan Kearney. He went by the moniker "Turtleboy."

Soon the Genduso scandal had made it, if not to the *Globe*, at least to the *Herald* (see Chapter 19).

Then it got worse. The colonel was Richard McKeon, a former detective in the Worcester County District Attorney's Office. He had worked there with a hack assistant district attorney named Tim "Let 'Em Go" Bibaud, who was rewarded with a district court judgeship. In the finest tradition of the hackerama, Bibaud's wayward daughter Ali was likewise handed a string of hack jobs, first in the district attorney's office, then later as a toll taker on the Turnpike.

Dan Risteen, Leigha Genduso's future good friend.

In 2017, she was pulled over by a young state trooper for OUI. Loaded to the gills, she told the trooper that her father was a judge and that she was a junkie who got the money for drugs by selling her body. (She described it much more graphically.) Then she offered the trooper a little something if he'd let her go.

The trooper recorded everything she said in his report and then the shit hit the fan. He was ordered to rewrite his report, which he'd already filed. He was told that if he didn't do what his superiors wanted him to do, to prevent embarrassment to their political cronies, that it could cost him his job. He was told the orders came directly from Col. McKeon and the secretary of public safety, another alumnus of the Worcester district attorney's office.

A lawsuit was quickly filed, with all the dirty laundry about the Worcester County hackerama spilling out, on the record. McKeon, before taking early retirement, admitted that "thousands" of arrest reports were routinely . . . amended . . . by the MSP. Soon following him out the door was Dan Risteen and the number-two statie, Francis Hughes.

Risteen and Hughes had been extras together in the famous movie about corrupt cops in Massachusetts, *The Departed*. Now they departed together, both going to work for future Teamsters boss Sean O'Brien.

Hughes's pension is now $177,078 a year, and he makes another $208,138 as the International Brotherhood's "chief investigator." Risteen's annual kiss in the mail from the Commonwealth is $163,038. He grabs $226,052 as O'Brien's "field services director."

Death, where is thy sting?

After the scandals of Leigha Genduso and Ali Bibaud, the floodgates opened. Everybody on the MSP started diming everyone else out.

Then came COVID. Whether by design or not, it became a pretext for the bad actors to rid themselves of honest troopers, who disproportionately refused to take the vaccine for either religious or health reasons.

In one case, a father who'd been convicted in the Troop E embezzlement scandal got to keep his pension, while his scrupulously honest son was fired (see Chapter 18).

Trooper Timothy Barry also refused to take the shot. He was both a Marine combat veteran and a Sunday school teacher, a third-generation cop. In 2020, when he was at the academy in New Braintree for training, he was summarily dragged out of class and fired in front of his fellow troopers, stripped of his badge, gun, uniform, and cruiser.

The enforcer was a lieutenant who had been arrested in Westfield in 2010 for assaulting his wife by shoving her head into an unflushed toilet that he had just defecated into.

Turtleboy had the gory details. The MSP seethed. They desperately wanted to get a look at his phone, to find out who was leaking information to him. (Spoiler alert: I gave Turtleboy the information.)

They fired a trooper from Bristol County who had been the subject of positive national news when he pulled over in his cruiser by the side of the road and shared his lunch with a homeless woman. A passerby saw it and took a photo, which went viral.

It may have been the MSP's best feel-good publicity since that 1958 cover of *The Saturday Evening Post*.

Turtleboy broke story after story about MSP corruption.

But it didn't help the trooper. He was fired for not taking the vaccine. (He later got his job back after getting the inoculation—in India.)

At the academy at New Braintree, the Class of 2020 was different because of the COVID panic that was being used to cleanse the MSP. Almost as soon as they went on the job, some got jammed up (see page 195).

More veteran troopers were arrested, including Daniel Griffin, one of the last remaining Mets on the MSP. He was charged in federal court with, among other things, destroying incriminating documents about the MSP conspiracy to steal federal overtime funds on the Turnpike.

These and many other scandals are covered in my columns for the *Boston Herald* reprinted in Chapter 18, "MSP: To Protect and Steal."

But the scandals haven't ended. In September 2024, at the academy in New Braintree, a twenty-five-year-old recruit, Enrique Delgado-Garcia, died a day after taking part in a "boxing exercise." The recruit had previously worked for Worcester County District Attorney Joe Early Jr., who had been involved in the Ali Bibaud scandal, and had been ordered by the State Ethics Commission to pay $5,000 to the trooper his office had attempted to intimidate.

Early recused himself from the investigation into his former employee's mysterious death. A special investigator was appointed, and by May 2025 he had charged the state $309,000 for his services. But there have been only murky explanations of the circumstances of Delgardo-Garcia's death.

Meanwhile, the new colonel of the MSP is settling into his new office in Framingham. On a trip to the State Police Museum in Whitinsville, some of the retired troopers presented him with a framed photo

Enrique Delgado-Garcia: The investigation continues . . .

of, you guessed it, the Norman Rockwell painting from 1958. It was even autographed by the little boy who posed, who is now over seventy years old.

It hangs behind his desk. But nobody at GHQ is operating under any illusions.

We're a very long way from Norman Rockwell.

Col. Geoffrey Noble with the Norman Rockwell painting behind him.

CHAPTER SEVENTEEN

# MSP Hall of Shame

Trooper Kristopher Carr, convicted in 2025 of motor-vehicle homicide while driving drunk in 2021. Fired.

Sgt. Gary Cederquist, convicted in the Commercial Driver's License (CDL) scandal. US attorney said he "chose bribery and extortion over his oath to protect the community." Made $331,620 in 2023 (legitimately). Retired January 2024. Pension: $8,850 a month. (His brother, Det. Lt. William Cederquist, remains on the MSP and made $439,600 in 2023 and $407,100 in 2024.)

Trooper Joel Rogers, convicted of bribery and extortion in the CDL scandal. Retired after indictment. Pension: $6,486 a month. Salary in 2023: $175,800.

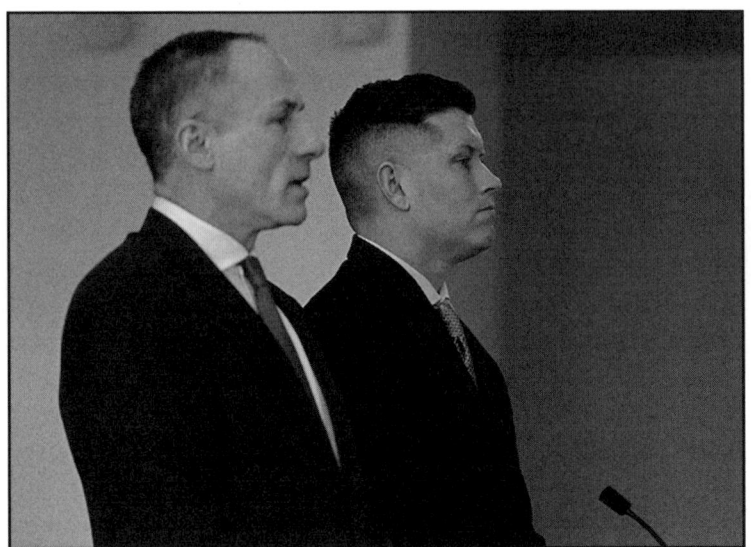

Trooper Terence Kent, shown here with his attorney, David Yannetti, charged with sexually assaulting a male motorist he stopped. Suspended, made $173,170 in 2023. He has two brothers on the job: Seamus and Michael Kent, who both made $178,920 last year. Not to be confused with Zachariah Kent, who was charged with twenty-three counts of shoplifting, stealing $1,000 worth of golf balls from Targets in Worcester County. Kent made $118,780 in 2024. He is now banned from all Targets.

Trooper Gregory Raftery, convicted in the Troop E embezzlement scandal. He made $219,670 in 2016 and was stripped of his $72,204.84-a-year pension in 2019. In 2025 he lost his appeal before the Supreme Judicial Court for restoration of his pension.

Trooper Calvin Butner, at his arraignment. He made $159,892.97 in 2022 and was sentenced to three months in prison. Pension: $6,020 a month.

Trooper Paul Cesan, convicted of embezzlement in the Troop E overtime scandal. He made $163,533 in 2016.

Lt. David Wilson, convicted in the Troop E embezzlement scandal. He made $259,475 in 2016. His pension of $105,492.24 a year was halted in 2019.

Trooper Matthew "Big Irish" Sheehan, accused of making racist posts on a police message board, was later charged with shooting an ATV driver on I-93 in Boston in 2018. He pleaded guilty to assault and battery with a dangerous weapon and was decertified as a police officer by POST Commission in 2025. No pension.

Trooper Eric Chin, convicted in the Troop E embezzlement scandal. No pension.

CHAPTER EIGHTEEN

# MSP: To Protect and Steal

### $584,072 Reasons the State Police Make Taxpayers Sick

*(Even by MSP standards, this was amazing. The highest paid state trooper last year was a guy who would have been fired from any real job back in 2011. He was accused of many other offenses over the years, but nothing stuck. Nothing ever does with the MSP. No wonder Michael Proctor wants his job back! If they won't fire Thomas McCarthy....)*

January 8, 2025

What made Milwaukee famous once made a loser out of MSP Capt. Thomas McCarthy.

Back in 2011, he was a Miller High Life drinker, according to police reports

The highest paid trooper of 2024: $584,072.

when he was arrested in Essex County for drunk driving. But McCarthy can afford a better brew now, much better, with the $584,072 he made last year at the MSP's F Troop at Logan Airport.

The headlines in the paper yesterday mentioned how McCarthy "blasts" past the MSP OT records, and "smashes OT ceiling."

Smashed, blasted—these seem like appropriate verbs to describe McCarthy, considering his squalid quarter-century-plus as a state trooper.

Somewhere, suspended Trooper Michael Proctor must be speed-dialing his lawyer before his upcoming "disciplinary" hearing, yelling, "If this bum doesn't get fired, why me?"

Let us return to a boozy Saturday night back in 2011. According to Saugus police reports, McCarthy was in his unmarked MSP Crown Vic on Saville Street in Saugus when a town cop smelled him reeking of alcohol. The local cop told McCarthy to turn off his engine.

"You've got to be kidding me!" McCarthy snarled. "I'm outta here."

Three cruisers trailed him as he unlawfully sped off, blew through a stop sign, crossed the yellow line "numerous times," and finally swerved onto Route 1.

As the OJ-like chase continued, McCarthy veered into the Square One Mall and skidded to a stop in what was then the Sears parking lot.

The Saugus cops again yelled at the future $584,072-a-year world's highest paid state trooper to turn off the unmarked vehicle and toss out the keys, but he refused. Finally he complied, staggered out of his Crown Vic, and was told he was under arrest.

"Are you kidding me?" he repeated. According to the report, he "resisted" being handcuffed. A search of his MSP vehicle uncovered a gun, an empty Miller, and two full containers of the Champagne of Bottled Beer.

Naturally, McCarthy was not given either a Breathalyzer or field sobriety test because . . . professional courtesy. An MSP supervisor called to the Saugus Police Department reported seeing signs of "intoxication"—two colloquialisms for which are "blasted" and "smashed."

The next Tuesday, the world's highest paid state trooper was a no-show at his own arraignment on drunk-driving charges. He was reported to be in a "facility"—in Florida. Because that's where the staties always go when they get a bad ice cube, to that sunny place for shady people. Just ask "the Foxboro Flasher." (See the next column.)

As corrupt as the MSP are, even they were appalled by McCarthy not even pretending to care about his OUI.

"The department is disappointed he saw fit not to show up at his arraignment," the MSP flack said. "Every person who gets arrested has to. Why he thinks he is any different is a mystery."

Not really. The world's highest paid state trooper knew then, and knows even better now that he's a millionaire. He's a state cop, and he can do whatever he damn well pleases, while still making $584,072 a year.

McCarthy got a hack judge to give him a continued without a finding (CWOF). He was suspended for a year and now makes, I repeat, $584,072 a year.

As Rudyard Kipling once wrote, "There comes a night/When the best get tight." But this was not a one-off for the world's highest paid state trooper.

In 2005, according to the MSP, after another disciplinary incident, he "forfeited 30 days."

In 2002, according to a Channel 25 report in 2014, the world's highest paid state trooper "crashed into another motorist at 4 a.m. in Reading. The other driver and his passenger both needed to be taken to the hospital.

"A witness tells State Police he saw McCarthy possibly throwing beer cans out of his car and 'was possibly operating under the influence of alcohol,' records show.

"The driver hit by McCarthy was later told that McCarthy ran from the scene. But the Reading police report doesn't even mention McCarthy's name."

A sergeant picked the tosspot trooper up at the accident scene and drove him to the barracks in Andover. She said she "observed no characteristic of alcohol intake."

Stop me if you've heard this one before.

Think about this: If you as a civilian got lugged for driving under, after being chased by three cruisers, do you think you'd get a pass on blowing in the bag, or on the Sidewalk Olympics (as in Saugus)? Would your name be excised from the incident report (as in Reading)? And would you now be making $584,072 a year . . . in the exact same job?

But wait, there's more, according to Channel 25, which got a look at his personnel file after a two-year struggle over public records concerning the disciplinary proceedings against corrupt cops. In 2000, a motorist stopped by the world's highest paid state trooper complained that he had "alcohol on his breath." MSP "investigated" and decided that the allegation was "false."

Of course it was!

In the 2014 story about the personnel records of dodgy dipso staties, Channel 25 referred to McCarthy as a "former captain." Now he's a captain again. He was demoted after the Saugus incident, then took the promotional exams to become captain again.

For the record, last year McCarthy's base pay was $224,007.22. He pocketed $349,815.27 in overtime. He grabbed another $10,250 in "other" pay.

Total: $584,072.

To coin a phrase, "You've got to be kidding me! I'm outta here."

## Trooper Accused of Exposing Himself at Gillette Stadium Quits

*July 28, 2020*

MSP finally got rid of one of their bad apples without handing him a multimillion-dollar pension package.

Yet.

You see, in the sordid world of the MSP, it's never really over until the kiss in the mail is rubber-stamped through.

C'mon down, ex-Trooper Andrew Patterson, also known as the Foxboro Flasher.

This is the thirty-two-year-old Lynn guy who went to a Luke Bryant concert in Foxboro in June 2019 and ended up getting charged with one count of lewd, wanton, and lascivious conduct.

Ex-Trooper Andrew Patterson, the "Foxboro Flasher."

According to the Foxboro police report, Patterson arrived in a state of extreme intoxication and proceeded to, among other things, pleasure himself while sitting in someone else's seat, after which he "started dancing" behind the grossed-out woman "and pretended to 'grind' on her."

A male concertgoer told police, "Patterson made a comment to him that he liked his beard, had a 'nice ass,' and that he could sit on his lap."

Patterson also grabbed some popcorn from the man with the nice rear end, after which he punched him in the face.

For his public service, the grateful citizens of the Commonwealth paid Patterson $149,746.47 in 2018.

Here are some of the witnesses' descriptions of Trooper Patterson in the police report:

"PATTERSON was extremely intoxicated and his speech was thick and slurred . . . Being inappropriate . . . could barely stand up . . . appeared to be in a daze . . . Thoroughly intoxicated and continued drinking."

All through this epic Kennedy-esque evening, Patterson's male victim was posting on Facebook, telling his friends about the guy who was "hitting on" him. He then described Patterson as a "sick bastard (who) even pulled out his (eggplant emoji)."

When Patterson later reeled off, the victim posted: "He's moved on to being a Joe Biden to the young girls in here. Honestly he's lucky I haven't smashed a chair on this frat boy."

The MSP: To Protect and Serve. Or, in the case of Patterson: To Protect and Overserve.

In the aftermath of his night on the town, Patterson was put on leave—paid leave, naturally, until the *Herald* obtained a copy of the police report four months later. The lewd-and-lascivious charge against him was dismissed in district court last fall, but Patterson seems to have never returned to the job.

And Thursday he "resigned." I asked the MSP whether he had been facing a dishonorable discharge.

In a statement, the MSP said they "can only confirm that he was discharged, not the type of discharge. He resigned as Internal Affairs case against him was in its disciplinary phase."

The staties said they had "no knowledge" of whether Patterson had yet applied for a pension, which would most likely be a disability pension (72 percent, tax-free) since he hadn't vested yet.

"He resigned. He faced various disciplinary outcomes, up to and potentially including termination, if the disciplinary phase of his investigation had run its course, but he resigned prior to its completion."

Patterson shot and killed a knife-wielding perp in the line of duty in 2015. He also has a Bronze Star from his combat tour in Iraq. Post-traumatic stress disorder (PTSD) would appear to be the ticket for early retirement at the age of thirty-three.

I called Patterson Tuesday (his cell-phone number is on the Foxboro Police Department report) and he referred me to his lawyer, Dan Moynihan of Stoneham.

"I'm not going to get into medical records," Moynihan said. "But if he has a medical issue, he will seek such a pension, as any public employee should."

In other words, count on it.

Patterson was accompanied on the night in question by his wife Rachel and another state trooper, Stephen Thomson. Trooper

Thomson's contribution to the evening's festivities came after his buddy punched the male civilian in the nose.

Thomson, according to the police report, "displayed a badge to him" and "made a comment about either himself or he and Thompson as being Troopers, and that he (the victim) is in big trouble now."

Thomson is still on the job—he made just over $237,000 in both 2023 and 2024.

Patterson, meanwhile, is on his own pension—$5,622 a month. He's been collecting since September 2020. The Foxboro Flasher is still only thirty-seven years old.

## Union Boss in the News

*August 21, 2019*

It used to be that criminals were the ones who were bribing cops to look the other way as they ran their racketeering enterprises.

SPAM boss Dana Pullman: He had a young girlfriend, believe it or not.

Now, if you believe what the feds said in Wednesday's criminal complaint about the state troopers' union, it's the cops who have been paying for protection to loot, plunder, and steal.

At the press conference announcing the indictment of Dana Pullman, the blubbery ex-boss of the State Police Association of Massachusetts (SPAM), an FBI agent said: "As president of SPAM, we believe Pullman wielded the union like a criminal enterprise, running it like an old-school mob boss."

Speaking of old-school mob bosses, Whitey Bulger used to say, referring to payoffs, "Christmas is for cops and kids." Now it's for cops, kids—and pols.

This is just the latest scandal to roil Governor Baker's pet police force. Consider the ongoing embezzlement scandal that's led to at least eight felony convictions of state cops, with thirty-eight more bent cops implicated—such a serious scandal that the MSP abruptly destroyed all the pre-2016 payroll records before the G-men wiped out the entire MSP.

Andrew Lelling, the US attorney, said Wednesday: "Pullman essentially took money from the pockets of his fellow State Police."

Is there no honor among thieves?

Not, apparently, in the MSP.

Check out the photo of the capo of this latest MSP racketeering enterprise—Pullman bears more than a passing resemblance to Jabba the Hut. Yet according to the feds' criminal complaint, Mr. Big was quite the Lothario—his wife was laundering kickbacks from the indicted lobbyist, while Pullman was jetting off to a Miami Beach love nest with "Individual No. 1" and spending $150 on caviar alone at a single $468 lunch at Marea, a high-end joint on Central Park South.

*Marea*, by the way, is Italian for "tide." I think it's safe to say it's now low tide for this latest MSP grift.

The State House politicians loved SPAM because of all the money the executive board was duking them. Playing whip-out with the cash was no problem for the notoriously cheap troopers, because, according to the feds, "PULLMAN at times encouraged members of the E-Board to submit (false) mileage expense reports to cover . . . political contributions they were expected to make."

Tens of thousands, in fact, to assorted pols in leadership, and of course Tall Deval and his lieutenant governor, Karyn Polito. The SPAM leadership took care of all the usual suspects—every Senate president back to Tom Birmingham, convicted felons, unindicted co-conspirators, hacks who became lobbyists (Mike Costello), assorted Timiltys, mostly ex-Senator Jim, Governor's Councilor Jen Caissie, two-fisted boozers like Brian Dempsey and Anthony Galluccio, disgraced ex-Lt. Gov. Tim "Crash" Murray—in short, every shady, dodgy, unemployable hack the union needed to keep its own rotten scams going.

Let's look at some numbers from the Office of Campaign and Political Finance, starting with the indicted lobbyist, Anne Lynch.

She contributed more than $75,000 to assorted hacks, two of whom committed suicide during scandals (Senator Brian "Multiple Choice" Joyce of Milton, Middlesex High Sheriff James DiPaola).

Like Lynch, Loverboy Dana Pullman was a registered lobbyist, meaning he couldn't give more than $200 to any hack per calendar year. But he still managed to hand out $33,875 in 177 different payouts.

His scorned-woman wife, Melissa, gave $10,800 to politicians in thirty-two different payments.

Tim Babbin, former SPAM vice president made 101 contributions to assorted pols for $25,125.

Andrew Daly, the union's ex-treasurer, who according to the criminal complaint tried to stop Pullman's crime spree, made $31,725 in contributions. (By the way, he's from Holden—Worcester County, same place as the Pullmans, Polito, the Bibauds, Crash Murray, et al.)

Ed Hunter, SPAM secretary, made 166 contributions, $41,300.

This is all public record—open and gross hackery.

Don't state troopers have to pass a physical every year? And qualify on the gun range? How long has it been since Pullman took either test? I'm told that if a statie is placed on no-duty status, he loses the use of a state police cruiser.

Oddly, in November 2017, Pullman spent $21,371 as a down payment on the lease of a new Chevrolet Suburban SUV "without the approval or knowledge of the E-board."

We're pretty sure much of this was common knowledge, up to and including ex-Colonel Richard McKeon, who was not, to put it mildly, a big fan of Pullman, the "Gangster of Love."

I wonder what McKeon told Dan Bennett, then secretary of public safety (and another Worcester hack), and I also wonder what Bennett told Tall Deval.

I can already hear Tall Deval answering reporters' questions about this latest scandal on his watch. Somebody cue the Sgt. Schultz sound: "I know nooooooooothhing!"

## Is the State Police Motto "To Protect and Overserve"?

*June 18, 2021*

The MSP—the latest casualty of Governor Charlie Baker's lunatic lockdowns.

Not that the troopers weren't a complete corrupt mess before 2020, but the "Panic" just accelerated their ethical collapse.

Take the most recent MSP hires—please! And read them their Miranda rights while you're at it.

If you saw the list in the *Herald* Thursday of the latest troopers who've been dishonorably discharged, you may have figured out that at least three of the fourteen had less than a year on the job.

And there's a fourth one from that class, down in Attleboro, suspended, awaiting trial on charges of domestic abuse of his girlfriend.

Last year's class at the academy in New Braintree was apparently rudely interrupted by the governor's hysterical overreaction to a seasonal flu. Kinda like all schools were, the difference being that they don't give you a badge, a gun, a car, and a million-dollar career when you graduate from middle school.

Let's start with Nidu Andrade (badge number 4418)— "probationary employee—inappropriate texts sent."

Andrade is why the *Herald* a couple of weeks ago filed the FOIA request for the dishonorable discharges. We'd heard about his, uh, inappropriate texts, but we couldn't nail down the perp's name.

Now that we have the name, we'll try to get you the actual report. Parental discretion advised.

By the way, don't get Nidu Andrade confused with ex-Lieutenant David Andrade, most recently in the news last year when he was dragged into court in Bristol County and charged with stealing $11,500.

The headline: "State Police Commander Was Allegedly Cruising in Bermuda When He Claimed to Be Working."

"Is Andrade collecting a pension?" you ask. Of course he is—$94,948 a year. Tax free. He's forty-eight years old.

Nidu Andrade, on the other hand, doesn't get a kiss in the mail. Nor does another member of the Class of 2020, Cody Lee (badge number 4545)—"off-duty incident ethnic slurs used."

This was in Revere, all recorded after Lee and a Hispanic man left a barroom. Lee used both the n-word and the s-word, and thus forfeited his chance to become a multimillionaire by age forty.

C'mon down, Michael Atton (badge number 4422). He too went on the job last year and has now "resigned during the pendency of two internal affairs investigations."

His problems began when Wrentham Police arrested him for allegedly beating his second wife, the mother of his two young children.

Another new hire in 2020 was one Joel Devine. He graduated from the academy in May 2020 and last summer threatened to kill his girlfriend, whom he began dating when she was eighteen, four times, or so say the Attleboro Police.

Trooper Devine (he's suspended) also allegedly throttled her during a vacation last Christmas in the Bahamas. (They love the big-money vacations in the islands, these staties, almost as much as they love their distilled spirits.)

Devine is a former Lexington cop. A lot of these bust-outs were small-town Barney Fifes who apparently dreamed of making the big time, or should I say big money. The Andrade with the pension started out as a New Bedford cop.

Then there's Dwayne Correia (badge number 3562), dishonorably discharged after losing his firearm during a late-night tryst with a female acquaintance in Providence.

Correia was a Raynham cop before he became a globe-trotting, gun-wielding lover boy. He was fired for "disabled geotab AVL—theft of firearm while out of state."

That "geotab AVL" reference—think GPS. Those records are what the feds have been using to pick off these crooked cops for embezzling federal funds, first in Troop E out on the Pike and soon in another one of these rotten MSP outfits known as . . . well, I'll keep that one under my Smokey Bear hat for now.

I just wonder if the feds are talking to any of the local trucking companies . . . The irony is, if these crooked state cops had just remained in their small towns, they could still be working the same grifts. The MSP just got a little too greedy, which is why they're getting knocked back down to size.

You know the old saying, Pigs get fat, hogs get slaughtered.

Meanwhile, life goes on in the hackerama. Next shoe to drop will be when charges are filed in the death of the Dedham High teenager who drowned in a pool on property owned by a retired state trooper who's collecting an annual pension of $131,961.

Once the Dedham Police Department incident report is filed with the court, including a list of witnesses, we'll have a better idea of how many staties were in attendance when alcohol was allegedly being served to minors.

Any superior officers? Anybody on the governor's security detail? At high school graduation parties, you always invite fat cats who can bring a check, and who better to take care of your college-bound kid than an MSP multimillionaire?

We'll know soon, but probably not today. Today was Bunker Hill Day, and Saturday is the newest public-sector holiday, Juneteenth, which means the ultimate hack dream has finally been realized—a four-day weekend, paid for by all us who work for a living.

But fourteen staties didn't make it to the promised land of the four-day weekend. On this day, remember them, and also the motto of the MSP: To protect and overserve.

# Trooper Laughing All the Way to the Bank

*April 17, 2022*

Meet the DeJongs, father and son, both former MSP troopers.

If at this late date you still don't understand just how profoundly corrupt Massachusetts is, consider the tale of the two DeJongs.

Daren, age sixty, is a convicted felon, so crooked he needs a corkscrew to get into his trousers in the morning.

While on the now-defunct Troop E, he embezzled more than $63,000 in federal funds for Turnpike overtime he didn't work.

He pleaded guilty in 2019, yet he remains unsentenced to this very day. Despite his sordid criminal career, DeJong hasn't served a single day in prison for his highway robbery.

Even more outrageous, he continues to collect his state-tax-free hack pension of $6,374 a month, which is $76,492 a year.

Next, consider his son, Nathan, thirty, with a spotless record on the job.

Ex-MSP felon Daren DeJong, right, with his attorney, ex-Middlesex County sheriff Brad Bailey.

A week ago Friday, on April 8, Nathan S. DeJong (badge number 4108) received a "dishonorable discharge" from the MSP: "On or about January 19, 2022, in the city of Framingham, (he) did fail to conform to work standards established for the member's rank, title, or position. This occurred when Trooper DeJong failed to receive COVID-19 vaccination as a condition of continuing employment."

In other words, he was terminated for refusing to submit to Governor Charlie Baker's insane obsession with getting a vaccine. He is out of work and unlikely to ever get another job in law enforcement, at least in the Commonwealth.

That's what the "dishonorable" discharge was about—shooting the wounded. That'll teach those damn deplorables!

Yet his crooked father is still a free man, stuffing his pockets full of state cash every month.

Who says crime doesn't pay? Who says cheaters never prosper? In Massachusetts they damn well do prosper, and Daren DeJong is Exhibit A.

Here's how the hacks work the pension scam for convicted felons: Until the perp, in this case Daddy DeJong, is sentenced, the State Retirement Board doesn't even schedule a hearing to discuss terminating the sticky-fingered cop's kiss in the mail.

On those exceedingly rare occasions a hack does lose his pension, he can drag out the appeal month after direct-deposit month, even longer if he can get an ex-wife to file an appeal to keep her own share of the felonious spouse's ill-gotten gains.

You know what they call this grift in the hackerama? Professional courtesy. Because, you know, it could happen to anybody, getting their hands (and feet) caught in the cookie jar.

This week when I obtained the list of the twelve troopers fired for their refusal to join the Church of COVID, the name "DeJong" looked familiar.

Then I recalled that I'd written a column asking why his father hadn't yet been sentenced. That was in February 2020—twenty-six direct deposits ago. When I wrote it, the old man was grabbing $6,284 a month, $90 less than he's pocketing now.

I assumed that surely Daren DeJong must have done at least a few months by now. Way back in 2019, when he pleaded guilty, the feds were demanding a six-month sentence, a wrist slap to be sure, but still more than most of the crooked millionaire troopers were getting, which was nothing.

So I went to the Bureau of Prisons website, but DeJong's name didn't show up. That means he's never been incarcerated. I called his lawyer, who confirmed that his client was still awaiting sentencing.

You know the old saying: Justice delayed is justice denied. So I asked DeJong's lawyer if a sentencing date had even been set.

"Nope," he said.

I checked the docket in federal court. The last entry for DeJong was dated July 15 of last year—apparently a routine response by the prosecutors to something or other. Since then, nada, unless you want to count those nine more direct deposits to felon DeJong's bank account of $6,374 the first of every month.

DeJong should be crying all the way to the Big House. Instead he's laughing all the way to the bank.

And his son, who did nothing wrong, is fired by Charlie Baker. For the crime of not bending a knee to the Deep State.

Daddy DeJong has made more money in his life of crime than most gangsters, who didn't have the added edge of carrying a badge. According to the state comptroller, Daddy pocketed $200,416 in 2016 with all his overtime and phony-baloney details out there on I-90.

The kid never earned more than $97,000 or so before he was fired. So much for honesty being the best policy.

Daddy initially admitted to embezzling $14,000. But suddenly, after the statute of limitations expired, the very ethical MSP decided to cough up a lot more damning records, and it became clear that DeJong had robbed the taxpayers of $63,000.

Here's how the miracle discovery was reported in court: "The MSP reported to the government it had 'discovered' a 'number of boxes' with these materials. What has not been reported is how these materials were discovered, who discovered them, why they were not previously located, or what state these materials were in when they were discovered."

The answer to all the above questions is . . . Massachusetts.

In January 2020 DeJong's sentencing was postponed by Judge Mark Wolf because he wanted further investigation of the racketeering enterprise d/b/a the MSP. DeJong is fine with that, as long as the kiss in the mail keeps on coming.

I just hope he's whacking up the pot with his son Nathan. It's the least he can do, because he obviously didn't raise the kid right. If only Nathan had stuck to stealing, like the old man, instead of sticking to his principles, he'd probably already be on the fast track to detective or sergeant.

Instead he's fired. For the crime of not wanting to take a worthless vaccine that might in fact make him sick.

I told you this was a very Massachusetts story.

In the halls of justice, the only justice is in the halls.

## Looking for Love in All the Wrong Places

*May 15, 2021*

On the home page of his lovey-dovey wedding website from 2019, ex-State Trooper Dwayne Correia (badge number 3562) includes this sappy bromide from Nicholas Sparks: "Marriage is about becoming a team. You're going to spend the rest of your life learning about each other, and every now and then things blow up."

Things blew up big-time for Dwayne Correia last August 11.

It was such a bad day for this week's disgraced state cop that the MSP wrote a twenty-three-page report on his sordid misadventures in Rhode Island (where he'd gotten married, on Goat Island, almost exactly one year earlier).

Even though Correia was forced to resign, with a dishonorable discharge, the corrupt MSP fought desperately to stop release of the damning report, dragging their jackbooted feet for more than two months.

Last August 11 was a very busy day for Correia, who is also a former Rhode Island state cop, married to a local cop in Bristol County. First, according to the report, he drove to MSP headquarters in Framingham "to sign his 'Disposition without Hearing/Waiver of Right to Trial Board' (waiver) for a previous investigation that occurred at SP Middleboro on February 25, 2020."

In other words, he was disposing of another little problem he'd had on the job. So Dwayne was ready for a celebration.

As he later confessed, Correia told his bride he'd be working that evening. Then he unplugged the GPS on his unmarked cruiser so that the brass wouldn't know where he was. He drove south in his uniform, then ducked into a Raymour & Flanigan's furniture store to change into street clothes.

He had female companionship awaiting him in Providence—a woman who later told the troopers she'd "dated" him (her word) in college although they were "currently just friends."

Let's call his friend "Ms. X."

At the Capitol Grill in Providence the trooper and Ms. X met a third person, and in two hours ran up a $763.49 tab, including a $200 tip, for martinis, wine, and food.

Ms. X had conveniently rented a room at the Renaissance Hotel, where Correia parked his unmarked cruiser. The report says he removed a backpack. He left his service firearm in the car, which he left unlocked. Correia also neglected to activate the anti-theft alarm.

I guess he was in a hurry to get upstairs.

Correia then spent the entire night with Ms. X. On September 1, she told the investigators that he stayed with her overnight "because he had had too much to drink."

On October 6, in a second interview, Ms. X changed her story. Asked if Correia had really stayed over because he was drunk, "She stated no, that they were going to hang out."

Hang out. That's her (second) story and she's sticking to it.

At 4:22 a.m., as Correia and Ms. X were still hanging out, surveillance video shows three yutes prowling the hotel parking lot, testing car doors to see if any idiots had left their vehicles unlocked. They quickly broke into idiot Correia's unmarked MSP cruiser and stole his fully loaded Smith & Wesson.

At 6:05 a.m., after his all-night hang out, Correia came downstairs and discovered his gun missing. According to the Internal Affairs report, he never went back on the job, using vacation days for the rest of the month until the gun theft was discovered.

He did, however, use his state credit card to fill up his cruiser with gasoline. And he did drive into Boston on August 15 to meet Ms. X at the upscale Liberty Hotel "for a couple of hours" after playing a round of golf.

Over dinner, the soon-to-be-busted trooper "mentioned being overwhelmed with his marriage, house move and child whom he was having shortly with his wife."

By August 31, a woman—it's not clear if it was Ms. X or the third person at the pre-hang-out $763 dinner in Providence—informed another trooper that Correia was in deep trouble.

"She stated that she did not call Trooper Correia's wife because she didn't want her to be emotional that Trooper Correia was confiding in [redacted] with this information and not his wife."

On September 1, Lt. Col. Richard Ball "received information" that Correia had lost his gun. At the time, Ball was running the Division of Field Services.

Less than three months later, Ball had retired, with an annual tax-free pension of $113,446.

Everybody was running away from Correia now. It's all about protecting their phony-baloney jobs. The investigators tried to set up a "formal interview" with at least one of his MSP pals. To which Correia's buddy "declined to be interviewed and stated he was no longer friends with Trooper Correia and had nothing to say."

When he was finally asked about how he lost his weapon, Correia responded in classic modern MSP fashion: "I've been advised by my attorney not to answer that question."

The gun was recovered, and Correia has now suffered that rarest of MSP punishments—actually losing his job.

One suggestion for Badge 3265 now that he's unemployed: Trooper, change that syrupy quote on your wedding page to something more appropriate. May I suggest a classic country song from Faron Young: "Loving Here and Living There and Lying In Between."

Coming soon: More tawdry tales from your MSP.

# Massachusetts Troopers Gone Bad, Worse, and Criminally Charged

*September 22, 2021*

Could ex-state trooper Nidu Andrade (badge number 4418) be the dumbest hire yet by the corrupt, drug-addled, skirt-chasing, spouse-abusing, embezzling, gun-selling, knee-walking drunk, sticky-fingered MSP?

For starters, is it ever a good idea to send an unsolicited photo of one's private parts to a woman you just met—on a police call?

If you're a Fox News host, sexting can get you fired. If you're an ex-congressman, it can land you in the prison known as FMC Devens in Ayer.

If you're probationary trooper Andrade, it gets you bounced from the job after less than a year.

No worries, though. As he puts it in one of his texts to his would-be gal pal: "It's fine I'm dead too lol."

LOL—laughing out loud. A digital conversational fallback for pedestrian minds, like Nidu's.

"I was being silly lol."

By now you know the basics about Trooper Andrade's short, squalid career. He took a shine, as they say, to a victim—a woman he met on the highway while responding to a domestic abuse call. He began texting her, as the report notes.

"During the conversations she was asked about her bra size, was told he was off-duty, was told she could talk to him about anything and was asked to send pictures of her 'parts.'"

"Well nice lol."

To break the ice, Trooper Andrade commented on her cleavage, speculating that she was "D cup if I cold (sic) guess."

Spelling is another problem for Nidu. *Could* becomes "cold." He misspells *you're* as "your."

As Nidu continued his courtship, the woman "confirmed that she received a photo of a penis, which she said was his penis and which she never asked for. She confirmed that this was the only picture she had received from him."

Andrade was really into photographs—his that he sent and hers that she didn't.

"Revealing picture lol . . . Your new profile pic lol."

She was asked by the investigator if the X-rated snapshot was the trooper's, and she answered yes.

After which the investigator observes, "NOTE: It is not known how [redacted] knows that or if she was speculating."

"I gues (sic) it depends on what your (sic) looking for lol."

For the record, Andrade was a member of the academy's Panic Class of 2020.

One of his classmates has already been cashiered for "off-duty ethnic slurs used" and another "resigned during the pendency of two internal affairs investigations."

None of these bent staties are to be confused with the Foxboro Flasher. Or the trooper fired after he lost his gun while shacking up with his girlfriend in a no-tell motel in Providence, or the married sergeant who was collared in New Hampshire while making a run for the state line after allegedly using his gal pal "as the heavy bag in his home gymnasium work," as Ring Lardner once put it.

Then there's Matthew Kelley (badge number 3979), cited for "improper storage of contraband," shortly after he was hospitalized for what was described as a "medical emergency." He quickly resigned.

Everybody makes mistakes, but do these crooked cops have no common sense whatsoever?

What about that famous old aphorism variously attributed to different sages? "Never write when you can speak, never speak when you can nod, never nod when you can wink . . ."

And never, ever send anybody an unsolicited photo of your Johnson. Or even solicited, for that matter.

John "Zip" Connolly, the FBI agent who was convicted of murder in an organized-crime hit in Florida, once made an instructional video for the FBI academy in Quantico. He advised the next generation of corrupt G-men how to avoid . . . well, his own fate, as it turned out.

"Don't ever let them," Zip lectured, speaking of criminals, "get you where they have anything on you."

I still have that instructional video. I'd be glad to send it to the academy. For a price, of course.

We got a tip on Trooper Andrade's courting rituals last May, but our sources couldn't come up with his name. So we started filing random Freedom of Information Act (FOIA) requests. In the late spring, the MSP brass finally coughed up his name, and the fact that he'd been fired.

"Now that we have a name," I wrote, "we'll try to get you the actual report."

That was June 17. The staties finally coughed up the report on Monday, September 20—three months after we asked for it. It had been written May 4. I don't know what the delay was. Maybe the MSP scanner broke and they couldn't get any repairman to drive out to Framingham to fix it.

Next up is Trooper Matthew Kelley, Mr. Improper Storage of Contraband. They never admitted he was gone until we spotted it in an obscure court filing out of Bristol County.

Kelley's been out almost three months now, but the investigation continues, or so the MSP claims.

"So might as well chat lol," as Nidu used to say.

MSP says it will be handing over the final report on Kelley's medical emergency as soon as it's finished.

Lol.

## Conviction Won't Stop These Thieving Massachusetts State Police Troopers

*December 16, 2023*

Christmas in the hackerama is the most wonderful time of the year. Santa Claus knows who's been naughty or nice. But if you're a crooked cop, old St. Nick will never, ever put a lump of coal in your stocking.

That $10,913-a-month kiss in the mail just keeps on coming, more than three years after you're indicted, month after felonious, thieving, sticky-fingered month.

This morning let's consider two very naughty little boys who did their stealing as members of the MSP.

Ex-Lt. Daniel Griffin and ex-Sgt. William Robertson started embezzling thousands of dollars in federally funded overtime in 2015. After years of stealing, when the stench got so bad, the feds say they "took steps to avoid detention by shredding and burning records."

The two crooked cops were indicted more than three years ago. And yet they weren't convicted of conspiracy, wire fraud, and theft from government programs until last week in Worcester.

So much for a speedy trial. Which has been very convenient for these career criminals with badges, because all these years, while they were awaiting trial, getting continuance after continuance after continuance, they've been collecting their tax-free state pensions.

According to the State Retirement Board, both pocketed their first pension checks on December 31, 2020—almost immediately after their indictments.

For three years now, while under indictment, Robertson has been grabbing $7,992 a month—$95,899 a year.

Griffin, an even more audacious public-sector fraudster, has been collecting $130,956 a year—$10,913 a month. He went out on disability.

I kid you not. Disability! Since when is kleptomania an officially recognized disease?

In 2019, despite Griffin's breathtaking career of crime, the MSP exonerated him of every charge. It was so outrageous that the feds mentioned it in their presentencing memo to the judge. They described him as "the poster boy of State Police corruption." This was before Michael Proctor, obviously, but at the time it was true.

Now the two bent cops have finally reached their inevitable destinations—convicted of multiple felonies, looking at thirty-plus years in durance vile. So now their obscenely bloated pensions will end immediately, right?

Wrong! And this is where this morning's Christmas miracle begins, worthy of a Hallmark Yuletide TV movie. For the crooked troopers, *It's A Wonderful Life*. Perhaps it's not *Miracle on 34th Street*, but surely we are witnessing *Miracle at the State Retirement Board*.

Because, you see, just because they're convicted felons, cops who stole a hot stove and then came back for the smoke, that doesn't mean their pensions automatically cease.

Under state law, a conviction is not considered final, even though it is, until after sentencing. That won't be until . . . March 20, 2024, although I'm guessing there will be another delay or two or three so that the monthly wire transfers to the robbers can continue ad infinitum.

You ask why the legislature would pass such a preposterous law, to enable hack thieves to continue stealing even more money from the Commonwealth after they're convicted of stealing. You know the answer: professional courtesy.

Once the sentences are handed down, whenever that is, the matter of revocation of pensions goes before the State Retirement Board. And of course the board will just automatically terminate the pensions at its next monthly meeting, right?

Wrong again! The proposed revocations will go before a hearing officer, who will no doubt hear arguments from the arrogant millionaire cop thugs that it would be terribly unfair to strip them of their ill-gotten gains because, again, professional courtesy. Another contention the future jailbirds will probably make is that if they are stripped of their kisses in the mail, it's only proper and fitting that their "contributions" to the system be refunded to them.

As if they haven't already grabbed more than they paid in, since their simultaneous indictments and "retirements" back in 2020. According to the Retirement Board, their first checks went out December 31, 2020.

Do the math. For Sgt. Robertson, that's $96,000 times three, or about $288,000. The "disabled" Lt. Griffin has pocketed $130,000 times three, or $390,000.

It's not the Retirement Board's fault, though. They are just following the law, as appalling as it is.

Just before their trial started in Worcester, Griffin pleaded guilty to multiple other felonies, including four additional counts of wire fraud and eleven counts of filing false tax returns.

Hunter Biden could not be reached for comment.

While Griffin was embezzling public funds and shredding documents and filing memos saying the incriminating evidence had been "inadvertently discarded or misplaced," he was also making $2 million running a "security" business on the side.

The feds say he "hid" $727,000 in revenue from his company and used the corporate income to pay for his second home on the Cape, as well as for golf club expenses and assorted automobiles.

Griffin also pleaded guilty to defrauding the Belmont Hill School of $175,000 in financial aid he wasn't eligible for. He had two sons and he told the hoity-toity woke school (deep-state alumni include General Thoroughly Modern Milley and Admiral Richard, er Rachel Levine) that he had no money in his family's 529 college-fund account.

In fact, the greed-crazed Griffin was sitting on $254,847. In addition to the "security" company and the organized embezzlement, he was also "part owner of several Boston gyms." Perhaps all his rackets were just Griffin's way of coping with his . . . disability.

In 2017, after one of Griffin's sons "only" got $28,750 in aid from the comrades at Belmont Hill, the trooper became incensed, according to the original indictment. "GRIFFIN sent a series of emails to the financial aid office complaining that he was being honest about his financial means; that other families were abusing the system by hiding monies . . . and making significant cash 'under the table.'"

Honest? You can't make this stuff up. Belmont Hill coughed another $4,000 in aid to young Griffin.

By the way, just before he was indicted, way back in October 2020, Griffin took a "buyout" of $91,800. That's on top of the $200,000-plus he made every year, legally. It's one thing to feed at the public trough. Lt. Griffin licked the plate.

His political hero was Willard Mitt Romney, who also sent his sons to la-de-da Belmont Hill. Griffin donated $1,075 to Pierre Delecto.

When the federal heat started coming down, the feds say that Griffin ordered his underlings—"Troopers 1, 2, and 3"—to destroy all the evidence. "GRIFFIN told Trooper 1, in sum and substance, 'Don't tell them (the G-men) bleeping anything.'"

Today is December 17. Two weeks from today, Griffin will receive at least his thirty-seventh monthly kiss of $10,913 from the taxpayers. On January 31, he'll pocket another $10,913. And on February 29, and on March 31, and on April 30 . . .

Santa Claus only comes once a year. We take care of the Dan Griffins and William Robertsons and all the rest of the sleazy hacks 365 days a year.

It's Christmas, baby, and don't you forget it. As Tiny Tim would say, "God bless us, everyone!" Especially all the payroll patriots who just keep stealing and stealing and stealing.

(Postscript: The pensions of Griffin and Robertson were finally suspended in September 2024, pending final resolution of their appeals.)

## Massachusetts State Police Not Making the Grade

*August 8, 2021*

This culture of corruption and cover-up in the MSP must be eradicated, once and for all.

Who do these jackbooted thugs think they are—the FBI?

Our local multimillionaire highway robbers need to go back to the pizza-delivery gigs they had before they got into the rackets. And that's what the MSP is now, organized crime, a massive racketeering enterprise of grifts, shakedowns, gun trafficking, drug deals, drunk driving, girlfriend-beating, embezzlement, etc.

And if a trooper is busted, most of the time the only "punishment" he gets is a lifetime six-figure annual pension at age forty-five or fifty, tax-free if he can scam a "disability," which most of these sticky-fingered crooks can.

C'mon down, ex-Trooper Matthew Kelley, late of the "gang unit." I think that means he was in the gang.

Kelley's tawdry career ended in ignominy in early May, after he suffered what the brass at first described as a "medical emergency."

This week, almost three months after the *Herald* began asking the MSP to confirm what we already knew as fact, they finally copped to the fact that Kelley had been dishonorably discharged for "improper storage of contraband."

But at first they wouldn't even say what the contraband was. Finally they admitted, "the contraband was narcotics."

So Kelley had a "medical emergency," after which he was fired for "improper storage" of narcotics. Hmmmm, I wonder where exactly Trooper Kelley was improperly storing the narcotics.

The *Herald* knew all this almost instantly—there are still some honest troopers out there, and they know how to get in touch with us.

On Kelley, we just needed an official confirmation from MSP. That was three months ago.

The troopers' stonewalling on Kelley began as soon as the first inquiry was made. The "medical emergency" was grudgingly acknowledged by a hack flack, with a one-sentence addendum: "I have nothing further to add."

We began filing FOIA requests, which by law are supposed to be answered in ten days. When the phone didn't ring, we knew it was the MSP.

Kelley vanished from the state payroll immediately. May turned into June. We filed more FOIAs, got more nonresponses. At the end of June, we learned that Kelley had, ahem, resigned, which seemed a rather harsh punishment for a "medical emergency."

We asked the MSP to confirm his termination. No response. We filed more FOIAs, to no avail.

As recklessly lawless as the MSP has become, they sometimes include a formal notice of dishonorable discharge in the orders of the day. Kelley, though, got a good, thorough leaving alone.

We kept making calls, perusing court documents. We assumed that Kelley had made arrests, and that at some point even the sleazy MSP was going to have to let the perps he'd lugged know about his "medical emergency" and subsequent termination.

If you're a real reporter—and there aren't many left—you know what to do next. You google Kelley's name, find out who he's been arresting. Once you have the defendants' names, you get the docket numbers of their cases and pull the latest filings. It may take a while, but eventually you may hit pay dirt.

It happened last week, in an obscure discovery motion filed July 26 in Bristol Superior Court. The attorney general listed seventy-nine different pieces of evidence in a criminal case and then at the bottom of page 4 dropped this news: "Please also be advised that Matthew

Kelley, who was dishonorably discharged from the MSP on June 28, 2021, participated in the car stop . . ."

Bingo!

So it was finally public record. But the MSP asked for still more time to confirm—as if three months of stonewalling and foot-dragging since the "medical emergency" wasn't enough.

We have more questions about other troopers for the MSP. This fired probationary trooper Nidu Andrade—to whom exactly were his "inappropriate texts sent?" Was it someone he met on the job? Under what circumstances?

When will you release Andrade's actual texts? We need some more comic gold from you bent grossly overpaid clowns.

Another question: What percentage of state troopers applying for "disability" are approved? (The over-under line in Vegas is 100 percent.)

Does the very ethical MSP use the same medical board as the rest of the state? If not, why?

Do any state troopers (retired and/or current) have any children who are about to be tried in criminal cases in Suffolk County?

Should the academy at New Braintree add more courses for the recruits, teaching them, for example, how a GPS can be used against them in a court of law if they're embezzling federal overtime money?

Also, shouldn't MSP recruits be instructed in the latest trends in drug trafficking, namely, the use of pill presses to produce counterfeit prescription tablets, and how what you presume to be a safe FDA-approved opioid might in fact be fentanyl, which could lead to an unforeseen medical emergency?

By the way, Gov. Charlie Baker vows to get to the bottom of this pandemic of corruption among his dear pals on the MSP.

Rest assured, the governor will leave no stone unturned, except the ones all his crooked cops are hiding under.

# CHAPTER NINETEEN

# Trooper Leigha Genduso, Badge Number 3800

### Leigha Genduso's Past Should Have Kept Her off State Police Force

*March 7, 2018*

Is anyone going to lose his or her $150,000-a-year state pension over this Leigha Genduso scandal?

That's always the ultimate question in the hackerama—how is whatever-it-is going to affect my kiss in the mail?

Among all the multiple scandals in Massachusetts law enforcement, this one seems different. Some cops will always go bad, just like people in any other line of work. But usually police don't go over to the dark side until they've had their badge and their gun and their cruiser (and in Leigha's case her K-9) for a while.

From Scuttlebutts bar to the MSP's K-9 unit.

Think bent G-men Zip Connolly, H. Paul Rico, Vino Morris, and a host of others, or trooper Richard Schneiderhan, or BPD detective/hitman Bill Stuart. Corrupt as they all were, they were at least nominally clean when they were sworn in.

Not Leigha. Her infamous past was there for all to see. And somebody has to answer for this, or should, although I have my doubts about the ongoing MSP internal investigation into how she was hired.

At her boyfriend's trial, she admitted under a grant of immunity to committing a host of major felonies—kingpin-level drug dealing, perjury, income-tax evasion, and money laundering. But even if you put all that aside, what exactly were her qualifications for being a state trooper?

She was a cocktail waitress at Scuttlebutts in Salem. Period.

Oh, I forgot, she's also a web designer of sorts. When her gangster boyfriend, Sean Bucci, decided to set up a website to identify law enforcement informants, she's the one who came up with the name—WhosARat.com.

Here's what the cops said about Leigha's website: "Although BUCCI posted a disclaimer that the website's intent is to assist in criminal defense, it clearly has an underlying intimidation aspect."

Nice, huh?

This website—which is still around—was such a big deal that the fat thug Bucci actually appeared on Geraldo Rivera's TV show in 2007. You can still watch the segment on YouTube. When asked about the peril posed to informants by being listed as rats, Bucci replies: "Don't come crying because you're on a website, because you've already done the damage. You already signed up for the program. Deal with it."

Nobody noticed any of this? Nobody? Leigha Genduso was in the crosshairs of a major federal drug kingpin takedown—I count at least six local and state cops, six DEA agents. And you're telling me nobody realized that this gangster's moll—the Bonnie to Sean Bucci's Clyde—had gone on the job and was making $151,000 a year?

Has anyone seen Sean Bucci lately? He was sentenced to 151 months, and the feds seized $2.7 million in assets. This proud "Irish Italian," as he described himself, much to the chagrin of all Irish and Italians, has been out of prison since October 2015.

Do you suppose Bucci ever hooks up with his ex? Probably not, considering his public disdain for rats and snitches, which Leigha Genduso most assuredly is, in addition to all of her other attributes.

And where is Governor Charlie "Tall Deval" Baker on all this? I know he's got a whole host of other scandals in state government that he's very busy ignoring, but consider how quickly he moved against the state trooper known as "Big Irish."

I'm not defending Big Irish's rude comments on that cop website. But seriously, if making asinine comments in an internet chat room becomes a firing offense, there's not going to be anybody left to bag groceries at Market Basket, let alone patrol the Southeast Expressway.

Meanwhile, wherever she's stashed now, Leigha still has a listing on a "talent" website: "Age 36 Female Boston MA. Height 5′3″. Weight 116 lbs. Body Type Petite. Ethnicity Caucasian. Hair Color Brown. Eye Color Brown."

As for her résumé, the website notes that Leigha has "not yet provided this information."

One final question for Leigha: Is Scuttlebutts hiring?

## Latest Trooper Scandal Adds to "the Departed" from Force

*February 28, 2018*

The departed—that's what you can call all the thousands of drug convictions erased from the books after the epic misconduct of Massachusetts law enforcement these last few years.

First it was the corrupt state crime lab chemists Annie Dookhan and Sonja Farak faking thousands of criminal drug analyses. And now we have the case of MSP Trooper Leigha Genduso, who departed from the payroll last week after it was revealed that before she became a statie, she had admitted in federal court to perjury, money laundering, and kingpin-level drug dealing.

This gangster's moll was in the K-9 unit. Why do I see a lot more drug convictions . . . departing?

Yesterday I asked the MSP and the Executive Office of Public Safety how many cases Genduso had testified in and whether her rap sheet was ever disclosed to the assorted defendants, as required under law and legal ethics.

The EOPS responded with three words: "No comment. Thanks."

Genduso's dearest friend in the state police was Lt. Col. Dan Risteen, who also departed the payroll last week, after news about his playmate's rap sheet was published.

The departed Risteen, ironically, is a real expert on *The Departed*—he had a bit role in the 2006 Boston mob/corrupt cop movie of the same name. He played "Crack House Cop #1." Risteen was joined in that scene by "Crack House Cop #2"—Francis Hughes, then an MSP lieutenant.

Ironically enough, last November Hughes departed from the MSP payroll as abruptly as his pal Risteen during that other recent state police scandal, the brooming of an OUI case involving the junkie-prostitute daughter of a hack judge from Worcester.

The departed are really stacking up—the burgeoning scandals have also claimed Lt. Col. Richard McKeon and Maj. Susan Anderson, neither of whom appeared in *The Departed*.

So how long do you think it will take before the first motion to dismiss a guilty verdict based on Genduso's testimony? I'm guessing the briefs will be stacked up by St. Patrick's Day.

To set the stage for all the departures, let's consider trooper Genduso's admissions, under oath, about her lies to the grand jury, specifically about a money box containing $275,000 in cash from selling illegal drugs.

Q. Ms. Genduso, you lied to the grand jury about what you did with that box of money. We've established that already, right?

A. That's correct.

Next, the lawyer asks the future state trooper about her sworn testimony that she delivered a bag of cash to a lawyer at a sub shop in Lynn.

Q. And you made up that story?

A. Well, not technically.

Q. You just said that you just left out a few things, right?

> A. Right.
>
> Q. But in fact, you actually made up a few things, too, didn't you?
>
> A. Well, what I was just about to say is that I did meet him at a sub shop in Lynn prior to that.
>
> Q. With a bag full of $50,000?
>
> A. No. No. But with a bag full of money that he gave me.
>
> Q. Oh, with a bag of money that he gave you.
>
> A. It was actually $5,000.

Think about it—not only is every last person Trooper Genduso testified against going to be getting out of prison, but they'll also be suing the Commonwealth. Do you blame them? A lot of taxpayer money will soon be . . . departing.

> Q. You talked about taking $50,000 in cash out of the money box yourself?
>
> A. That part was a lie, correct.
>
> Q. Thank you. And putting the $50,000 into a paper bag. That's what you told the prosecutor and the agent here?
>
> A. Yeah.
>
> Q. That didn't happen, did it?
>
> A. No, it did not.
>
> Q. And you told them that you then traveled to a sub shop in Lynn with the bag of $50,000?
>
> A. Right.
>
> Q. Which did not happen, did it?
>
> A. Right.
>
> Q. And gave that money to Atty. Zerola, $50,000 cash, that you had taken out of the box of money. And that did not happen, did it, ma'am?
>
> A. Nope, it didn't.

They could make a movie about the corruption in the MSP and how many of the bent brass are going to be fired now that they're busted. Too bad the perfect title is already taken—*The Departed*.

(Postscript: Attorney Frank Zerola, to whom Genduso handed $5,000 in cash at the sub shop in Lynn, was found guilty in state court in 2023 of raping a twenty-one-year-old woman. He was sentenced to five to ten years in prison.)

## Suspended Trooper Leigha Genduso Can Always Go Back to Old Job

*July 4, 2018*

Leigha Genduso, call me! I have an idea for your next career.

Actually, my suggestion is that you go back to your pre-MSP job—dealing drugs.

Let's face it, you were always much more qualified to be a drug dealer than a state trooper. And the beautiful thing now is, after all these years you were on the wrong side of the law, it's finally legal to sell weed, or soon will be anyway, as soon as the hacks get around to issuing the licenses.

As for all the other sordid crimes you admitted committing before you became a state trooper—money laundering, income-tax evasion, "perjurizing," as you put it—those are all still illegal. But hey, they were illegal when you were selected for the "elite" MSP after the proverbial nationwide search.

Think about it, Leigha, no more having to wrap the ten-pound bricks of ganja in Christmas gift wrap, like you did in the old days when you were living in the gangster's house while you were applying for the MSP. No more of those white-knuckle deliveries to Worcester, glancing nervously into the rearview mirror for flashing blue lights.

As readers may recall, despite her career as a mobster's moll, Trooper Genduso enjoyed a meteoric rise through the ranks of the very ethical MSP. By age thirty-six, she was making $145,000 a year—not too shabby for a former cocktail waitress at Scuttlebutts in Salem with a GED. And she was in the K-9 unit, which usually takes years to make, but then, she was a real crack trooper. Just ask her dear friend, Lt. Col. Dan Risteen.

Sadly, her life of crime was exposed in the endless scandals that have forever tarnished the once-sterling reputation of the MSP. She is suspended without pay and recently resurfaced at a different bar in Essex County, one that opens at 7 a.m. Nothing like a little eggs 'n' legs, right Leigha?

Someone shot some sneaky photos and videos of her behind the tap the other night. They're posted at turtleboysports.com. Her hair is cut very short, she's wearing flat shoes and a backless blouse—not bad considering she turned thirty-seven in April.

I agree with one of the commenters on the site—Leigha looks better as a brunette than a blonde, and likewise, bartender is a much better fit for Leigha than state trooper.

The other day, I called her latest gin mill and asked for La Genduso.

"She ain't here," said the woman who answered the phone, who sounded like she was simultaneously chewing gum and smoking a Chesterfield King. "She works nights. Who's dis?"

An old friend, I said.

"Well, call her on her cell phone then," she said.

I lost the number, I said. Can you give it to me?

"Who are you?"

I used to buy drugs from her, I said. That was a lie, but it got the woman's attention.

"I don't give a (bleep) what you used to do!" she shrieked, and slammed down the phone.

Oh well, give me a call, Leigha. We can catch up. Does your old boyfriend, the gangster, stop by for a Hoodsie, now that he's finally out of prison? Do you have visitation rights for your K-9, Kojak?

Seriously, Leigha, think about getting back into the drug business. You know the old saying: When one door closes, another one opens. Look on the bright side, Leigha, at least the cell door never closed on you, and you got to be an MSP trooper.

And at least you didn't "work" in Troop E. If you had, you might have been indicted by now. Being fired is no fun. Being indicted is worse, much worse.

# Dealer's Moll Turned Statie Pens a Page-Turner

*January 25, 2019*

Remember Leigha Genduso—the poster gal for the rampant corruption of the MSP?

Genduso is the Shrewsbury BFF of Lt. Gov. Karyn Polito—check out their multiple smiling photos together online. Genduso got her badge and her gun after admitting in open court to being the longtime live-in moll of a drug kingpin, during which time she (a) lied under oath to a grand jury, (b) sold multiple kilos of hydroponic weed, (c) engaged in money laundering of hundreds of thousands of dollars in drug proceeds, and (d) evaded federal and state income taxes.

Genduso was hired after a nationwide search during which none of the MSP sleuths noticed any of the aforementioned crimes of the girlfriend of a state police major.

Genduso's boyfriend retired as soon as she was busted and is, at fifty-five, collecting a pension of $159,000 a year. And Leigha has now penned her, uh, memoirs online. If you want a one-line review, Oscar Wilde summed it up well when reviewing an earlier work of art: "It would take a heart of stone not to laugh."

The title of her seventy-plus-page tome is *The Demons Behind Me*, which is pretty feeble, but most of the better titles have already been taken, like, *White Punks on Dope*, or *Third Rate Romance, Low Rent Rendezvous*, or *The Cops Are Robbers*, or *Drinkin' Doubles Don't Make a Party*.

Before her stellar career in organized crime and then law enforcement, Genduso cut quite the swath in the local hospitality industry, working in such five-star establishments as Scuttlebutts, Funky Murphy's, and Centerfolds, a sanctuary for weary businessmen.

But she had this recurring problem: DEA agents kept showing up at whatever bucket of blood she was tending bar. But Genduso tries to see the glass not as half empty, but as half full—with Jameson Irish whiskey, her drink of choice when she's thinking of committing suicide. At least at a strip joint, she rationalizes, there are worse things than being under surveillance for drug trafficking. "I guess," she writes, "if you are going to have DEA agents following you, you may as well be in an establishment where its (sic) more of a judgment-free zone, right?"

My only regret—other than wasting an hour of my life chuckling over Genduso's criminality and illiteracy—is that in the roster of the evil men who ruined her life, I only rank a distant third.

The person most responsible for destroying Leigha's life, she believes, is her ex-con ex-boyfriend, Sean Bucci, whom she ratted out into a multiyear sentence for drug dealing. Once Bucci (Bureau of Prisons number 24784-038) got out of prison, her damning testimony was quickly leaked to a "white-trash blogger"—Aidan Kearney, also known as Turtleboy.

And that was the end of her $150,000-a-year gig as one of the MSP's dozens, if not scores, of crooked cops, not to mention her cop boyfriend's career, and his best friend's, and the colonel's . . .

The erstwhile brass are all getting a kiss in the mail of at least $13,000 a month. Genduso, on the other hand, says she is making $20 an hour working at a security company—a crooked ex-cop working with a bunch of wannabe mall cops.

I picked up the Genduso story early on, especially after she was taken off the job and went back to slinging booze at an all-day gin mill in Danvers.

"Howie Carr began calling the bar relentlessly asking if I was working, when I was working, saying, 'I'm looking to buy some weed from Genduso!' and then cackling about it the next day live on his podcast like he's some king champ for stalking me and saying what he said."

The same day I printed a column in the *Herald* about the MSP Trooper of the Year's new job, a brawl broke out when some of her thug ex's pals showed up.

"My other favorite stalker, Howie Carr, jumped in on it saying he was to take the recognition for that because of his non-stop phone calls into the bar. I was in the press once again."

But do I get any credit? No, even though I try to keep her name in the news, mentioning her every time another statie gets arrested, she complains.

Oh well, Leigha, I don't hold a grudge.

One last thing: Whatever strip joint you work at next, Leigha, never forget the motto of the proud law enforcement agency you once represented, nay, symbolized, with such distinction: To Protect and Steal.

## CHAPTER TWENTY

## FBI

It is ironic that it was the intervention of the FBI and the Department of Justice that likely saved Karen Read from conviction for a crime she did not commit.

Ironic, because over the decades, agents in the Boston office of the FBI have, among other things, either set up or actually participated in at least six organized-crime murders, had two agents go to prison as Mob hitmen, and framed four innocent men for a gangland hit, sending them to prison for more than thirty years.

At least six G-men took payoffs from cocaine-dealing serial killers. In return they performed all sorts of services, including supplying the mobsters with forty pounds of C4 explosives that they planned to use for, among other things, killing a reporter. (Namely, me.)

These weren't just one or two bad apples. The corruption in the Boston office went on for more than forty years. At one of the organized-crime trials in which he testified, serial-killing gangster Stevie Flemmi was asked about his dealings with the Boston FBI. "Which FBI are you talking about?" he asked. In other words, which generation? The original corrupt agents who recruited him all retired eventually, moving into more important jobs despite their corruption.

And then they were succeeded by a new generation, just as corrupt.

The most corrupt of all the Boston agents, even worse than hitman John "Zip" Connolly, was H. Paul Rico, a native of the upscale suburb of Belmont. He got his break in the FBI in 1961, when J. Edgar Hoover, at the behest of Attorney General Robert F. Kennedy, announced that the Bureau would be going after organized crime.

**Rico, H. Paul**      "Ric"
Football 2, 3
AMBITION: To come back and find everything the way I left it
PET PEEVE: Cards
*"A form more active, light and strong
Ne'er shot the ranks of war along"*

H. Paul Rico's 1943 yearbook, Belmont High School.

Rico died in prison awaiting trial for a Mob hit.

To take down La Cosa Nostra, the agents were allowed to recruit non-Mafia gangsters as sources. Suddenly Rico's career was taking off. He became a force in organized crime because he came across like a gangster.

One of his nemeses, Tulsa Police Detective Mike Huff, tracked him for twenty years after Rico set up the murder of a Tulsa millionaire. Finally, Huff had to fly to Florida to meet the special agent he'd heard so much about.

"I thought I'd be meeting some great lawman," Huff recalled later. "After about five minutes, I realized I was talking to the Godfather."

In the 1960s, Rico partnered with Dennis Condon, a Charlestown native. The biggest organized-crime crew in Charlestown, the McLaughlins, were embroiled in a bloody gang war with the gang next door in Somerville, which would become known as the Winter Hill Gang.

The McLaughlins didn't like Rico and Condon. As part of Hoover's mandate, the FBI could install "gypsy wires"—unauthorized, illegal bugs and wiretaps of gangster hangouts. Rico used to fly down occasionally to Washington, DC, where he'd get his picture taken with Hoover and his gay lover, Clyde Tolson. It would appear in the Boston papers the next morning.

One morning, after returning from DC, Rico was sitting on the wire into the McLaughlin headquarters. He heard the head of the gang, Punchy McLaughlin, joking about Rico posing with Hoover and Tolson, and then speculated, in obscene detail, what Rico had been doing with the two confirmed bachelors who ran the FBI.

Rico went wild. He swore he would kill them, or get them killed, in the ongoing Irish Gang War. First, he brokered the shift of Stevie Flemmi's crew from loyalty to the McLaughlins to Winter Hill.

Another of the McLaughlin brothers, George, had gotten drunk

Dennis Condon, from corrupt FBI agent to Governor Dukakis's executive secretary of public safety.

and murdered a bank teller at a christening. When Rico and Condon discovered where he was holed up, they went to Stevie Flemmi's corner store in Roxbury and asked if he could get them a throw-down, untraceable gun.

Stevie was amenable—they were all on the same team, after all. But why? he asked. Rico told him that they were planning to bust into McLaughlin's hideout that night, throw down the gun, and claim they'd had to kill him while he was resisting arrest.

Flemmi got them the gun, a .38 revolver. The next morning, he picked up the *Record American* and there on the front page was a photo of McLaughlin being taken into custody—alive. That afternoon, Flemmi asked Rico what had gone wrong.

According to Flemmi's own statement in his official DEA-6 confession, Rico had recruited five agents. Four of them were "capable"—they'd go along with anything he suggested, up to and including murder—but that he wasn't sure about the fifth one. So they'd nixed the murder plan.

Flemmi never got his throw-down back.

In 1965, the FBI was starting the Witness Protection Program. The first big name to be recruited in Boston was Joe Barboza, a Portuguese hit man who operated out of East Boston. In March 1965, he was involved in the murder of a small-time hoodlum named Teddy Deegan.

According to documents the FBI grudgingly released under a federal court order more than thirty years later, Rico knew who was going to murder Deegan—before the murder. He confirmed the killers two days later, but they weren't arrested.

Rico and Condon decided to protect Barboza and one of his friends, Jimmy "the Bear" Flemmi, Stevie's brother. Stevie had already become an FBI informant, so protecting his brother could just be written off as professional courtesy.

But it was not only about protecting Jimmy Flemmi. Barboza falsely put rivals of his into the death car just to settle old scores. Louie Greco was a World War II veteran who had moved to Florida by the time of the murder. But he'd make the mistake of punching one of Barboza's crew in the mouth. He was convicted and died in state prison thirty years later.

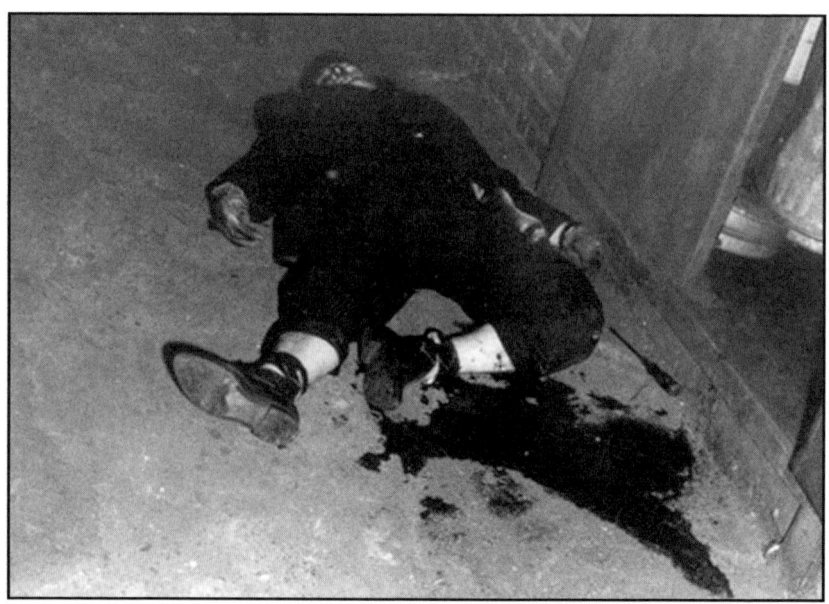

The 1965 murder of Teddy Deegan—covered up for forty years by the FBI.

Joe "the Horse" Salvati was a go-fer in the North End. When Barboza was in jail he sent a couple of his guys around trying to raise bail money. The Horse had refused to chip in $300. At trial, Barboza put him in the front seat. Because witnesses had said they'd seen a bald guy in the front seat (Jimmy Flemmi), Barboza said Salvati had been wearing a bald wig that night.

For $300, Salvati did more than thirty years in prison. All four were convicted and sentenced to death or life in prison.

The FBI had a mandatory retirement age of fifty, and Rico and Condon were getting close. To keep their lucrative rackets going after they reached fifty, they needed new blood to keep their connections current.

The next generation would be John "Zip" Connolly of South Boston. He had recently joined the FBI at the behest of outgoing House Speaker John McCormack of South Boston, a longtime friend of both the Bulger family and J. Edgar Hoover.

In 1972, Connolly was stationed in New York and desperate to get back to Boston. So Rico arranged for him to collar a Boston mobster on

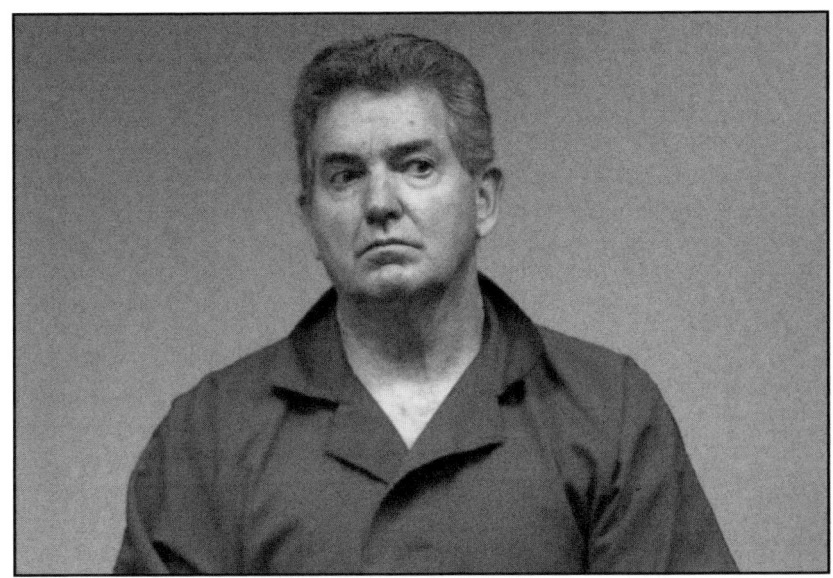

John "Zip" Connolly, FBI agent, Mob hitman.

the lam—the partner of Rico's informant Stevie Flemmi, who was also a fugitive after a Mob bombing. But Stevie abruptly decided to leave New York for Montreal a few days before Connolly arrested his friend.

Flemmi had gotten a heads-up to flee from Rico, his longtime friend and criminal associate. When he called Flemmi, Rico would always identify himself as "Jack from Boston."

Once he arranged for Flemmi's return to Boston, Rico retired to a "security" job with a jai-alai company. Condon got a hack state job as executive secretary of public safety for Gov. Michael Dukakis, a "reform" Democrat.

In the early seventies, on orders from J. Edgar Hoover himself, Rico had tried to recruit Whitey Bulger as a source. If a criminal became a confidential source, he was afforded some protection. Designation as "top echelon" was even more significant. In 1976, at Connolly's urgings, Bulger officially became a snitch of the FBI. He was paired with veteran "top echelon" informant Stevie Flemmi. They were both in what had become the Winter Hill Gang, a loose confederation of non-Mafia gangsters.

Connolly saw his FBI job as protecting Bulger and Flemmi, period. When they killed a Revere nightclub owner whom they had been told was an FBI informant, the feds convened an emergency meeting to figure out who had murdered their informant.

"Only the Mafia kills like that," Connolly lied. For that deception, the gang gave him a large diamond ring. It was the first of hundreds of thousands of dollars he took from the Mob. Other agents began taking payoffs as well.

To protect their new paymasters, the FBI arrested or drove away all the hoods above Bulger and Flemmi in the Winter Hill Gang, and after that the local Mafia. By 1982, thanks to the FBI, the two top figures in the Boston underworld were Whitey Bulger and Stevie Flemmi.

Bulger and Flemmi took care of "their" agents, and not just with money. After they hit the retirement age of fifty, often they got jobs with companies or public agencies connected to Whitey Bulger's brother Billy, the president of the Massachusetts Senate.

Meanwhile, H. Paul Rico had gotten a job as director of security for a company called World Jai Alai, which ran frontons in both Florida and Connecticut. The company was owned by a Tulsa millionaire named Roger Wheeler. His financial guy was a local Mob wannabe named John Callahan.

Callahan cut Bulger and Flemmi in on various rackets at the Connecticut fronton under the guise of providing "protection" from the five Mafia families in New York. In those pre-cocaine days, $10,000 a week was a huge underworld score, and soon the Boston crowd was dreaming of seizing the whole company.

There was only one problem: Wheeler didn't want to sell. So Callahan and the FBI's boys approached an unstable local hood named Brian Halloran to murder Wheeler. He turned them down, but there was a problem. Halloran had other criminal charges pending against him. He began hinting to honest FBI agents that he had some very hot information.

At the time, Connolly was taking a year off to attend Harvard University on a mid-career program. His superiors in the FBI had written glowing recommendations to Harvard on his behalf. But he took time out from his studies, such as they were, to get word back to Bulger about Halloran's threats to turn informant.

Bulger quickly murdered Halloran and another man outside a bar on Northern Avenue in 1982. Everyone knew that Connolly had set them up.

At Bulger's trial, in 2013, one of his defense witnesses was an ex-FBI agent named Robert Fitzpatrick, who as Connolly's superior in the Boston office had always written glowing reviews of his performance.

However, after his retirement, Fitzpatrick had written a preposterous book full of alleged FBI exploits that put him at the center of every major FBI case since Martin Luther King's assassination. He also gave himself twenty-twenty hindsight.

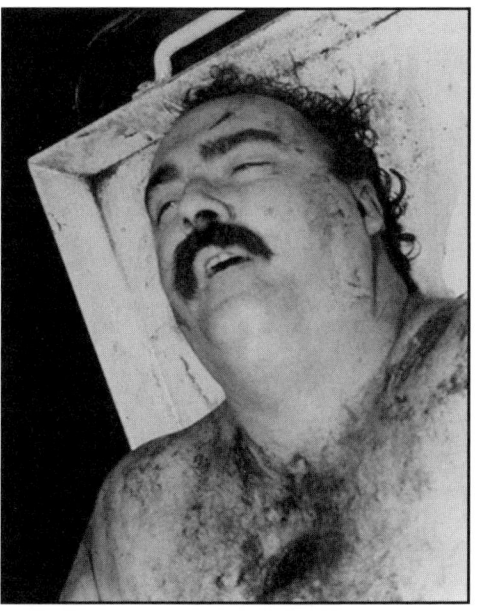

Brian Halloran, set up by the FBI for Whitey Bulger to murder.

On cross-examination, a federal prosecutor asked Fitzpatrick about his statement in his book about how soon he had known Connolly was involved in gangland murders: "I knew full well that Halloran was killed because Connolly had told Bulger he was talking, making him a direct accessory to murder."

Yet that same year, Fitzpatrick had written yet another gushing review of Connolly's performance: "His performance has been at the level to which we should all aspire to attain, but few will realistically reach."

The federal prosecutor read Fitzpatrick's glowing praise of Connolly back to him, then paused for a moment before asking his next question: "After those murders in May of 1982, you didn't call up Harvard and tell them that John Connolly might not be Harvard material after all, did you?"

"I don't recall," Fitzpatrick said. After Bulger was convicted in 2013, he was indicted and convicted on six counts of perjury.

FBI agents and former agents continued to set up more murders to cover up their involvement in the World Jai Alai case.

After eliminating Halloran, the crew resumed their plans to grab the company by murdering the CEO. The assignment was given to two fugitive members of the gang, Johnny Martorano and Joe McDonald, who had been on the lam for years.

The two veteran hitmen went to Tulsa, where they shot Wheeler in the parking lot of a private golf club. Rico had conveyed his schedule of his employer through Flemmi to Martorano. Martorano later said he knew the information had come from a cop because Wheeler's complexion was described as "ruddy."

"I never heard anybody but a cop use the word 'ruddy,'" Martorano said.

Meanwhile, the four men falsely convicted of murdering Teddy Deegan in 1965 remained behind bars. As early as 1973, a Mafia turncoat

FBI agents set up the 1981 murder of Roger Wheeler in Tulsa.

named Vinnie Teresa pointed out in a best-selling book that the men had been framed by the FBI. Nothing happened.

All through the 1980s, every year petitions for commutations or pardons would come before the Governor's Council, an elected body in Massachusetts. The US attorneys in Boston—including future Gov. William Weld—would write letters to the councilors opposing release of the innocent men.

One of the US attorneys was William Mueller, who would eventually become FBI director and then run the investigation into the Russian-Trump "collusion" that never happened (see Chapter 21).

By this time Connolly had a new boss in the office, John Morris. Bulger nicknamed him "Vino," because once when meeting with the gangsters at a downtown hotel to give them an update on the FBI's Mafia investigations, he got so drunk that Bulger had to drive him home, with Flemmi following in Morris's unmarked FBI vehicle.

As Whitey and Stevie moved into cocaine dealing, the payoffs to their G-men escalated. At Connolly's later murder trial in Miami, one of the secretaries in the Boston office recalled opening a bottom drawer in his desk (he seldom appeared at work). She was surprised to see a number of unopened government paychecks that he hadn't even bothered to cash.

Flemmi later estimated Connolly took $235,000 in Mob payoffs over the years. He once bragged, "I'm in the gang!" He bought a yacht and a vacation home in the ritzy Cape Cod town of Chatham.

Connolly began to fancy himself a role model for the younger agents. He made a training video for the FBI training academy in Quantico, Virginia, about how to handle organized-crime informants.

His takeaway: "Never try to out-gangster a gangster."

Meanwhile, his pal Vino Morris was promoted to director of the training academy.

Bulger's reign of terror in Boston began winding down by 1990. His cocaine ring in South Boston was broken up. John Connolly was distraught, desperately trying to find out if "Jimmy" was going to be arrested. (The answer was, no.)

But at their court arraignments, it quickly became evident that many of Bulgers dealers had state or city jobs. It became an issue in the governor's race, and the Bulger's candidate was upset by a Republican. Connolly abruptly decided to retire and take a job as director of security for Boston Edison.

By that time, the younger agents in the office had begun calling him "Cannoli," because of the way he dressed like a capo in the Gambino crime family of New York.

By then it was clear that something had gone very wrong in the Boston FBI office. Whitey Bulger fled ahead of a federal indictment in 1994, after a tip from Connolly, just before his arrest. He would be a fugitive for sixteen years. The FBI tried to find him, but had no success. When the cold case was turned over to the US Marshals in 2010, it took them about six months to arrest him.

Two of the four men framed by Rico, Condon, and the FBI in 1965 had died in prison. But the two who hadn't were finally released from prison. In 1997, Congress held its first hearings on FBI corruption in Boston, and Rico was called to testify. When asked by a Connecticut Republican how he felt about the frame-up, Rico snarled: "Whaddaya want from me, tears?"

It would get worse. In 2002, finally, authorities in Tulsa decided they had enough evidence to indict Rico for setting up the murder of Roger Wheeler in 1981. Det. Mike Huff was sworn in as a police officer in Miami-Dade so that he could personally make the arrest.

When Rico opened the door and saw Huff standing there with a warrant in his hand, he literally shit his pants. He was flown back to Oklahoma and died a couple of months later in a prison hospital.

In 2002, the men framed in the Deegan murder sued for their wrongful thirty-five-year imprisonment. By then, the FBI director was Robert Mueller, the former acting US attorney in Boston. He scoffed at the lawsuit, saying all the exculpatory evidence was merely "fodder for cross-examination."

Zip Connolly was convicted in federal court in Boston on racketeering charges in 2002. He was convicted in state court in Florida in 2007 for the murder of John Callahan. He was finally released from prison in Florida in 2021.

According to Connolly's lawyer, he was terminally ill with melanoma, and had less than a year to live. In 2025, he is back in Massachusetts, still alive and collecting a pension from the FBI.

Meanwhile, a third generation of Boston FBI agents became embroiled in scandal. Peter Strzok was briefly an agent in the Boston office in the late 1990s, and later became a counterintelligence agent in the Washington office. Like John "Vino" Morris before him, he began cheating on his wife with a woman in the office—married FBI lawyer Lisa Page.

In 2016, he was one of the agents who concocted the operation "Crossfire Hurricane"—the hoax falsely accusing Donald J. Trump of "colluding" with the Russians to defeat Hillary Clinton. Strzok and his sidepiece Lisa Page were consumed with hatred for Trump, and Strzok was part of the cabal on the seventh floor of the Hoover building who conspired with the CIA, Democrat candidate Hillary Clinton, and left-wing media to concoct what many consider the greatest political scandal in American history.

It was Strzok, the former Boston agent, who created the original document to open the "investigation," out of whole cloth, just the way his predecessors Rico, Connolly, and Morris had done in earlier years.

In *The Hill*, a former FBI executive described the fantastically corrupt document that Strzok created: "In a normal, legitimate FBI Electronic Communication, or EC, there would be a 'To' and a 'From' line. The Crossfire Hurricane EC had only a 'From' line; it is from a part of the FBI's Counterintelligence Division whose contact is listed as Peter Strzok.

"The EC was drafted also by Peter Strzok. And, finally, it is approved by Peter Strzok. Essentially, it is a document created by Peter Strzok, approved by Peter Strzok, and sent from Peter Strzok to Peter Strzok.

"On that basis alone, the document is an absurdity, violative of all FBI protocols and, therefore, invalid on its face. An agent cannot approve his or her own case; that would make a mockery of the oversight designed to protect Americans. Yet, for this document, Peter Strzok was pitcher, catcher, batter, and umpire."

Peter Strzok was fired from the FBI on August 10, 2018.

The Boston FBI office traditions continued.

# CHAPTER TWENTY-ONE

# "Not So Honorable"

*In 2017, Robert Mueller was the special counsel running the "Russian collusion" investigation against President Donald Trump. Since the charges were completely false, the probe basically amounted to a cover-up of the origins of the hoax, in the Hillary Clinton campaign of 2016.*

To falsely portray Mueller's cover-up "probe" as being at least somewhat legitimate, the Democrat-controlled mainstream media went into overdrive, trying to portray him as an honorable man. I knew that was not true. He had been spectacularly unsuccessful prosecuting Hells Angels in California in the 1970s.

Then he moved to Boston where he was briefly acting US attorney in the 1980s, while the four innocent men framed by the FBI in the Teddy Deegan hit remained imprisoned.

Even though they were innocent, and everybody knew that they were, he did nothing to get them out of prison. Years later, after their release (two had died in prison), they sued. By then Mueller was FBI director, but he refused to turn over exculpatory material that was by then over thirty years old.

As you will see next, Judge Nancy Gertner threatened him with sanctions to turn over the documents. She was rightly outraged by his refusal to help right a terrible wrong. In the end, the four men or their estates received a judgment of $102 million.

In 2018, Alan Dershowitz pointed out Mueller's indefensible behavior in the Boston FBI frame-up. And now-retired Judge Gertner, a rabid Democrat partisan, began defending the man she'd been threatening to find in contempt a dozen years earlier.

I went down to the state archives in Dorchester and pulled the files on the case and then wrote a lengthy column about it for the Daily Caller *in June 2018.*

Reprinted with permission by the *Daily Caller*.

## Not So Honorable: Docs Show Mueller's FBI Denied Justice to Four Innocent Men

As FBI director in 2002, Special Counsel Robert Mueller directed his agents to oppose the pardons of four wrongfully imprisoned men because exculpatory evidence was merely "fodder for cross-examination," newly revealed FBI documents show.

Four years later, the four men, or their estates, were awarded $102 million by a federal judge in Boston for their wrongful decades-long imprisonment due to FBI misconduct.

Mueller ordered the Boston FBI office to answer a request to him from the Massachusetts Advisory Board of Pardons for an "official version" of the imprisonment of the four men for a gangland murder in Chelsea, Massachusetts, in March 1965.

The four men—Louie Greco, Henry Tameleo, Peter Limone, and Joe Salvati—were convicted in state court in Boston of murdering Edward "Teddy" Deegan, a small-time hoodlum, in an alley during a bank burglary.

Within days of the murder, Boston FBI agents knew the identities of the actual murderers, and reported the information to J. Edgar Hoover in Washington. But they allowed a Mob hitman they had flipped, Joseph Barboza, to settle some old scores by falsely testifying that the four men had taken part in the gangland murder he had helped arrange with others.

In 2002, lawyers for one of the innocent men, Louie Greco, were seeking a posthumous pardon for him from the State of Massachusetts. Greco, a decorated World War II veteran, had been living in Florida at the time of the murder, but was nevertheless convicted on Barboza's perjured testimony.

Greco died in 1995 after serving twenty-eight years in prison for a crime he did not commit.

Another Boston gangster later testified to a congressional committee that after the 1967 trial, one of the FBI agents bragged about framing Greco and said, "How does Louie Greco like going from Miami to Death Row? He wasn't even there!"

Louie Greco, died in prison after being framed by FBI.

For thirty-five years, the FBI refused to release the evidence exonerating the wrongfully imprisoned men on the grounds of "national security." It was finally released in 2000 as part of an investigation into corruption in the Boston office of the FBI.

After the state pardons board asked Mueller for the Bureau's version of its actions, a Boston FBI agent, Charles Prouty, wrote back on May 9, 2002, that "FBI Headquarters in Washington, D.C. has directed the office to respond."

While conceding that the damning FBI reports contained "impeachment material," Mueller's FBI still contended that the innocent men might in fact be guilty, despite the FBI's own reports to the contrary.

"This does not necessarily mean, however, that Limone or any of the other defendants is innocent—it merely means that they are entitled to a new trial."

Deegan was murdered on March 12, and the FBI office sent memos to Bureau headquarters in Washington on March 15 and March 19 identifying the real killers—and with no mention of the four men who later won the $102 million judgment.

Mueller, however, tried to convince the Massachusetts authorities that his own Bureau's documents did not mean that the four men had been railroaded.

"Much of the FBI confidential source information relates to the individuals who were involved in the Deegan murder as principals," Mueller's deputy said, underlining the word. "This information is not necessarily inconsistent with the crimes for which the defendants were convicted."

Prouty did not mention the fact that Greco had moved from Boston to Florida before the murder. Mueller's agent also did not point out that the siblings of victim Deegan, who had grown up in Boston's West End with Limone, had earlier written the state parole board in support of Limone's release. The Deegan siblings told the Parole Board that Limone had warned his childhood friend Deegan to be careful because of the murder contract out on him.

Michael Albano, a former member of the Massachusetts Parole Board and onetime mayor of Springfield, worked for years to free the innocent men.

"Even after the facts of the FBI cover-up were revealed," he said last week on *The Howie Carr Show* after reading the letter, "the FBI continued the cover-up with the approval and authorization of Director Robert Mueller III."

This newly rediscovered letter is the latest indication of Mueller's role in what may have been the FBI's greatest scandal ever, at least until the current Spygate controversy, which has led to Mueller's ongoing "investigation" of President Trump.

John Cavicchi, the Greco attorney who found Mueller's FBI letter in his case files last week, said it had "outraged" him all over again.

"After all those years," Cavicchi said Sunday, "the feds still couldn't admit that they had engineered this gross miscarriage of justice. Why couldn't Mueller, who was in Boston while this frame-up was going on, admit the Bureau's culpability, then apologize and just settle the civil suit?"

In Boston, the four men were always widely known to be innocent. As early as 1973, a Mafia turncoat wrote in a local best-selling book how they were framed by the FBI and its star Mob informant, hitman Joe "the Animal" Barboza, one of the actual killers of Deegan.

Mueller was an assistant US attorney in Boston in the 1980s as the imprisoned men futilely tried to get their convictions overturned. Greco passed a lie detector test on live national TV.

But the FBI was adamant that they should remain behind bars. Mueller served briefly as US attorney in Boston in 1986–87. Both his predecessor and his successor as US attorney wrote letters to state authorities demanding that the innocent men not be released.

Albano, the former parole board member, has said that he has seen a similar letter written by Mueller during his brief stint as US attorney. But that letter, if it ever existed, appears to have disappeared from state files.

Still, Alan Dershowitz, the retired Harvard Law School professor, recently described Mueller as "the guy who kept four innocent people in prison for many years . . . right at the center of it."

Nancy Gertner, the now-retired federal judge who presided over the civil case for damages that ended with the $102 million award, then wrote an op-ed piece in *The New York Times* accusing Dershowitz and Fox News host Sean Hannity, among others, of "smearing" Mueller.

Gertner, who was appointed to the bench by her Yale Law School classmate Bill Clinton, claimed Mueller "had no involvement in that case."

However, in December 2006, during the civil trial, Judge Gertner wrote a show-cause order accusing Mueller of stonewalling production of exculpatory evidence—"a serious problem," she wrote.

"This is a case about, inter alia, informant abuse, about the failure to disclose exculpatory evidence bearing on the innocence of the four plaintiffs, about FBI agents allegedly 'hiding the ball,' not disclosing critical information that would have exonerated the plaintiff . . . and not doing so for nearly 40 years."

She continued, "Given those accusations, the position the FBI is taking is chilling . . . This Court is not remotely satisfied."

Gertner said she had been asked by the innocent men to hold the FBI in contempt of court and that she had taken their motion "under advisement."

"In order to make that decision," she wrote, "the Court ORDERS that this matter be brought to the personal attention of the Director of the FBI."

In other words, Robert Mueller III.

Six days later, attorneys for the Justice Department filed a notice of compliance, saying, "This matter has been brought to the personal attention of the Director of the FBI; counsel for the United States have been provided with unredacted copies of the FBI documents on plaintiffs' trial exhibit list . . ."

And so Mueller avoided being cited for contempt for court.

During the 1980s, in addition to the annual letters from the US attorney in Boston, local FBI agents lobbied state authorities to keep the innocent men behind bars. According to Albano and others, two local G-men would go directly to the State House to lobby members of the Governor's Council, which considered commutations and pardons.

Another former member of the Governor's Council recalled how the two agents liked to speak directly to the politicians, rather than leave behind a paper trail.

The two FBI agents were John Morris and John "Zip" Connolly. Morris has since admitted taking $7,000 in payoffs from gangster Whitey Bulger and his partner Stevie Flemmi, the younger brother of "the Bear," who actually murdered Deegan in 1965.

Both Flemmi and Bulger, whose brother was the Democrat president of the Massachusetts Senate, were longtime "top-echelon" informants of the FBI. Flemmi has testified to the Drug Enforcement Administration that he and Bulger at one time had six Boston G-men on their underworld payroll. Both Flemmi and Bulger are serving life sentences in federal prison; Bulger was convicted of eleven murders and Flemmi of five.

At Bulger's 2013 trial, Morris admitted telling Connolly about a gangster who was about to flip and testify against Bulger in 1981. Connolly, despite being a midlife student at Harvard at the time, got the message to Bulger, and the gangland chieftain gunned down the informant and another man in South Boston.

Connolly, the Harvard man, is currently serving a forty-year sentence in a Florida prison after being convicted of orchestrating a different gangland hit in Miami, to cover up still another organized-crime murder, at a golf course in Tulsa, Oklahoma.

That Oklahoma murder was set up by a third corrupt Boston FBI agent, H. Paul Rico, who was one of the two agents who engineered the frame-up of the four innocent men back in 1965. Rico died in a prison hospital in Tulsa in 2003 after being arrested in Florida and brought back to the Sooner state to stand trial on murder charges.

Asked for a statement about the 2002 letter Mueller authorized to be sent to the Advisory Board of Pardons, Mueller's office on Friday declined comment.

In the Greco family's 2002 plea for a posthumous pardon, their lawyer wrote: "Louie Greco died an innocent man, despite numerous unheeded pleas of innocence. His innocence was known prior to trial, yet he was tried, convicted and sentenced to death. Now, the truth is being revealed and those responsible are facing a Congressional and Justice Department investigation. It is time for Massachusetts to officially acknowledge the wrong done to Mr. Greco and his family and remove this blot from his name."

But after receiving the letter from Mueller, the board rejected the family's petition in July 2003.

Finally, in the waning days of his administration in December 2014, Governor Deval Patrick issued a proclamation laying out the facts of the corrupt frame-up by the FBI and Greco's innocence.

"Any stigma and disgrace," the governor wrote, "is hereby removed."

Greco had been dead nineteen years. He spent the last twenty-eight years of his life in prison for a crime he did not commit—a fact Robert Mueller knew but adamantly refused to acknowledge even after Greco's death behind bars.

"Even the dead," Michael Albano said, "can't rest in peace with this FBI memo."

# CHAPTER TWENTY-TWO

# Fred Weichel: Another Norfolk County Frame-up

Like Karen Read, Fred Weichel was charged in Norfolk County with a murder he did not commit.

They did it as a favor for James "Whitey" Bulger, the serial killing gangster from South Boston.

Bulger was always worried about up-and-coming street guys in Southie. Uneasy lies the head that wears the crown—especially in the underworld. He'd gotten control by eliminating a guy named Donald Killeen. His partner Stevie Flemmi had engineered a hostile takeover of his own in Roxbury with a guy named Wimpy Bennett.

Fred Weichel, thirty-six years in prison

Whitey kept a close eye on Weichel. He was a young guy, twenty-eight, but very tough. Tough enough to have been used as a strong-arm man when Whitey was taking over cocaine dealing in South Boston by getting all the independents "in line."

As insulation, Whitey recruited an old-time Southie wiseguy named Billy Shea to round up the cocaine dealers. And Shea brought in two fearsome South Boston hard guys—Tommy Nee and Fred Weichel.

Shea would cruise the streets of Southie, with Weichel in the front seat and Nee in the back. At Whitey's murder trial in 2013, Shea explained how he and his crew got the dealers in line: "We'd pull up, pull them over—'Get in the car.' If they didn't get in, I would explain to them that this was daylight, you notice it's daylight, the next time you see us, it will be nighttime, you won't have a chance to speak."

Weichel and Shea would be in the front seat, so the dealer would get into the back with Nee. What he'd immediately notice on the seat, covered with a towel, was an automatic weapon. Intimidation. "Nee or Weichel wouldn't have to say too much. The criminal element in Boston knew who was dangerous and who wasn't. They knew."

If they seemed too frightened by the firearm, Shea would tell them, "Don't mind that, it's for a piece of business later on. It was all show, dog and pony."

Mission accomplished, Whitey began wondering what to do with the freelance thugs. Nee was too dangerous—too "capable"—to keep around. Bulger kept tabs on his whereabouts, which he dutifully passed to his corrupt FBI agent/hitman John "Zip" Connolly. Nee was finally arrested by the feds in 1981. Out on bail, he was shot to death outside the Pen Tavern. Whitey had nothing to do with it, but was reportedly ecstatic when he got the news.

But he still had to deal with Weichel, whom he didn't like. Too tough, had a tough brother—not Whitey's kind of guy.

"Jim Bulger didn't really care for Freddie," Bulger gravedigger Kevin "Two" Weeks testified decades later.

The opportunity to take him off the board finally came around in 1980. A twenty-five-year-old drunk named Robert LaMonica was shot to death in Braintree—Norfolk County—in May 1980.

Weichel had what appeared to be a perfect alibi—he was drinking in Triple O's, Whitey's bar in the Lower End, which he had taken over from the Killeens after murdering the gang boss in Framingham and scattering the remaining Killeen crew members.

But Weichel had to go. Cops found a teenager who'd been drinking beer, in the dark, 175 feet away from the scene. Police convinced him to identify Weichel as the shooter. BPD fabricated evidence against him. (The city later paid him $3 million.)

Most significantly, Whitey himself stepped in. Ostensibly, he was trying to protect the real killer, Tommy Barrett, whose family he knew. That's the way he always operated. He was just trying to help. But he really wanted to get rid of Weichel, once and for all.

So he drove his blue Chevy Malibu to the D Street projects, where Weichel lived. He honked the horn, and Weichel knew who it was. Everybody in the Town knew that car. Whitey gave him an ultimatum: "If you ever mention Tommy Barrett's name, I'll kill you," he said. "And if I can't get you, I'll get your mother and your sister . . . He said he was going to cut my head off and kick it down the street like a head of lettuce."

The district attorney of Norfolk County was Bill Delahunt. He'd gone to parochial school with another member of Whitey's gang, Johnny Martorano. He the usual type of go-along-to-get-along prosecutor who gets elected in Norfolk County.

Weichel was convicted in 1981 and sentenced to life without parole. In 1982, Barrett wrote a letter to Weichel's mother, confessing to the crime. But Weichel at first didn't know about the letter, and then later still feared Whitey's wrath enough to not release it.

In 1996, District Attorney Delahunt was elected to Congress. He wasn't old enough to start collecting his state pension—unless district attorneys could be reclassified as "Group 4" police officers, who under state law could begin collecting a decade earlier, at age fifty-five.

So Delahunt filed legislation to grab his state pension a decade sooner. The bill had to be approved by the state Senate. Billy Bulger had by then become president of the University of Massachusetts. But he maintained firm control of the Senate through his hand-picked new president—Tom Birmingham, the son of a corrupt Boston City Hall official whom Billy had defended in a criminal case involving payoffs to the family of a Mob hitman named "Suitcase." The new Senate president had been named after his uncle, a minor Charlestown wise guy murdered by the Winter Hill Gang in 1969.

No one in the Senate raised any objections to taking care of Delahunt, the guy who'd done such a solid for Whitey Bulger for disposing of Fred Weichel once and for all.

Delahunt's new $59,000 pension (in addition to his Congressional salary) was portrayed as secondary to the legislature's charitable attempts to get a pension for the young family of a Suffolk County prosecutor who'd been recently murdered by a gangbanger. In fact, it was mostly a payoff to Delahunt for services rendered.

Weichel languished in prison through the decades. He couldn't attend his mother's wake or funeral in 2000. At one point, he was stabbed in the arm and face. Another time he had his jaw broken when he was beaten "with a sock with an object in it." In 2013, after Whitey's capture, he admitted that he knew Weichel wasn't the killer. But he refused to testify on his old rival's behalf.

Finally, in 2017, his conviction was overturned and he was released from prison. A judge ruled that Delahunt had withheld a report exonerating him, in much the same way that the same office would do with Karen Read in 2024, refusing to acknowledge the report by the top accident-reconstruction experts in the United States that proved that Read's SUV didn't strike, let alone kill her boyfriend John O'Keefe.

Weichel sued the state for his thirty-six years of wrongful imprisonment. Then-attorney general Maura Healey argued against paying him anything, saying that even if Weichel did not kill LaMonica, he knew who did and had a duty to identify the real murderer.

He won the case and the jury awarded him $33 million, even though settlements under the state's wrongful-conviction law are capped at $1 million—about $28,000 for each of his lost thirty-six years.

He filed a federal lawsuit and last year, after Karen Read's first trial, which ended with two acquittals on murder charges that Norfolk County decided to ignore, Fred Weichel settled with the Town of Braintree, where he was arrested, for $14.9 million.

The lawsuit had alleged that Braintree Police, BPD, and the MSP had fabricated evidence against him, much as Karen Read contended that the police had planted pieces of broken taillight near the death scene in her case in order to send her to prison for a crime that she didn't commit. The state had already agreed to pay Weichel about $1.3 million for the MSP's role in the frame-up.

With Bulger and Delahunt both dead, Weichel's lawyers could lay out the theory he'd been afraid to offer more than four decades earlier.

"Bulger had a reason to falsely implicate someone," the motion said. "Bulger was dating Veronica Barrett, whose son, Thomas Barrett, later confessed to committing the murder. Bulger also may have wanted to set up (Weichel) to take pressure off himself because police investigated ties between him and LaMonica."

And of course, there was the fact that Bulger also wanted to get rid of any potential rivals. If he could get the cops to do his dirty work for him, so much the better.

Weichel now lives modestly in South Boston. As for Whitey, he was beaten to death in 2018 at a federal prison in West Virginia, by inmates wielding socks containing heavy locks—the same type of makeshift weapon that had almost killed Weichel decades earlier.

One of Whitey's killers had been a hitman for the Mafia in Springfield, Fotios "Freddy" Geas, a former guard in the Hampden County House of Correction. Geas hated Whitey for, among other reasons, framing Fred Weichel.

This is as close to justice as anyone ever gets now in Massachusetts.

# CHAPTER TWENTY-THREE

# Rotten Boroughs

## Watertown Police Accused of Arresting Behavior

Rep. John "Get Off My" Lawn.

*November 17, 2020*

The Watertown Police Department is putting the "sex" back in Middlesex County. It's a small town, Watertown, so small, in fact, that the police chief and the state rep are brothers. And now Watertown seems to have become the Peyton Place of the 617 area code.

It's all outlined in a lawsuit filed in Middlesex Superior Court by a former WPD detective, Kathleen E. Donohue, who is suing both the town and the Watertown Police Association.

Among her accusations: She had a five-year-long "sexual relationship" with now-Chief Michael Lawn beginning in 2009. He's the brother of state Rep. John Lawn, a hack Democrat lifer who's the chairman of some rubber-stamp committee at the State House.

"[Now-Chief Lawn] used the power of his position and isolation he knew Det. Donohue was experiencing to invite her to engage in an intimate relationship with him. She could not and did not resist," the suit alleges.

The star-crossed WPD lovebirds continued, as the old song goes, livin' here, lovin' there, lyin' in between. "Lt. Lawn's professional support for Det. Donohue waxed and waned with their relationship, which ended after his wife learned about it," the suit states.

In some towns, that might be a problem. But not in Watertown. Nevertheless, after all the third-rate romances and low-rent rendezvouses ended, there were recriminations.

"For instance, one day in April of 2015, Lt. Lawn texted Det. Donohue, among other things, the following: 'I'm (bleeping) out of my mind'; 'You know what (bleep) off'; 'Call your lawyer;' '(Bleep) you;' 'Good bye, take me down. U don't own me. Get that'; 'I want u out of my life.' He angrily told her that she had ruined his career," the complaint states

That wasn't true, of course. His brother John was and is the state rep from Watertown. In 2015, Chief Ed Deveau decided to retire. Deveau, by the way, also appears in Donohue's complaint, in paragraph 57: "On information and belief, Chief Deveau had himself participated in activities creating a hostile work environment for women WPD officers. On information and belief, his misconduct included his exposing himself to a woman officer as well as engaging in other forms of harassment and disparate treatment."

Rotten Boroughs | 247

In 2015, "seeking to protect himself and his future," Lawn asked his boss, Capt. Thomas Rocca, to relieve him of his job running the detectives' division.

"On information and belief, Capt. Rocca, as well as Lt. (James) O'Connor, knew of the relationship between Det. Donohue and Lt. Lawn. Lt. O'Connor and Lt. Lawn are cousins."

Cousins? In Watertown? I told you it was a small town.

"In or around June 2015, Lt. O'Connor took over command of the Detectives' Division from Lt. Lawn."

Another nationwide search, cousin!

She no longer worked for him, but according to the lawsuit, the future chief "continued to disparage Det. Donohue in communications with her directly . . . His language continued to bear the mark of sexism and hostility: He wrote '(Bleep) u'; 'Bitch'; 'Go (bleep) yourself' and phrases similar."

Based on his stellar record, Lawn was soon promoted to chief.

In December 2016, the chief and his former gal pal "talked as both of them sat in their separate cars."

The suit goes on: "His reaction was alarming: The Chief slammed his hands on the steering wheel of his vehicle, threw his cell phone on the floor, yelled at Det. Donohue and drove away."

Well, as long as there were no hard feelings . . .

Donohue was basically forced out of the department, a process that her thirty-six-page suit details at some length. As part of her complaint, she recounts what she says male WPD cops have gotten away with:

"Another male officer, during his tenure on the force, forged identities in order to obtain controlled substances illegally. On information and belief, he was not emergently suspended."

"Another male officer lied directly to the Chief about being present on a detail when he was in fact getting a haircut. On information and belief, he was not emergently suspended."

Who did these cops think they were, state troopers?

In paragraph 153 we meet still another cop at the Watertown Middle School who "was alleged to have engaged in inappropriate conduct towards a female staff member and female students. As alleged, this patrolman encouraged female students to cut class to sleep in his office, showed them a sexually charged video and an inappropriate internet site.

"It was further alleged that the patrolman spent time off campus with one student who was a victim of sexual abuse, gave her money, and encouraged her to call him 'Daddy.' That same officer was also alleged to have punched a student."

Maybe the other student refused to call him Daddy. At any rate, that cop wasn't fired, the suit alleges.

I called Chief Lawn Tuesday and left a message asking him if he wanted to comment on his alleged sexual relationship with Det. Donohue and all the other charges she made. He did not return the call.

I then called Rep. Lawn to ask him if he wanted to comment on the scandalous allegations his married brother's ex-girlfriend was making against his brother the chief, and whether he thought it might be time for a good housecleaning at the WPD.

Mr. Chairman likewise did not return my call.

Watertown—putting the "sex" back in Middlesex County.

## Rep. Lawn Inducted into State House Alcohol of Fame

*July 17, 2025*

What the McAlberts are to the Town of Canton, the Lawn family is to Watertown. A bunch of privileged, drunk bullies lording it over everybody, costing the taxpayers millions and generally embarrassing the hell out of the decent, law-abiding citizenry.

By now, you've heard about the drunkard Democrat state rep, John Lawn, just inducted into the State House Alcohol of Fame. He was arrested by Boston cops for OUI early Wednesday morning after getting smashed and then smashing into half the cars around the State House, after which he informed cops, "I am a state rep," and then asked for an Uber—three times.

The Watertown wastrel yesterday took "full responsibility" for his actions and then pleaded not guilty. So much for taking full responsibility . . .

Here's something you may not have noticed in the BPD incident report, about what happened after the reprobate rep was taken to the Nashua Street jail. The intake nurse asked him for a urine sample and handed him a cup.

"While going into the cell," the BPD report states, "the suspect placed the urine sample cup on the counter inside the cell and attempted to pee into the cup while it was on the counter."

Just how drunk were you, Mr. Chairman?

"Officers asked the suspect to do it at the toilet. The suspect proceeded to pee into the cup and after he finished urinating, he emptied the contents of the cup into the toilet and gave the empty cup to the nurse."

Talk about a bad ice cube . . .

"Officers observed that the suspect may have urinated on himself as there were wet spots on his shirt and pants."

For this the statesman is paid $135,060 a year, because he is a committee chairman. How much would we have to pay him if he didn't wet himself after getting knee-walking drunk? He also flunked the Sidewalk Olympics, including the one-leg stand.

It's hard to stand on one leg when you're legless. I thought every legislator knew that.

Another Lawn, another scandal. They're Watertown's political wannabees—Kmart Kennedys, as they used to be called. And of course to be Kmart Kennedys you need to have multiple kinsmen slurping at the trough for big bucks.

It's the hackerama!

Meet the solon's sibling, Sheila Lawn, "Sis." She used to be married to Dennis Lehane, the writer. Now she's "first assistant clerk magistrate," in Brighton District Court, for $145,734 a year. Apparently she's been out-hacked for the job of clerk once or twice.

Ya can't win 'em all, even if you're a Lawn.

Next, we have brother Michael Lawn, the former police chief of Watertown. Working for the WPD was the only job he ever had, or so he said when he retired in July 2022, which was four months before his former cop girlfriend won $4 million in a state lawsuit against the town for sexual harassment.

The plaintiff's name is Kathleen E. Donahue, and in her suit she says Michael Lawn "invited her to engage in an intimate relationship with him. She could not and did not resist."

Relationships with the Lawns never last long. Just ask Dennis Lehane. It's a wonderful department, positively Canton-like. Instead of everybody being named Albert, everybody's a Lawn or an O'Connor. As the chief mentioned in his farewell interview after all his years on the job: "Being able to work with my Dad, being able to work with my sister—who was here for a few years, and more recently with my nephew . . ."

I checked the state comptroller's payroll yesterday. By an incredible coincidence, since 2022, the year he retired and his ex-gal pal got $4 million from the town, on the state payroll there's been a Michael Lawn listed as a "per diem security staffing specialist Trial Ct."

He made $37,390 last year working part-time. So far this year Lawn has pocketed $12,839.

Rep. Lawn appeared in court yesterday. He was represented by Timothy Flaherty of Cambridge, who also represents horny Cambridge City Councilor Paul Boner, I mean Toner, the accused john. Like Chief Lawn before him, Boner was just trying to put the "sex" back in Middlesex County.

Lawn's lawyer Flaherty is the son of former House speaker and convicted felon Good Time Charlie Flaherty.

Flaherty was suspended from the bar a few years back. Something about witness tampering. But now he's back. By the way, Flaherty himself is a politician of sorts. He tried to run for the State Senate after then-incumbent Anthony Galluccio went down on a rap for, you guessed it, drunk driving.

Jailuccio, as he was known after he was locked up in Billerica, was the hack who while on house arrest claimed he was still testing drunk on the breathalyzer because of his toothpaste. Jailuccio never specified whether he was brushing with Arm and Hammered, or Michelob Ultra Brite, or maybe Harvey's Bristol Gleam.

Why didn't John "Get Off My" Lawn think of that?

But Jailuccio is yesterday's drunkard. The tosspot du jour is John Lawn. He is a hack's hack, as you can see from his state campaign finance reports. Just this year alone, at least eight former legislators have donated to the drunkard Democrat. Not to mention a bunch of other lobbyists who list their job titles as "regulatory affairs" or "government relations" or "policy advisor."

On March 31, the Boston Police Patrolmen's Association (BPPA) PAC gave Rep. Lawn $500. On Wednesday morning, members of that very same union arrested their patron.

That right there is a hard fall, for any hack. You know you're having a bad night when your own cops put the cuffs on you.

What made Milwaukee famous has made a loser out of John Lawn.

## How's Indictment, ex-Methuen Police "Don" Joe Solomon?

Ex-chief Joe Solomon was making $326,272 a year—in a city of 53,000.

*September 30, 2023*

An indictment is always a disappointment, so why is this man smiling? But what does ex-Methuen Police Chief Joseph Solomon care? His motto is, If you're indicted, you're invited.

How did he run the Methuen Police Department, you ask? Like "the don of an organized-crime family," according to one of the several scathing reports about him over the years.

Don Solomon was paid $326,272 a year as chief. Plus he got to run a business on the side—"security." He got a "night deferential." He didn't have one police car, he had two.

The second cruiser was used by Chief Solomon to smoke cigars in. Or so said one of the dissident city councilors, who by the way happened to be a Lawrence Police Department officer. You can't be a real organized-crime don unless you smoke cigars.

As he stuffed holiday envelopes full of bribes for his bent feds and crooked local police, Whitey Bulger used to quip, "Christmas is for cops and kids!" For Joseph Solomon, the capo di tutti capi of the Methuen Police Department, every day was Christmas.

When they eventually build a Massachusetts Corrupt Cops Hall of Fame, Solomon should be inducted as a charter member, alongside Zip Connolly, H. Paul Rico, and Gerry Clemente.

He was fired once, in 2008. But this being Massachusetts, the Don was ordered rehired, and he got back pay of $195,000 for his, uh, wrongful termination. And he resumed what the state now says was his life of crime in uniform.

He was charged this week by a state grand jury with a laundry list of corruption charges, including perjury by written document, uttering a forged document, procurement fraud, and a host of violations of the civil-service laws.

Solomon was basically running his own personal hackerama out of the Methuen Police Department. Everything was done with the connivance of the local political establishment, which made the current Boston City Council look like the Good Government Association.

For a long time, Methuen City Hall was in fact *King Solomon's Mines*. And there was plenty of gold in them thar hills.

You know, it's one thing to feed at the trough. It's another thing to lick the plate.

Chief Solomon never got that memo. Or maybe he was too busy taking all those junkets to sunny places for shady people. Or negotiating his next contract, with the $20,129 kiss for his very prestigious college degree, not to mention collecting a salary that was eventually supposed to rise to $375,548 a year. Think of what his pension would have been then.

In a city of 53,000, Solomon was making more than the police chiefs/commissioners of, among other places, New York, Chicago, and Houston.

He was, of course, a "counter-terrorism expert." He terrorized the taxpayers of Methuen.

The attorney general put out a bare-bones press release about his indictment Thursday night. The actual charges apparently won't be filed until next week in Salem.

There's also a 203-page report detailing Solomon's looting spree that was written by a former state police officer who now runs a private-detective agency. Like the indictment, it's not totally public yet either, but a few parts have been leaked.

Solomon was described as running the department through "humiliation, fear, intimidation and retaliation."

The Methuen Police Department, the ex-trooper said, was "a textbook case of public corruption."

Apparently the new attorney general and the new district attorney of Essex County agreed.

If you check out Solomon's political contributions, you can learn that his favorite payroll patriot was Diana DiZoglio, who is now calling herself the "reform" auditor of Massachusetts.

She pocketed at least $1,550 from Don Solomon. I'm sure it had no connection to the fact that one of the Methuen city councilors also had the last name of DiZoglio.

Other than handing them cash, how was Solomon able to get the local yokels to go along with his highway robbery? Well, the guy who was indicted with Don Solomon is a former city councilor who had been put on the department. The councilor had no credentials for the job so they just forged them—at least according to the indictment.

Two of the patrolmen were the sons of city councilors. A former mayor, Jim Jajuga, who used to work for the other Bulger brother Billy as a state senator, had a son who was a captain.

When Jajuga was elected mayor, Solomon "gave" him a brand new Chevy Tahoe SUV with tinted windows. It was a gift, so-called, from the police department.

According to a report by the state inspector general, two city councilors were on the short list to be hired as cops. And what jobs!

The last police contract the Don was mixed up in would have paid captains as much as $459,906 a year, lieutenants $289,834, and sergeants $181,298.

Plus overtime and details.

The union totally rewrote that pact after the city's negotiators had agreed to a real contract. It was so outrageous that the union's lawyer emailed one of Solomon's caporegimes, Griftin' Greg Gallant, that he just hoped the city "doesn't bring its calculators" when it signed off on the heist.

Most of this stuff is at least two years old. I had thought Solomon et al. were going to skate. This is, after all, Massachusetts. But then Thursday night the news was released. I put City Councilor D.J. Beauregard, one of the real reformers, on my radio show for a victory lap.

Some of Solomon's stooges immediately took to social media to accuse Beauregard of being "giddy" about the fall of the Don. He pleads guilty to glee.

"They were screwing 53,000 taxpaying residents of Methuen for years," he said. "Yeah, I'm happy there's finally maybe going to be some justice."

There's an election coming up in Methuen on November 7. Some of the Don's soldiers—or their children—are trying to resurrect their squalid careers. Again, this is Massachusetts. No matter how corrupt, you can always run again. Look at the Kool-Aid Kult on the GOP state committee.

As for Methuen, is it too late for Kendra Lara and Ricky Ricardo Arroyo to head north to run write-in campaigns for the City Council? They'd be perfect additions to the Solomon Crime Family.

Rotten Boroughs | 255

# The "Smiley-Face" Case Is No Joke

*December 17, 2024*

Let's say you are locked up in jail after being convicted at trial. As you sit in your cell studying your case files, you notice that your thirty-three-year-old female prosecutor was writing official documents to your fifty-six-year-old male trial judge and then scrawling a cute little hand-written "smiley face" at the bottom. Do you think if you saw that your prosecutor had written a smiley-face note to your judge, you might want to call your lawyer?

C'mon down Gerson Pascual-Santana, who by the way happens to be a person of color, unlike the thirty-three-year-old female prosecutor and the fifty-six-year-old male judge, who are white. So now the "smiley-face" case will soon be heard by a single justice of the Supreme Judicial Court (SJC).

And the Massachusetts criminal justice system has another massive black eye.

The hack judge in question—Douglas Darnbrough—has already resigned. His young female friend remains on the job. If I could, I would insert a smiley face here for her!

Judge Douglas Darnbrough, left, in happier times, 2019.

Her name is Karlyn Butler. For a while she remained unidentified, but now it's public record. Looking for love in all the wrong places—those are the allegations, anyway.

The only problem for Butler's bosses in the Bristol County District Attorney's Office is that they've told so many different stories about who did and who didn't do what to whom, and most of them contradict what the previous filings said.

Pascual-Santana was convicted in March 2023 of molesting his preteen stepdaughter, a charge he continues to deny adamantly to this day.

The first eyebrows were raised when the blond thirty-three-year-old Butler asked for two years in jail and one year of probation for Pascual-Santana. Her fifty-six-year-old friend gave the person of color three and a half years to serve and eight years' probation. The maximum allowed under law!

And so Butler's boss, elected DA Tom Quinn, got to issue a glowing press release about how tough he is on crime.

All was well until a few months later, when anonymous letters began circulating in legal circles in New Bedford. They're all now in the public record, detailing how "Darnbrough is having an affair with one of the prosecutors [name redacted]."

This cost a hack judge his job.

"They have been in an affair since the end of 2022," said the anonymous writer. "They go to the Carmines (sic) restaurant in New Bedford every Tuesday after work."

Tawdry Tuesday, I guess you'd call it. Or maybe Two-Timin' Tuesday.

The letters kept coming. Defense lawyers started demanding to see the cell phones of both the judge and his young friend.

On September 21, 2023, the judge stopped coming to the courthouse. On October 10, he was reassigned to Plymouth District Court. He lasted at Plymouth until October 12—three days.

On November 2, Darnbrough sent a letter of resignation to Governor Maura Healey, effective November 10. Then he sent a second letter to Healey, re-resigning, this time effective December 30.

This was shocking because state judges never quit, especially with no pension in the works, and now Darnbrough is out, O-U-T. (No smiley face for him.)

Darnbrough is the typical failed lawyer who fantasizes about becoming a judge. He has the usual judge's second-rate education—Bryant College, Southern New England School of Law. He finally scored a minor hack sinecure as an assistant clerk magistrate in Taunton in 2013.

His record was so lackluster that his judicial appointment was about to fail in the Governor's Council in 2016. Governor Charlie Baker had to step in to break the 4–4 tie. And this is what the taxpayers got for their money. Thanks Charlie!

There is no way a payroll patriot like Darnbrough would have ever given up his $207,855-a-year early retirement unless there was no other option.

As for Butler, she claimed there was nothing to the letters, or the smiley face, and is still employed by the district attorney.

Keep your friends close . . .

The problem for the district attorney now is the sequence of stories his office has told. That chronology is outlined in an amicus brief on Pascual-Santana's appeal by the ACLU, the New England Innocence Project and the Massachusetts Association of Criminal Defense Lawyers:

"Unsigned letters arrive and allege that a judge and prosecutor engaged in an improper relationship and ex parte communications.

"After the letters arrive, the judge is absent and then resigns.

"The DA's office initially suggests that no investigation was conducted.

"The DA's office concedes a duty to investigate and claims that the DA's office in fact did conduct an investigation.

"The DA's office reverses course and claims it was the Trial Court that conducted the investigation, but provides no evidence of that investigation or its findings.

"The District Court refuses to reconsider its order denying discovery from the Trial Court and refuses to order any additional discovery from the DA's office . . ."

In conclusion, the ACLU et al. argue that "there is no evidence that any entity within the Commonwealth conducted any investigation into these allegations, the district attorney's office's shifting unsworn representations are no substitute for such evidence, and a remedy is therefore warranted."

Like, releasing Pascual-Santana. And then maybe turning over the cell phones of the fifty-six-year-old disgraced ex-judge and his femme fatale. This case is, as the anonymous writer says, "just the tip of the iceberg."

Who is this anonymous writer? Call her Madam X. Is she a "woman scorned?" The district attorney's office seems to know who "she" is. In a January 29 filing, the district attorney mentions an "in-person confrontation" Madam X had with La Butler.

Madam X knows the make, model, and color of both lovebirds' cars. She knows the ins and outs of the love nest known as the courthouse. Cue the smiley face again as Madam X writes about the young female prosecutor.

"She put a smiley face on the continuance request. This is of significance because Judge Darnbrough was the only judge who allowed or denied the continuance requests. So she knew he would see the smiley face on the continuance request."

At one point, the district attorney's office said they couldn't identify her because of "protection of confidentiality for witnesses to preserve future investigatory techniques."

A few weeks later the whistleblower excuse was gone. Now, they said, it was "criminal harassment" and "the investigation" continues.

Why isn't there more interest in this X-rated case in state-run Boston media? Again, the guy who's locked up in North Dartmouth is a Dominican, a person of color. There are serious questions about how he ended up there, at the hands of certain unsavory Caucasian bad actors.

I thought such outrages mattered. But maybe everyone in the Bristol County District Attorney's Office and the Trial Court gets a pass because they're all . . . Democrats.

Can I get me a smiley face here?

## CHAPTER TWENTY-FOUR

# High Sheriffs in Low Places

In the torrent of unending law enforcement scandals, they're easy to forget, but sheriffs do exist in Massachusetts. And they get into trouble, maybe not as much as the BPD and MSP, but regularly nonetheless.

The first sheriff indicted in 2025 was Steve Tompkins from Suffolk County. He was charged by the feds with extorting a cannabis company into selling him stock in a pre-IPO deal, and then, when the value plummeted, demanding immediate repayment of his initial investment.

Tompkins was arrested in Florida—it used to be that Massachusetts gangsters were lugged in the Sunshine State. Now it's cops.

Tompkins was appointed by Governor Deval Patrick in 2013, after he contributed $1,750 to the Democrat. A native of New York, he'd been the driver for the previous sheriff, Andrea Cabral, who after leaving government got involved with the emerging marijuana industry.

Like many sheriffs, Tompkins had been involved in scandals throughout his tawdry tenure. He was fined a total of $14,800 by the State Ethics Commission over the years for a variety of infractions, including hiring his own niece in violation of state anti-nepotism laws.

In 2024, Tompkins made $215,430 as high sheriff.

There's an old joke about sheriffs: They have to deal with the dregs of society . . . and then there are the inmates.

As mentioned earlier, one former corrections officer of note "Fotios 'Freddy' Geas was briefly a guard at the Hampden County House of Correction. Then he became a hitman for the Mafia in Springfield. His most notable hit: James "Whitey" Bulger, whom he murdered with a lock in a sock in a federal prison in West Virginia in 2018.

Sheriffs often have more mundane criminal problems. Nantucket Sheriff Richard Bretschneider was arrested in 2006 and charged with violating a restraining order taken out by his wife. He retired in 2010 due to ill health—the voters got sick of him. Since January 2011 he's been collecting a pension of $5,958 a month.

Here are some photos of ethically impaired Massachusetts "high sheriffs."

High sheriff of Middlesex County, James DiPaola, committed suicide in Maine in 2010 at age fifty-seven after becoming embroiled in several scandals.

Hampden County Sheriff Nick Cocchi, arrested at MGM Springfield Casino in September 2024, charged with drunk driving in his county SUV, which he left running outside the entrance with a missing tire before he ran inside the casino. Case continued without a finding.

High sheriff of Suffolk County, Steve Tompkins, under federal indictment for allegedly extorting a marijuana company endorsing Michelle Wu for mayor of Boston 2021.

Tompkins, in baseball cap, attends Mayor Michelle Wu's "No-Whites-Allowed" Christmas party at the city-owned Parkman House in 2023. Next to Tompkins is Conan Harris, an ex-con who did ten years in prison for drug trafficking and is now married to US Rep. Ayanna Pressley.

High sheriff of Middlesex County, "Honest" John McGonigle, appointed to fill a vacancy by Gov. Michael Dukakis. Convicted on federal racketeering and tax-evasion charges in 1994.

Sheriff of Essex County, Charles "Chuckles" Reardon, left, appointed to fill a vacancy by Gov. Michael Dukakis. Convicted in 1996 on various federal corruption charges.

Indicted high sheriffs Howard Fitzpatrick of Middlesex and Fred Sullivan of Suffolk at a Harvard University commencement. Both beat raps of "negligence" after high-profile escapes from their respective jails.

High Sheriffs in Low Places | 265

# Epilogue

Karen Read announced a movie deal with a company called LBI a few weeks after the verdict. She will be partnering with her attorney Alan Jackson.

Alan Jackson wrote a letter to BPD Commissioner Michael Cox, demanding that Officer Kelly Dever be placed on the Brady List of police officers whose testimony lacks credibility.

He mentioned her conflicting stories, first to the FBI in 2023, and then on the witness stand at the second trial, about whether she saw two key police figures in the case loitering around Karen Read's SUV for a "wildly long time," as she told the feds.

"Either Officer Dever lied about having a false memory," Jackson wrote, "or she actually suffers from a condition that subjects her to fake memories. In either case, her credibility and reliability as a law enforcement officer are irreparably compromised.

"If she lied under oath," Jackson continued, "Officer Dever is guilty of perjury. If she truly suffers from false memories, she is unfit to serve as a police officer."

On September 1, Dever resigned from the BPD. The news was announced late on a Friday night, after the newspapers' deadlines had passed.

Alan Jackson issued a statement the next day:

"Ms. Dever's departure from the BPD is a reminder that those who betray the public trust cannot remain its guardians."

A few days after the trial ended, Sgt. Yuriy Bukhenik was transferred out of the Norfolk County District Attorney's Office to MSP headquarters in Framingham. He was temporarily assigned to the "Division of Standards and Training" pending a more permanent reassignment.

As predicted, after the trial, Shanon Burgess, the prosecution's "accident reconstruction" expert who lied about his education and confused multiple simple facts during his comic testimony, disappeared from the website of his employer, Aperture.

Now, the joke in my column about Burgess's post-trial employment had really come true—seventeen years of college down the drain.

Immediately after the not-guilty verdict, Brian Albert and the rest of the McAlberts gave self-serving interviews to ABC News, claiming to be victims of the Free Karen Read movement.

Brian Albert, now collecting a $100,000 pension from the City of Boston, said he would have "taken a bullet" for the late John O'Keefe. But he added he couldn't be bothered coming out of his house that morning "in his underwear," as he put it, only because as a BPD officer, he had no authority to take part in an investigation by a different police department.

I quickly tweeted out a BPD police report from 2019 describing how Albert took part in a fugitive investigation with . . . the Canton Police Department. That tweet was seen by 250,000 people—a record for me. People still seem angry about what happened to Karen Read.

In early August, Michael Proctor had a hearing before the state Civil Service Commission, appealing his firing. He accused the MSP of slow-walking his demands for documents he claimed he needed to prove that he had suffered "disparate treatment" by being fired while other troopers committed worse violations and weren't terminated.

The next day, Michael Proctor appeared at a hearing in Dedham about a murder case he'd investigated in Milton. The attorney for defendant Myles King accused Proctor and prosecutor Adam Lally of doing exactly what Proctor had charged the MSP with the previous day—failing to produce the evidence King needed to defend himself in a timely fashion.

Michael Proctor 2025: Not letting his firing affect his appetite.

Proctor appeared to have put on about fifty pounds since the first trial. As he waddled out of the courthouse, his nemesis Turtleboy asked him: "How's the diet goin'?"

As Turtleboy continued to fight the criminal charges pending against him, including witness intimidation, the district attorney's "special" prosecutor—that seventy-three-year-old retired judge with two state pensions worth $203,000 a year—said he would need weeks to examine what he described to the judge as "5,000 pages of discovery."

He turned over everything to Turtleboy's attorneys, who began looking at the 5,000 pages. They quickly discovered that 4,000 of the pages were blank, and hundreds more were totally redacted.

One of the emails showed that Ken Halloran, the former state trooper, boyfriend of the governor's sister, and nephew of slain gangster Brian Halloran (see photo on page 229), had a son named Paul Halloran. Paul Halloran avoided serious criminal charges in 2022 after assaulting a young hockey ref during a game in Foxboro—Norfolk County.

The case was bagged just before Christmas in 2022 after the Hallorans hired as their lawyer a former governor's councilor named Terry Kennedy. Meatball Morrissey's prosecutor said Halloran was a good boy who had just been elected to the student senate at Suffolk University. The young ref had sent a letter of complaint to Meatball, included in the released emails, which Meatball never bothered to respond to. The ref is now suing young Halloran, who has a summer job working for the state.

Also included in the discovery was another email sent out by Morrissey to his payroll patriots the morning Matthew Farwell was arrested by FBI agents for allegedly murdering Sandra Birchmore. Despite the years-long scandal involving the suicide ruling by Norfolk County, Morrissey appeared stunned by the news.

"Is there any truth to this?"

District Attorney Morrissey turned seventy-one in early August, and, for the first time in years, he did not hold a birthday fundraiser in Quincy.

Since January, he'd only received a single donation, of $200, from a lobbyist who used to be the counsel to a state House speaker convicted of obstruction of justice.

At press time, he still has $422,276.64 in his campaign account if he decides to seek reelection in 2026.

A DNA test on Sandra Birchwell's unborn baby showed that Matthew Farwell, the former Stoughton police officer jailed and charged with murdering her in Canton in 2021, was not the father of her child.

Robert Devine, a former deputy chief of police in Stoughton also accused of sexual abuse of Sandra Birchmore prior to her murder, was the subject of a hearing before the Peace Officers' Standards and Training (POST) Commission as to whether he should be allowed to retain his police certification in Massachusetts.

The hearing officer for the POST Commission was a retired judge named Kenneth Fishman, a former attorney for mobster Stevie Flemmi, who testified that he bribed at least five FBI agents and multiple police officers during an underworld career that included at least fifty gangland hits, some with police officers.

Robert Mueller, the former FBI director and acting US attorney in Boston who took part in the cover-up of the framing of four innocent men in Boston for a gangland murder they did not commit, was subpoenaed to appear before a congressional committee investigating the Jeffrey Epstein scandal.

It was reported that Mueller would be unable to give sworn testimony because he has been living for several years in an assisted-living memory facility.

In August, at the arraignment of corrupt Suffolk County Sheriff Steve Tompkins, he was represented by Karen Read's appeal attorney, Martin Weinberg, who has been representing corrupt cops for at least forty years. (See the Gerry Clemente photo on page 110.)

A few days later, Tompkins did what all indicted Massachusetts law-enforcement officers always do whenever they're arrested—he announced he had developed "a serious medical issue," as Weinberg described it.

The High Sheriff said he would be stepping aside until trial—but would continue collecting his $191,000-a-year paycheck as he fights this suddenly-diagnosed medical malady.

Two months after her acquittal, Karen Read finally got her SUV back from the MSP. Its electronic system had been totally destroyed.

Weinberg: My client is innocent.

Meanwhile, the district attorney's "special prosecutor" filed a new motion in court to get the passwords for two of Read's confiscated cell phones. Morrissey still wants to charge her for "witness intimidation" of the McAlberts, even though one grand jury earlier in 2025 had refused to issue such an indictment.

Yet another Norfolk County lawman, Sheriff Patrick McDermott, was charged in a political scandal. A Democrat, he agreed to pay $7,500 in penalties and hand over tens of thousands of dollars in campaign cash to resolve state allegations that he had improperly used $31,000 from his political account for personal use.

Even the *Globe*, which traditionally looks the other way at Democrat corruption, felt compelled to give some honest perspective to McDermott's scandal:

"He is at least the third Massachusetts sheriff to be accused of breaking the law over the last year," the *Globe* noted. "The last three presidents of the Massachusetts Sheriffs' Association have now faced allegations of misusing campaign funds, drunken driving or extorting a cannabis company."

In late August, after conferences with her new team of local attorneys preparing for her pending civil lawsuits in state court against

Karen Read's first post-trial sit-down interview, with author and Alan Jackson.

the MSP and certain individuals, Karen Read and Alan Jackson came to my radio studio in Needham for a live hour-long appearance.

At the end of the hour, I asked Karen Read if she had anything she wanted to say directly to District Attorney Morrissey and the MSP. She considered her response for more than five seconds before finally speaking:

"You lost, you lost big time. And you know what you did. You know what you've done."

To be continued...

# Acknowledgments

Putting together any book like this is a team effort, especially in such a short time since the not-guilty verdict for Karen Read on June 18.

Thanks as always go to my wife, Kathy, the mailroom manager, who came up with the title *Mass Corruption*, which works. On my staff, producer Taylor Cormier did a splendid job designing the book cover and also in obtaining rights to many of the photos listed below. Cloe Amaral, the digital manager of my radio network, collected all the photos, put together the columns in a well-organized fashion, and did a great job running the social-media campaign to promote the book's release.

Thanks also to my show's two producers for all their hard work, Jarred Diglio and Matt McElwain.

I also greatly appreciate the permission from my newspaper, the *Boston Herald*, to use the excellent news photographs, as well as the assistance of *Herald* editor Joe Dwinell.

Also, thanks to Jennifer Welsch of JLW Publishing Services, who handled production, and our printer, Kase Printing, of Hudson, New Hampshire. They both do a great job, and they do it quickly.

Most of the photos in this book came from the *Boston Herald*, or from public sources like police departments, including mug shots.

Other photos include:

Michael Proctor, Associated Press, page 269
Jailbird Chris Albert, Associated Press, page 48
Brian "Lucky" Loughran, Associated Press, page 49
Joseph Paul, Associated Press, page 49
Daniel Whitley, Associated Press, page 51
Yuriuy Bukhenik, Associated Press, page 25
Jill Daniels, courtesy Aidan Kearney, page 82
Gerry Clemente, Getty Images, page 110
Patrick Rose, Getty Images, page 128
Kelly Dever, Associated Press, page 130
Robert Twitchell, Getty Images, page 139
Leonardo Johnson, Getty Images, page 162
Terence Kent with David Yannetti, Getty Images, page 182
Calvin Butner, Getty Images, page 183
Paul Cesan, Getty Images, page 183

# Index

Albano, Michael, 237–238, 240
Albert, Brian, *48,* 56, 68, 114, 268
   Brian Higgins and, 142
   Greg Long and, 120–121
   not interviewed by MSP, 152
Albert, Chris, 2, 27, *48,* 77, 79–80, 83, 116–117
Albert, Colin, 68
Albert, Julie, 77
Albert, Kevin, 2, 56, *57,* 114, 117
Alessi, Robert, *4,* 71
   testimony of Shanon Burgess and, 17, 19–20
Anderson, Susan, 216
Anderson, Tania Fernandes, *120,* 135
Andrade, David, 196, 204–206
Andrade, Nidu, 195–196, 206, 212
Angiulo, Jerry, 127
Atton, Michael, 196

Babbin, Tim, 194
Bailey, Brad, *198*
Baker, Amy, 98
Baker, Charlie "Tall Deval," 194, 195, 199, 200, 212, 215
   Douglas Darnbrough and, 258
   Leigha Genduso and, 215
Ball, Richard, 203
Ballou, Joseph, 166–167
Barbadoro, Michael, 91
Barboza, Joe, 225–226, 235, 238
Barrett, Tommy, 243, 245
Barrett, Veronica, 245
Barry, Timothy, 177
Beauregard, D. J., 255

Beland, Lynn, 87
Bennett, Dan, 195
Bennett, Willie, *121,* 121–122
Berkowitz, Ken, 36, 113, 122–123, *123,* 131
Bibaud, Tim, 175–176
Birchmore, Sandra, 24–25, 38, 97, 113, 114, 150–158, 270
Birchwell, Sandra, 270
Birmingham, Tom, 194, 243
*Boston Finest, 139*
*Boston Globe*
   on dangerous BPD vehicle pursuits, 133
   defense of prosecutors in Karen Read case, 15
   on the Genduso scandal, 175
   on Hank Brennan, 64
   on John Connolly, 127
   Leonardo Johnson case and, 163
   on Patrick McDermott, 272
*Boston Herald,* 89, 178, 221, 275
   on dishonorably discharged officers, 195, 210–211
   on the Genduso scandal, 175
   on the Karen Read trials, viii, 64
   on MSP marijuana scandals, 173
Boston Police Department (BPD), 1–2
   arrests of detectives of, 127–128
   dangerous vehicle pursuits by, 132–133
   deep flaws of, 119–120
   framing of Fred Weichel by, *241,* 241–245
   framing of Leonardo Johnson and, *162,* 163–168

gay population shakedown by, 124–125
hall of shame, *136–139*
Internal Affairs and Anti-Corruption Divisions of, 128–129, 133–135
Irish Gang War and, 109–110, 125
Juston Root shooting by, 160–161
lying by Kelly Dever of, 131–132
wrongful arrests by, 121–122
Bradley, Heather, 96
Brady, Jennifer, 95–96
Brady, Tom, *95,* 95–96
Brennan, Hank, *9,* 18–21, *37,* 41, *63*
confusion of, 36–40
courtroom humiliations of, 67–70
mangled vocabulary of, 70–74
relationship with Michael Morrissey, 65–66, 87–88, 94
representation of Whitey Bulger, 37–40, 63–67, 94
testimony of Kelly Dever and, 131–132
testimony of Steve Flemmi and, 66–70
Bretschneider, Richard, 262
Brooks, Immanuel A., 133
Bucci, Sean, 214–215, 221
Buckley, William, 99
Bukhenik, Yuriy, 46, 68–69, 87
Free Karen Read campaign and, 105–108
lies of, 30–33
need for translator, 27–30
salary of, 54
testimony of, 24–27, *25*
transfer after end of Karen Read's trial, 268
Bulger, Billy, 88, 89, 92
as Senate president, 127, 228, 239, 255
Bulger, James "Whitey," ix, x, 37–40, 55, 92, 126
Brian Halloran killed by, 174, 229–230
cocaine dealing by, 231
FBI tipoff of, 172
Fred Weichel and, 241–245
as fugitive for sixteen years, 232
Hank Brennan and, 63–64, 94

influence on the Karen Read case, 64–67
John Connolly and, 228, 239
Michael Morrissey and, 88
murder of, 262
murder of Teddy Deegan and, 239–240
recruited as FBI source, 227
Burgess, Shanon, 17–21, *18,* 23, 72, 268
Butler, Karlyn, 257
Butner, Calvin, 171, *172, 183*

Cabral, Andrea, 261
Caissie, Jen, 194
Callahan, John, 228, 232
Cannone, Beverly, 2, *8,* 91, 92, 132
brother of, hired to defend Chris Albert, 80
confusion of, 23
definition of exculpatory, 77, *94*
instruction to not mention federal grand jury, 78
running cover for Hank Brennan, 94
Canton, court proceedings in
"false memory" in, 129–132
Sandra Birchmore and, 150–158
as sideshow, 76–79
Canton Police Department, 122, 268
crimes committed by, 114
ducking of responsibilities by, 101–104
lying by Kelly Dever of, 131–132
Carey, Richard, 166, 167
Carney, Jay, 65
Carpenter, Ronald, 83
Carr, Howie
coverage of the Genduso story, 221
post-trial interview of Karen Read and Alan Jackson, *272,* 272–273
on wrongful imprisonments under Robert Mueller, 237
Carr, Kristopher, *180*
Carrasquillo, Nelson, *139*
Casper, Denise, 40
Castruita, Chenee, 155
Cavicchi, John, 237
Cederquist, Gary, *181*
Cederquist, William, *181*

Cesan, Paul, *183*
Champagnie, Patrick, 133–135
Champagnie, Triston, 133–135
Chin, Eric, *185*
Clemente, Gerry, 110, *110,* 110–111, 113, 170–171
Clinton, Bill, 238
Clinton, Hillary, 233, 234
Cocchi, Nick, *262*
Collins, James, 98
Collins, Peter, 98
Condon, Dennis, 224, *224,* 224–225, 232
Connolly, John "Zip," 38, 88, 127, 205, 214, 223, 226–233, *227*
 attendance at Harvard, 228–229, 239–240
 convicted of murder of John Callahan, 232
 convicted of racketeering charges, 232
 joins the FBI, 226–227
 mob payoffs taken by, 231, 239
 murder of Brian Halloran and, 229
 protection of Bulger and Flemmi by, 228, 242
 released from prison, 233
 retirement from the FBI, 232
Conway, Daniel, 134
Conway, John A., 134
Coolidge, Calvin, 124
*Cops Are Robbers, The,* 110, 171
Correia, Dwayne, 196–197, 201–203
Cosgrove, Robert, 66, 92, 116
Costello, Mike, 194
COVID-19 pandemic, 99, 129, 156, 176, 178, 199
Cox, Michael, 121, 122, *130,* 133, 135
Cronin, John, 99
"Crossfire Hurricane," 233
Curley, James Michael, 124

Daher, E. George, 89
*Daily Caller,* 235
Daly, Andrew, 194
Daniels, Jack, 83
Daniels, Jill, 57, *82,* 83–85

Darnbrough, Douglas, *256,* 256–260
Davis, Ed, *123*
Deegan, Teddy, 225, *226,* 230–231, 232, 234
 wrongful imprisonment of four men for murder of, 235–240
DeJong, Daren, *198,* 198–201
DeJong, Nathan, 198–201
Delahunt, William, 126, 243–245
Delgado-Garcia, Enrique, 178
*Demons Behind Me, The,* 220
Dempsey, Brian, 194
Dershowitz, Alan, 235, 238
Deveau, Ed, 247
Dever, Kelly, 121–124, *130,* 131–132, 267
Devine, Joel, 196
Devine, Robert, 270
DiBona, Noel, 97–98
Dicicco, Dave, 54, 59
DiPaola, James, 194, *262*
*Distillations,* 165
DiZoglio, Diana, 89
Doherty, Henry, *138*
Donohue, Kathleen E., 247–249, 251
Dookhan, Annie, 162–168, *164,* 215
Downey, Paul, *136*
Doyle, Matthew, 98
Doyle, Steven, 98
Dukakis, Michael, 170, 171, 227, *264*

Epstein, Jeffrey, 271
Essex County Sheriff, *264*

Fanning, John, 54
Farak, Sonja, 163–168, *164,* 215
Farley, Matthew, 133
Farwell, Matthew, 25, 150–158, *151,* 270
Fauci, Anthony, 55
Federal Bureau of Investigation (FBI), 46, 79, 88, 112, 122–123, 145, 193
 Annie Dookhan and, 164
 Boston Mafia and, 222–233
 Boston Police Department work with, 125, 127
 Brian O'Hare and, 173
 cocaine dealing and, 231

Index | 279

crooked agents of, 36–39, 65,
  222–223, 236–237
under director Robert Mueller,
  234–240
expert witnesses hired by, 14, 41,
  42, 69
investigation of corruption in
  Norfolk County DA office, 53
Jen McCabe interviews by, 12
John Connolly and (see Connolly,
  John "Zip")
Karen Read case and, 97, 222
Michael Proctor and, 60, 87
murder of Brian Halloran and,
  229–230
murder of John Callahan and,
  228, 232
murder of Roger Wheeler and, 228,
  230, *230,* 232
murder of Teddy Deegan and, 225,
  *226,* 230–231, 232, 235–240
Nick Gianturco of, 36–39, *37*
people framed for murder by, 41
Russiagate hoax and, 117, 231, 233,
  234–235
Sandra Birchmore case and, 151,
  153–158
targeting of Martin Luther King, Jr.,
  by, 55
text messages discovered by, 3
Whitey Bulger case and, 20, 172
witnesses lying to, 12, 45, 129–131
wrongful imprisonment of Louie
  Greco, 225, 235–240, *236*
Fishman, Kenneth, 270
Fitzpatrick, Howard, *265*
Fitzpatrick, Robert, 20, 39, 229–230
Flaherty, Charlie, 99, 251
Flaherty, Timothy, 251
Flemmi, Jimmy "the Bear," 225
Flemmi, Stevie, ix, 37–39, 66–70,
  125–127, *126,* 270
  Boston FBI and, 222–227
  cocaine dealing by, 231
  John Morris and, 231

  McLaughlin brothers and, 224–225
  murder of Teddy Deegan by, 239–240
Floyd, George, 118
Flynn, Ray, 121, 127
Foley, Leah, xii
Foxboro Flasher, 189–192, *190*
Fuhrman, Mark, 77

Galluccio, Anthony, 194, 251–252
Gay population shakedown by BPD,
  124–125
Geas, Fotios "Freddy," 245, 262
Genduso, Leigha, 175, *175,* 175–176, *213*
  bad boyfriends of, 214–215, 221
  drug convictions erased due to
    testimony of, 215–218
  hired by the MSP, 220
  infamous past of, 213–215
  life after being a trooper, 218–219
Gertner, Nancy, 234–235, 238–239
Gianturco, Nick, 36–38, *37*
Goldberg, Deb, 167
Gotti, John, 132
Greco, Louie, 225, 235–240, *236*
Griffin, Daniel, 178, 207–210
Guarino, Nicholas, 17, 36–38, *37,*
  113, 152

Halloran, Brian, 174, 228–229, *229,*
  269–270
Halloran, Ken, 174, 269–270
Halloran, Paul, 269
Hamilton, George, 126
Hampden County Sheriff, *262*
Hannity, Sean, 238
Harris, Conan, *263*
Harris, Kamala, vi, 94
Hawkins, Ralph, 114
Healey, Maura, 55, 163, 167, 174, 244
Higgins, Brian, 57, 122, 131, *141*
  cross-examined by David Yannetti,
    144–146
  embarrassing texts of, 140–141
  as fat, drunk, and stupid, 143–146
*Hill, The,* 233

Hoover, J. Edgar, 55, 223, 224, 226, 227, 235
*Howie Carr Show, The,* 237
Huff, Mike, 224, 232
Hussey, Deb, 88

*Improper Bostonians,* 125
Irish Gang War, 109–110, 125

Jackson, Alan, 1, 3, *4–8,* 93, 267
   on evidence in Karen Read case, 100–101
   on Michael Proctor, 169
   post-trial interview of, *272,* 272–273
   on reasonable doubt, 40
   testimony of Brian Higgins and, 141
   testimony of Joseph Paul and, 14
   testimony of Kelly Dever and, 131–132
   testimony of Michael Proctor and, 54
   testimony of Yuriy Bukhenik and, 28, 31, 33–35
   on use of word "nefarious," 11–12
Jajuga, Jim, *255*
Johnson, Leonardo, *162,* 162–168
Jordan, Joe, 127
Joyce, Brian, 194
Jury, Karen Read, 40–43
Justice, Buford T., 29

Kaczmarek, Anne, 166–167, 168
Kearney, Aidan "Turtleboy," 21, 44, 83, 89, 92, 117, 175, 221, 269
   blog about the Karen Read case, 79
   targeted as fall guy, 81, 83, 84
Keating, Bill, 88, 96
Kelley, Matthew, 205, 206, 210–212
Kennedy, Robert F., 223
Kennedy, Terry, 270
Kent, Michael, *182*
Kent, Seamus, *182*
Kent, Terence, *182*
Kent, Zachariah, 116
Killeen, Donald, 88, 241
King, Edward J., 170
King, Martin Luther, Jr., 55, 229

King, Myles, 268
Kotkowski, Jeff, 54

Labadini, Joseph, 98
Labadini, Matthew J., 98
Labadini, Michelle, 98
La Cosa Nostra, 224
Lally, Adam, 23, 35, 81, 268
LaMonica, Robert, 242, 245
Laposata, Elizabeth, 72
Lawn, John, *246,* 247, 252
   drunk driving arrest of, 249–250
Lawn, Michael, 247–249, 250–251
Lee, Cody, 196
Lee, Daniel, 79
Lehane, Dennis, 250, 251
Lelling, Andrew, 193
Lenes-Davila, Kevin, 133
Limone, Peter, 235, 236–240
Little, Elizabeth, *4, 6*
Long, Gregory, *120,* 120–121
Loughran, Lucky, *49,* 60, 79–82
Lyons, Mary, 115, *115*

MacPherson, Eric, 134
Mafia, Boston. *see* Federal Bureau of Investigation (FBI)
Marathas, Jason, 83
Marathas, Nick, 83–84, 85
Mariano, Ron, 89
Martorano, Johnny, 172, 230
Massachusetts State Peace Officer Standards Training (POST) Commission, 118
Massachusetts State Police (MSP), v–viii, 104–108
   Andrew Patterson of, 189–192, *190*
   continued corruption even after conviction, 206–210
   corruption of, 169–179
   Daren DeJong of, *198,* 198–201
   dishonorable discharges from, 195–197
   Dwayne Correia of, 196–197, 201–203
   hall of shame, *180–185*

Index | 281

lack of progress in eradicating
culture of corruption at, 210–212
Leigha Genduso of (*see* Genduso,
Leigha)
Matthew Kelley of, 205, 206,
210–212
Nidu Andrade of, 196, 204–206, 212
police union, 173–174, 192–195
reforms of, 109, 171
salaries of, 170
Thomas McCarthy of, *186,* 186–189
Mattaposett Police Department, 115
Maxon, Heather, 71
"McAlberts," the, 11–13, 27, 31, 33,
43–45, 83, 249, 272
as bar regulars, 84
as male chauvinists, 53
Proctor and, 56
McCabe, Jennifer, viii, *10,* 11–12,
35, 77, 79
lying by, 129, 147–149
McCabe, Matt, 12–13
McCarthy, Thomas, *186,* 186–189
McCormack, John, 226
McDermott, Patrick, 95–96, 272
McDonald, Joe, 230
McGonigle, John, *264*
McGraw, David, 84
McKeon, Richard, 175–176, 195, 216
McLaughlin brothers, 224–225
Mello, Ken, 87
Metheuen Police Department, *252,*
252–255
Michlewitz, Aaron, 117
Middlesex County Sheriff, 194, *264, 265*
Moore, Chris, 54
Moran, Terry, 45
Morris, John "Vino," 38, 88, 214, 231,
233, 239
Morrissey, Michael, vi, viii, *9,* 18, *75,*
*86,* 270, 271–272
Bill O'Donnell and, 96–99
chasing white whales, 85–90
defense attacks on, 81
Juston Root case and, 160–161

Karen Read's statement to, 273
as male chauvinist, 55
Nick Guarino case and, 38
relationship with Hank Brennan,
65–66, 87–88, 94
Sandra Birchmore case and, 152, 158
testimony of Andrew Rentscler and,
41–42
testimony of Judson Welcher and,
21–24
testimony of Yuriy Bukhenik and,
24–27
Moynihan, Dan, 191
Mueller, Robert, 232, 270–271
Nancy Gertner and, 234–235, 238–239
wrongful imprisonments under,
235–240
Mueller, William, 231
Murray, Tim, 194

Nee, Tommy, 242
Nelson, Ronald, *137*
*New York Times, The,* 238
Nicholson, Russ, 109–110
Noble, Geoffrey, *51,* 105, *179*
Norfolk County Bar Association, 91–92
Norfolk County grifter leaders, 93–96

O'Brien, Gerard, *138*
O'Connell, William, 88
O'Connor, James, 248
O'Donnell, Bill, 96–99
O'Hare, Brian, 173
O'Keefe, John, v–vi, 1–3, 11, 25–26
cell phone of, 16
sneakers of, *25,* 25–26
vehicle of, 34–35

Page, Lisa, 233
Pascual-Santana, Gerson, 256–260
Patrick, Deval, 240, 261
Patterson, Andrew, 189–192, *190*
Patterson, Rachel, 191
Paul, David, 16
Paul, Joseph, 13–17, 19, 29, *49*

Police officers, 109–118. *see also*
  Boston Police Department (BPD);
  Massachusetts State Police (MSP)
  court cases against, 115–117
  dishonorably discharged, 195–212
  drunk driving by, 115, 118,
    125–126, 187
  embezzlement by, 198–201, 207–210
  male chauvinism among, 53–56
  outside jobs of, 112
  overtime work by, 112
  retirement pensions of, 111–112
  thefts by, *110,* 110–111, 113, 170
Police reforms, 109, 171
Police unions, 173–174, 192–195
Polito, Karyn, 194, 220
Ponzo, Chris, x–xii
Ponzo, Joe, x–xii
Prescott, John, 77
Presidents Golf Course, 98
Pressley, Ayanna, 55, *263*
Proctor, Michael, 1–2, 15, 22, 45, *47,*
  *52,* 76, 207, 268, *269*
  Bukhenik's testimony on, 31
  continued certification of, 118
  cross-examination of, 77
  firing of, 28, 32, 59–61, 169–170
  under investigation, 33
  investigative mistakes of, 55, 117
  John O'Keefe's clothes and, 165
  as male chauvinist, 53–56
  misogynistic messages about Karen
    Read, 61
  suspension and corruption of, 56–59,
    87, 89, 187
Prouty, Charles, 236, 237
Pulido, Roberto, *138*
Pullman, Dana, 173–174, *174, 192,*
  193–195

Quinn, Tom, 257

Raftery, Gregory, *182*
Read, Karen, case of, v–ix, *4, 8, 48,* 244.
  *see also* Testimony

  Canton police framing in, 101–104
  as corrupt Canton townie sideshow,
    76–79, 101
  defense team in, *4–8*
  Free Karen Read movement and,
    104–108, 268
  influence of the Whitey Bulger case
    on, 64–67
  mangled vocabulary of Hank
    Brennan and, 70–74
  movie deal after, 267
  as Norfolk County hackerama, 90–93
  post-trial interview on, *272,* 272–273
  prosecution team in, *8–9*
  reasonable doubt in, 40–43
  use of term "nefarious" in, 11–13
Reardon, Charles, *264*
Reasonable doubt, 40–43
*Record American,* 225
Rentschler, Andrew, 41–42
Richardson, Elliot, *125,* 125–126
Rico, H. Paul, 88, 125, *223*
  corruption of, 214, 223–226,
    228, 232
  murder of Teddy Deegan set up
    by, 240
*Rifleman,* 125
Risteen, Dan, 175–176, 216, 219
Rivera, Geraldo, 214
Roache, Buddy, 127
Roache, Francis "Mickey," 127
Robertson, William, 207–208, 210
Rocca, Thomas, 248
Rogers, Joel, *181*
Rollins, Rachel, *120*
Rombney, Willard Mitt, 209
Root, Juston, 97, *159,* 160–161
Rose, Patrick, 128, *128*
Russiagate hoax, 117, 129, 231, 233,
  234–235
Rutley, Jonathan C., 96

Salemme, Frank, 59
Salvati, Joe "the Horse," 226, 235
Saraf, Steve, *50*

Index | 283

Schiffer, Richard L., Jr., 101–103
Schneiderhan, Richard, 171, *172*, 214
Schoener, Walter, 116–117
Schultz, Sgt., 31, 195
Shea, Billy, 242
Shea, Joe, 98–99
Sheehan, Matthew, *184*
Sheriffs, Massachusetts, 194, 261–262, *262–265*, 271–272
Sisitsky, Alan, 88
Smigielski, Brian, *137*
Solomon, Joe, *252*, 252–255
State Police Association of Massachusetts (SPAM), 173–174, 192–195
Stoughton Police Department, 113–114
*Street Corner Society,* 109
Strzok, Peter, 233
Stuart, Bill, 125–126, 214
Stuart, Carol, 121
Stuart, Chuck, 121
Suffolk County Sheriff, 261, *263,* 271
Sullivan, Fred, *265*

Tameleo, Henry, 235
Taylor, Tim, 102–104
Teresa, Vinnie, 231
Testimony
   Andrew Rentschler, 41–42
   Brian Higgins, 143–146
   Brian "Lucky" Loughran, 79–82
   Jen McCabe, 129, 147–149
   Joseph Paul, 13–17
   Judson Welcher, 23–24
   Leigha Genduso, 215–218
   Shanon Burgess, 17–21
   Stevie Flemmi, 66–70
   Yuriy Bukhenik, 24–36, *25*
Thomson, Stephen, 191–192
Timilty, James, 124
Timilty, Walter F., 91

Tolson, Clyde, 224
Tompkins, Steve, 261, *263,* 271
Toner, Paul, 251
Torigian, Tim, *139*
Traub, David, 87
Trump, Donald, 45, 78, 129, 231, 233, 234–235, 237. *see also* Russiagate hoax
Tully, Brian, 46, *50,* 54, 57, 86–87
Twitchell, Robert, *139*

Unions, police, 173–174, 192–195

Walsh, Brian, 96
Watertown Police Department, 247–249
Weeks, Kevin "Two," 242
Weichel, Fred, 88, 126, *241,* 241–245
Weinberg, Marty, *110,* 271, *271*
Welcher, Judson, 23–24, 72
Weld, William, 171, 231
Wheeler, Roger, 228, 230, *230,* 232
White, Kevin, 127
Whitley, Daniel, *51*
Whyte, William A., 109
Williams, Paul, 114
Wilson, David, *184*
Winslow, Troy, 133
Winter Hill Gang, 124, 172, 224–225, 227–228, 244
Wolf, Mark, 201
Wu, Michelle, 117, 122, *263*
Wyshak, Fred, 40

Yannetti, David, 1, *4, 7–8,* 85
   Terence Kent and, *182*
   testimony of Brian Higgins and, 144–146

Zerola, Frank, 218